PUBLIC APPEARANCES / PRIVATE REALITIES

PUBLIC APPEARANCES
PRIVATE REALITIES

The Psychology of Self-Monitoring

Mark Snyder

University of Minnesota

W. H. Freeman and Company

New York

Library of Congress Cataloging in Publication Data

Snyder, Mark.
  Public appearances / private realities.

  Bibliography: p.
  Includes index.
  1. Self-presentation.   I. Title.
BF697.5.S44S59   1986   155.2   86-4822
ISBN 0-7167-1797-2
ISBN 0-7167-1798-0 (pbk.)

Contents

Preface

"Shall we clap into it roundly, without hawking or spitting or saying we are hoarse, which are only prologues to a bad voice," suggested Shakespeare in *As You Like It*. I agree, and so this preface will be brief. There will be no hawking and spitting here to explain what this book is about or why I wrote it. Not to fear, though. These matters of explanation will be dealt with soon enough, in the first few pages of the book, actually. Let me instead use this space to acknowledge debts of gratitude and offer words of appreciation. Having only one author, this book is something of a single-parent child. But, it does come from a large family whose members have contributed, each in their own way, to its nature and its nurture.

I could not have written this book without the insights gleaned from research on the nature of the self. Some of this research has been my own; some was the work of other investigators, including the many talented and dedicated graduate students who have joined me in my studies. Over the years, thousands of people have generously volunteered their time to participate in these studies and have bravely allowed us to peer through the windows of their lives. Not incidentally, more than a little financial support from the University of Minnesota, the National Institute of Mental Health, the National Science Foundation, and the Center for Advanced Study in the Behavioral Sciences has helped me do my research and write this book.

As the book went through its drafts, and there were more than a few, its form and substance have been shaped by the advice and counsel of students and colleagues. My editors and publishers join me in expressing special thanks to Phillip Shaver of the University of Denver and William Ickes of the University of Texas at Arlington, who read the manuscript and provided those most precious of commodities—constructive criticisms and tactful suggestions.

Mark Snyder

PUBLIC APPEARANCES / PRIVATE REALITIES

An Introduction to Self-Monitoring

The image of myself which I try to create in my own mind in order that I may love myself is very different from the image which I try to create in the minds of others in order that they may love me.

—W. H. Auden

THE GAPS AND contradictions between the selves we allow other people to see and the more private self only we personally are allowed to know have been the focal points of my explorations into the nature of the self. For well over a decade now, I have sought to understand the often tangled web that is woven of the public appearances and private realities of the self. Why, I have asked myself, do some people follow Auden's example, appearing to be living lives of public illusion, when others are content just to "be themselves," without constantly assessing the social climate around them? Why do the public and private person seem to mesh so well for some, when others project a kaleidoscope of changing appearances?

My attempts to answer these questions have grown out of a long-standing fascination with the differences between reality and illusion. I was struck by the contrast between the way things often appear to be and the reality that lurks beneath the surface—in novels, on the stage, and in people's actual lives. In J. D. Salinger's *Catcher in the Rye,* 16-year-old Holden Caulfield found himself repulsed by the pretense of adults who talked as if they loved each other but whose unloving actions spoke louder than their words. For centuries now, theatergoers have been charmed by *Tartuffe,* Moliere's comedy about a man who changes from one self to another with the ease of a chameleon changing colors, masquerading as a paragon of religious virtue while busily robbing other men of their property and their wives.

These contradictions between public appearances and private realities appealed to both parts of my dual professional identity—the social psychologist and the personality psychologist. As a social psychologist, I wanted to understand the world of appearances as it operates in social relationships: How is the appearance built up? How is it maintained? What are its effects on the person who projects it and those around him or her? As a personality psychologist, I wanted to know where personality resides: Is it in the *persona*—the public face—or in the underlying private reality? I was also interested in exploring an older, more philosophical question: Is there a "real" me, an essential self beneath the various images that people project?

My concerns led me to develop the concept of *self-monitoring.* I have applied this concept both as a theoretical guide for asking questions about the nature of the self and the ties that bind personality and social behavior and as an empirical vehicle for answering these questions. I will begin this chronicle of my journey of investigation at the beginning—with an introduction to the concept of self-monitoring.

CHAPTER 1

The Construct of Self-Monitoring

■

There is a pretty woman on my television screen. Her name appears. It is
Lauren. Lauren looks pensive. "I'm very into attitudes," Lauren says. "I
have dozens of them sort of hovering in the closet in my room. They're all
part of a world I created for myself. But I'm never really sure who I am
in that world. Is there a real me inside, or am I only what you see?"
(*Minneapolis Star and Tribune,* April 28, 1983)

ALTHOUGH FEW OF us explicitly ask the question Lauren did in an
advertisement for Calvin Klein jeans, most people share an interest in
discovering who that one true self is that underlies the many roles they
play in the course of their lives.

For some people, discovery of the self comes easily; they have no
difficulty fulfilling the Socratic exhortation, "Know thyself." For others, a sense of identity is not so readily available. Many people turn to
the self-help sections of their favorite bookstores in search of paper-
bound recipes for discovering themselves, for liking themselves, for
respecting themselves, and for living up to the Shakespearean injunction, "To thine own self be true." For still others, the road to self-
understanding is torturous: They may undergo year after year of pain-
ful self-examination in psychoanalysis. Yet, as difficult as the quest for
the self may be, there are few people in this culture who would ques-

tion the assumption that there exists a self that is uniquely one's own, that distinguishes each person from all others, gives meaning to experiences, and brings continuity to life.

The Self: Public Appearances and Private Realities

Assumptions about the self, particularly that there is a true self, are some of our most cherished beliefs about human nature. But these beliefs are being challenged by the discoveries of researchers who study the self. Most people assume that each of us has one and only one true self, but this is not always so. Some people act as if they have not one, but many selves. Moreover, in spite of the widespread belief that the self is an integral feature of personal identity, for many people, it seems to be largely a product of their relationships with other people. These people exhibit striking gaps and contradictions between the *public appearances* and the *private realities* of the self. The public appearances created by a person's words and deeds may be the result of deliberate attempts to create images appropriate to particular circumstances in an attempt to be "the right person in the right place at the right time."

Just about everyone acts to control the impressions conveyed to others to some extent. But for some people, this strategy is a way of life. Some people are particularly sensitive to how they appear in social situations—at parties, job interviews, professional meetings—in circumstances of all kinds where they might be motivated to create and maintain an appearance. These people carefully observe their own performances and skillfully adjust their behavior to convey the desired image, acting like different people depending on the situation and their audience. It is as if they are actors for whom life itself is a drama in which they play a series of roles, choosing the self that best fits the circumstance at hand. Like Lauren, of the Calvin Klein ad, they have a closetful of "attitudes" they use to create public appearances that may or may not be backed up by the private reality of the "real me" on the inside.

The Concept of Self-Monitoring

There are differences in the extent to which people *monitor* (observe, regulate, and control) the public appearances of *self* they display in social situations and interpersonal relationships. The Laurens of the world are what I call *high self-monitors*. They monitor or control the images of self they project in social interaction to a great extent. *Low self-monitors,* in contrast, value congruence between who they are and what they do. Unlike their high self-monitoring counterparts, low self-monitors are not so concerned with constantly assessing the social climate around them. Their behavior is quite consistent: They typically express what they really think and feel, even if doing so means sailing against the prevailing winds of their social environments. They take the injunction, "To thine own self be true," seriously.

These self-monitoring propensities have profound effects, influencing people's views of the world, their behavior in social situations, and the dynamics of their relationships with other people. Although I began my research on self-monitoring by examining the extent to which people manage their *public* appearances of self, it has become apparent that self-monitoring is intimately associated with people's *private* beliefs about what constitutes a "self" as well. Accordingly, theory and research on self-monitoring have been able to provide some perspectives on the very nature of the self.

The Conceptual Ancestry of Self-Monitoring

Two questions provided the impetus for my explorations of self-monitoring: Do people actively attempt to control the images they convey to others during social interaction? What are the consequences of adopting or not adopting this strategic orientation to interpersonal relationships? When I began thinking about these questions, it very quickly became apparent that they had a rich and venerable heritage, one that was by no means confined to the annals of psychological inquiry. Indeed, the assumption that people try to influence their public appearances has cropped up time and again, both in literary allusion and in scientific discourse.

The "Life as Theater" Metaphor   "All the world's a stage," we are told by Jacques in Shakespeare's *As You Like It,* "and all the men and women merely players" in a theatrical performance in which they act out many parts in their lifetimes (II, viii, 139). In Cervantes' *Don Quixote,* the title character asks his companion, Sancho Panza (and us, as well):

"Tell me, have you not seen some comedy in which kings, emperors, pontiffs, knights, ladies, and numerous characters are introduced? One plays the ruffian, another the cheat, this one a merchant and that one a soldier. . . . Yet when the play is over and they have taken off their players' garments, all the actors are once more equal."

"Yes," replied Sancho, "I have seen all that."

"Well," continued Don Quixote, "the same thing happens in the comedy and intercourse of this world, where some play the part of emperors, others that of pontiffs—in short, all characters that a drama may have—but when it is all over, that is to say, when life is done, death takes from each the garb that differentiates him, and all at last are equal in the grave." (Part II, Book iii)

No less an authority on the theater than Sir Tyrone Guthrie has claimed that "we all spend a great deal of our lives in acting" (1971, p. 7). As for the form of this acting in the theater of life, Guthrie believed that it involved "pretending to be someone or something other than yourself, or even, while retaining your own identity, expressing thoughts or feelings which do not in fact correspond with your own thoughts and feelings at a particular moment" (1971, p. 7). As for the motivation behind this offstage and out-of-theater acting, Guthrie suggested that "most of it is done in a good-natured endeavour to lubricate the creaking mechanisms of social intercourse" (1971, p. 7):

Employees have to make a show to employers of being industrious and respectful, while employers have to make a show of being kind and just and taking an interest. "How's *Mrs.* Wetherbee? . . . Oh, not *again* (in a tone of extreme concern) . . . that's her second this winter." (With even deeper concern) "*Has* she tried those sort of inhaler things?" Fortunately at this moment the telephone rings and the actor can switch from the role of Considerate Employer to that of Jolly Fellow Rotarian and by the time the "kidding" and the roars of assumed laughter have run their dreadful course, old Wetherbee, thank God, has slipped out of your office and Miss Scales is ready to take dictation. Whereupon yet another Act begins: the iron-clad, ice-cold Man of Affairs creating order and profit out of chaos; and, at the same time, yet another impersonation: the Dominant Male allowing a Female to help him. . . . (1971, p. 7)

The Impression-Management Tradition   That people can and do control their public images is also a basic tenet of most, if not all, psychological and sociological theories of the self in social interaction. At the end of the nineteenth century, William James offered this psychological perspective on the social nature of the self:

> *A man has as many social selves as there are individuals who recognize him* and carry an image of him in their mind.... But as the individuals who carry the images form naturally into classes, we may practically say that he has as many different social selves as there are distinct *groups* of persons about whose opinions he cares. He generally shows a different side of himself to each of these different groups. Many a youth who is demure enough before his parents and teachers swears and swaggers like a pirate among his "tough" young friends. We do not show ourselves to our children as to our club companions, to our masters and employers as to our intimate friends. From this there results what practically is a division of the man into several selves.... (1890, vol. 1, p. 294)

James's notions have been echoed by successive generations of theorists (for reviews, see Gordon and Gergen, 1968; Schlenker, 1985). Symbolic interactionists—following in the footsteps of Cooley (1902), Thomas (1923), and Mead (1934)—have argued that the self is defined and "negotiated" through social interaction (for reviews, see Stryker, 1979, and Stryker and Statham, 1985).

Sullivan, a proponent of a brand of psychoanalytic theory called interpersonal psychiatry, suggested that "every human being has as many personalities as he has interpersonal relations" (quoted by Perry, 1982, p. 108). And, in a similar vein, role theorists have proposed that the self is a reflection of the social roles people perform (e.g., Biddle and Thomas, 1966; McCall and Simmons, 1978; Sarbin and Allen, 1968). As one theorist writing in this sociological tradition said:

> The self consists, from one point of view, of all the roles we are prepared to take in formulating our own lines of action, both the roles of individuals and of generalized others. From another and complementary view, the self is best conceived as a process in which the roles of others are taken and made use of in organizing our own activities. (Becker, 1968, p. 197)

Students of the self, working in a tradition known as "impression management," have taken as their theme the notion that people present different selves to different others. Erving Goffman, for one, analyzed the strategic presentation of self in everyday life (1955, 1959, 1963, 1967). He likened social interaction to a theatrical performance in which each person acts out a "line." A line is a set of carefully chosen verbal and nonverbal acts. Lines, however, can and do shift from situation to situation as different roles and expectations become salient.

Moreover, according to Goffman, people have many motives for trying to manage or influence the impressions they give others, in particular, the desire for social approval and the motive to control the outcome of the interaction. The person practicing impression management attempts to maintain an image appropriate to the current situation to secure a positive evaluation from the other person. To determine the best approach, alternative presentations of self are weighed. "A person determines how he ought to conduct himself during an occasion of talk by testing the potentially symbolic meaning of his acts against the self-images that are being sustained" (Goffman, 1967, pp. 38–39). A participant whose image receives social approval is said to be "in face"; one whose image fails is "out of face."

Goffman was a particularly prolific commentator on human nature (11 books in 25 years). He was also unusually insightful, a keen observer of the often subtle and difficult-to-notice maneuvers, routines, and rituals by which people manage their impressions in public. The "data" for his observations came not from the experiments and surveys familiar to most social scientists (in fact, his published works give no indication that he ever created any paper-and-pencil questionnaire measures of the phenomena he studied), but from his personal observations in everyday life. As one student of his work remarked: "He swam, in fact, in the same social sea as the rest of us, with the difference being that he had the capacity to make the most familiar observation a source of strange and fascinating insight" (Scheibe, 1985, p. 56).

Goffman had an eye as well for particularly revealing literary illustrations and novelistic examples. In *The Presentation of Self in Everyday Life* (1959), he introduces his ideas about the theatrical engineering involved in managing impressions by quoting at length from William Sansom's novel *A Contest of Ladies* (1956). In the book, the Englishman Preedy, making his first appearance on the beach while vacationing in Spain, manages without uttering a word, but instead by careful use of mannerisms and stage props (including his book, sandals, and beach bag), to appear to be, in quick succession and as it suited his purposes, Kindly Preedy, Methodical and Sensible Preedy, Big-Cat Preedy, and Carefree Preedy. Not incidentally, Preedy's image-fashioning activities are something of a caricature; but, for Goffman, Preedy was a prime defining example of the fashioning of identities by impression management.

From the perspective of Goffman and other impression-management theorists (see also, Alexander and Knight, 1971; Alexander and Lauderdale, 1977; Alexander and Sagatun, 1973), social interaction requires people to be aware of the interpretations others give their actions, to have a desire to maintain "face" and a large repertoire of self-presentational skills, and to be willing to use impression-management tactics. In short, people need the ability to control self-presentation (verbal and nonverbal) to foster desired images in the eyes of their beholders.

Impression management provides people with ritual formulas and rules for social conduct. As one theorist characterized it, with the guiding hand of social rules,

> the individual can navigate without fear in a threatening social world. He can even ignore the true attitudes of others, as long as he can get by them with the proper ritual formulas of salutation, sustaining conversation, farewells, and so on. The actor has only to be sure of the face-saving rules for interaction. Everyone is permitted the stolid self-assurance that comes with minute observation of unchallenging rules—we can all become social bureaucrats. (Becker, 1975, p. 61)

The description of the skilled navigator of the straits of social interaction as an actor is more than the mixing of nautical and theatrical metaphors. For the abilities that the impression-management theorists attribute to the successful social performer are precisely those that have been attributed to the successful stage performer (Metcalf, 1931). This convergence is, of course, to be expected from a theoretical framework that reflects the "life as theater" metaphor (for a review of this "dramaturgical" perspective, see Brissett and Edgley, 1975; for a critique, see Buss and Briggs, 1984).

Because of their focus on the stage-managed aspects of social intercourse, the impression-management theorists may seem to be "chroniclers of human superficiality" (Scheibe, 1985), relegating people to the status of "social bureaucrats," to use Becker's term (cf. Buss and Briggs, 1984). Goffman's obituary in the *New York Times* in 1982 characterized his main point as "People are essentially performers whose main business is fabricating an identity." Whether or not this is a fair characterization, the fact of the matter is that people do strive to influence and control the images others form of them during social interaction. To a greater or lesser extent, people seem to know what behaviors will create which impressions. At times, they seem able to perform precisely those actions that will create the desired images, often in the service of winning friends and influencing people. The techniques and tactics used (and sometimes exploited) have been meticulously and exhaustively catalogued (for reviews, see Gergen, 1971, 1977; Greenwald and Breckler, 1985; Jones, 1964; Schlenker, 1980; Snyder, 1981*a*; for a discussion of the pervasiveness of impression-management phenomena, see Buss and Briggs, 1984).

An Investigative Strategy for Self-Monitoring

As a psychological construct, self-monitoring carries on the tradition of these views of the self in social interaction, with particularly clear ties to the ideas of James and Goffman. If people can and do exercise control over their expressive behavior, self-presentation, and nonverbal displays of affect, how are these phenomena to be understood? How are their consequences to be discovered? How are their origins to be traced?

When I began my research on self-monitoring, I first tried to identify categories of people who differed consistently in the extent to which they could and did exercise control over their verbal and nonverbal self-presentation.

Why adopt such an investigative strategy? First of all, the differences in the extent to which people manage their public presentations of self are striking and undeniable. Some do it more often, and with greater skill, than others. Professional stage and screen actors can do more than most of us. Indeed, for many an entertainer, performing is a full-time preoccupation—in the words of Sammy Davis, Jr., "As soon as I go out the front door of my house in the morning, I'm on, daddy,

I'm on." Successful politicians have long practiced the art of putting on the right face for the right constituency. Onetime mayor of New York Fiorello LaGuardia was so skilled at adopting the mannerisms of different ethnic groups that it is easy to guess whose votes he was courting when you watch silent films of his campaign appearances. Today, candidates for public office routinely turn to media experts to help them acquire winning images (for discussions of politics and the media, see McGinniss, 1970; Shrum, 1977; Witcover, 1970). Media images have acquired such importance in presidential campaigns in the United States that, after losing his 1984 bid for the White House (to an incumbent with a Hollywood background), Walter Mondale said, by way of partially explaining his defeat, that he had never really warmed up to television.

Differences in mannerisms of various ethnic, national, and religious groups are often used to interpret their expressive behavior (all too often in stereotyped terms). Thus, we hear references to this or that group whose members "wear their hearts on their sleeves," who have "a stiff upper lip," or whose faces render them "inscrutable" to outsiders. In his book *The Italians,* Luigi Barzini reported in semiserious tones that "Orson Welles once acutely observed that Italy is full of actors, fifty million of them, in fact, and they are almost all good; there are only a few bad ones, and they are on the stage or in the films" (1967, p. 62).

In decidedly more serious tones, anthropologists have often characterized differences between cultures in terms suggestive of self-monitoring. Consider Ruth Benedict's characterization of Japanese life:

> They see the "whole duty of man" as if it were parcelled out into separate provinces on a map.... Each circle has its special detailed code and a man judges his fellows, not by ascribing to them integrated personalities, but by ... specifying the circle of behaviour he has not lived up to ... the particular province within which he violated the code. (1946, p. 137)

A society that places such a high value on rule following and role enactment may also be one with a correspondingly large proportion of high self-monitors in it. Indeed, Benedict has indicated that, in the Japan she studied, "the good player is one who accepts the rules and plays within them. He distinguishes himself from the bad player because of the fact that he is disciplined in his calculations and can follow other players' leads with full knowledge of what they mean under the rules of the game" (p. 154). This passage describes a person who displays a high amount of self-monitoring, one who has a highly developed awareness of the social world and who uses its dictates in following the rules of each circle of life.

We can all think of examples of highly skilled performers. Some of the more mercurial trial lawyers, the more flamboyant salespeople, and the more persuasive diplomats are the ones who come to my mind most readily. Needless to say, such highly skilled actors may be the exception rather than the rule. And, examples based on differences between ethnic, national, and religious groups are at best suggestive and sometimes misrepresentations. All too often, these examples lack documentation. The question really is: Within the *general* population, do people differ meaningfully in whether they can and do exercise intentional control over their self-presentations, expressive behaviors, and nonverbal displays of affect?

But how is this question to be answered? Often, psychological phenomena can be understood by focusing on those people who characteristically manifest the phenomena under investigation (Snyder and Ickes, 1985). For example, the study of prejudiced individuals has revealed a great deal about the nature of prejudice (Adorno, Frenkel-Brunswik, Levinson, and Sanford, 1950), the study of people with a high need for approval has been most informative about the dynamics of approval strivings (Crowne and Marlowe, 1964), and the study of Machiavellians has provided great insight into the nature of interpersonal manipulation (Christie and Geis, 1970). According to the logic of this investigative strategy,

> one could hardly study any particular social psychological phenomenon or process in individuals who rarely or never manifest that particular phenomenon or process. Accordingly, by identifying those individuals who typically manifest the ... phenomenon or process of concern, one gains access to the ideal candidates for investigating the social psychology of that phenomenon or process in action. That is, the identification of those individuals who characteristically manifest the phenomenon or process is undertaken, not as an end in and of itself, but rather as a means toward achieving the end of understanding an important social psychological phenomenon or process. (Snyder and Ickes, 1985, p. 885)

To apply this investigative strategy to self-monitoring, a way must be found to identify the two types of people—high and low self-monitors.

How, then, can differences in self-monitoring be captured? What are their consequences? Are there practical applications of self-monitoring? Where do self-monitoring propensities come from and how do they develop? What do theory and research on self-monitoring reveal about human nature? These questions define the agenda for investigations of self-monitoring. My answers and those of other researchers are contained in the chapters of this book.

CHAPTER 2

The Identification of Self-Monitoring

■

IN 1972, I developed the Self-Monitoring Scale as the first step in my empirical research on self-monitoring. With the help of the Self-Monitoring Scale, an instrument designed to reliably and validly measure self-monitoring propensities, it was possible to classify people as either high or low in self-monitoring. I, and other investigators, then could enlist their cooperation to study how and why self-monitoring is implicated in their lives as individuals and as social beings.

What kind of people are high and low self-monitors? The prototype of the high self-monitor is someone who is particularly sensitive to cues to the situational appropriateness of his or her social behavior and who uses these cues as guidelines for monitoring (that is, regulating and controlling) his or her expressive behavior and self-presentations. By contrast, the low self-monitor is less attentive to social information about situationally appropriate self-presentation and does not possess a highly developed repertoire of self-presentational skills. His or her expressive self-presentations seem, in a functional sense, to be controlled by inner attitudes, dispositions, and values, rather than to be molded and shaped to fit the situation.

The differences in these contrasting self-presentational styles recall the distinctions Allport (1961) once made between *expressive* behavior, that which is truly and spontaneously emitted, and *coping* behavior, that which is purposely controlled and consciously performed. In Allport's sense, the self-presentations of low self-monitors are expressive behavior and may be taken at face value—their words and deeds are typically accurate expressions of true underlying attitudes, feelings, and dispositions.

However, the activities of high self-monitors are, to use Allport's term, coping behavior and must be considered in relation to the goals of the self-presentations. Sometimes, the goal may be to display expressions that, although appropriate to the immediate circumstances, are not necessarily congruent with private attitudes and feelings. For example, jilted suitors may feign happiness at weddings even when feeling sadness over opportunities lost. And some marriage counselors may put on a show of interest and concern to mask their true feelings of apathy and boredom toward the troubled couple's all too common and mundane problems. At other times, the goal may be to communicate attitudes and feelings accurately, by means of an intensified expressive self-presentation. For instance, defense attorneys, in hopes of enhancing their chances for winning their cases, may exhibit exaggerated displays of confidence in their clients' innocence. Or job candidates may pretend to be more qualified and more confident of their suitability for a particular job than they really are.

The first goal will tend to *diminish* the relation between inner experience and outward expression (producing a *negative* relation when expressions diametrically oppose feelings and producing *no* relation when expressions have nothing to do with true inner events). The second goal will tend to *enhance* the relation between inner experience and outward expression (producing exaggerated *positive* relations). It probably would be wrong to say that high self-monitors lack feelings or that they are devoid of genuine inner experiences. Rather, like actors who feel sadness and happiness but control their tears and laughter, high self-monitors regulate and control the selves they present to others.

Constructing the Self-Monitoring Scale

How can self-monitoring propensities be identified? The Self-Monitoring Scale consists of 25 true–false self-descriptive statements that describe, among other things, concern with situational appropriateness of self-presentation (e.g., "At parties and social gatherings, I do not attempt to do or say things that others will like"), attention to social cues to situationally appropriate self-presentation (e.g., "When I am uncertain how to act in social situations, I look to the behavior of others for cues"), ability to control expressive behavior (e.g., "I can look anyone in the eye and tell a lie [if for a right end]"), use of this ability in particular situations (e.g., "I may deceive people by being friendly when I really dislike them"), and situation-to-situation shifts in expressive self-presentation (e.g., "In different situations and with different people, I often act like very different persons").

Although the items of the Self-Monitoring Scale describe these phenomena, an item does not necessarily refer to one and only one content domain. For example, the item "When I am uncertain how to act in a social situation, I look to the behavior of others for cues" has either explicit or implicit connections to at least four content domains: being concerned about situational appropriateness, attending to social comparison information, responding to interpersonal guidelines, and adopting this orientation in social situations. And the content domains themselves are not necessarily independent of each other. For example, using expressive self-control abilities presupposes that these abilities exist, just as attending to cues to situational appropriateness presupposes concern with that information. These features of self-monitoring and its measurement acquire particular significance when viewed in the context of the internal structure of the Self-Monitoring Scale (see Chapters 12 and 13).

Items of the Self-Monitoring Scale typically endorsed by high self-monitors include:

I would probably make a good actor.
In different situations and with different people, I often act like very different persons.
I'm not always the person I appear to be.

Moreover, high self-monitors report that what they say and do does not necessarily reflect what they really believe. Furthermore, they regard themselves as actors sufficiently skilled to display whatever self-presentation seems appropriate to their current situation in a convincing manner.

Low self-monitors claim, among other things, that:

I have trouble changing my behavior to suit different people and different situations.
I can only argue for ideas which I already believe.
I would not change my opinion (or the way I do things) in order to please people or win their favor.

In addition, low self-monitors do not believe that they possess the self-presentational skills that would permit them to adopt any orientation other than "being themselves."

The 25 items of the Self-Monitoring Scale are a set selected on the basis of an item analysis (using Anastasi's, 1968, D statistic) from a larger pool of items, using procedures designed to maximize the internal consistency of the measure (following guidelines suggested by Nunnally, 1967). Readers wishing further details on the psychometric construction of the Self-Monitoring Scale should see Snyder (1972, 1974). A complete listing of the items of the Self-Monitoring Scale, as well as instructions for administration and scoring, are contained in Table 2-1. The Self-Monitoring Scale is also available in Japanese, Arabic, German, Spanish, and Polish versions (e.g., Chemers and Ayman, 1985; Iwabuchi, Tanada, and Nakazato, 1982; Nowack and Kammer, 1984; Sara, 1982; Wojciszke, 1982).

The 25-item Self-Monitoring Scale is both internally consistent (with a Kuder-Richardson 20 reliability of +.66; Gangestad and Snyder, 1985) and temporally stable (with test-retest reliability estimates of +.83 for a one-month interval, Snyder, 1974; +.76 for a two-month interval, Kendzierski, 1982b; +.71 for a 2.5-month interval, Greaner and Penner, 1982; and +.77 for a 3.5-month interval, Kendzierski, 1982b). Moreover, scores on the Self-Monitoring Scale are relatively insensitive to conscious efforts to falsify results (Furnham and Henderson, 1982) and are independent of social desirability response sets (e.g., Paulhus, 1984).

Over the years, the distribution of Self-Monitoring Scale scores has remained remarkably stable. Thus, in a sample of 533 college students' scores collected in 1972, the distribution had a mean of 12.51, a median of 12, a standard deviation of 4.11, and a range of 2 to 24 (Snyder, 1972). In another sample of 1918 college students' scores col-

Table 2-1   The 25-Item Self-Monitoring Scale

1. I find it hard to imitate the behavior of other people.   (F)

2. My behavior is usually an expression of my true inner feelings, attitudes, and beliefs.   (F)

3. At parties and social gatherings, I do not attempt to do or say things that others will like.   (F)

4. I can only argue for ideas which I already believe.   (F)

5. I can make impromptu speeches even on topics about which I have almost no information.   (T)

6. I guess I put on a show to impress or entertain people.   (T)

7. When I am uncertain how to act in a social situation, I look to the behavior of others for cues.   (T)

8. I would probably make a good actor.   (T)

9. I rarely seek advice of my friends to choose movies, books, or music.   (F)

10. I sometimes appear to others to be experiencing deeper emotions than I actually am.   (T)

11. I laugh more when I watch a comedy with others than when alone.   (T)

12. In a group of people I am rarely the center of attention.   (F)

13. In different situations and with different people, I often act like very different persons.   (T)

14. I am not particularly good at making other people like me.   (F)

15. Even if I am not enjoying myself, I often pretend to be having a good time.   (T)

16. I'm not always the person I appear to be.   (T)

17. I would not change my opinions (or the way I do things) in order to please someone else or win their favor.   (F)

18. I have considered being an entertainer.   (T)

19. In order to get along and be liked, I tend to be what people expect me to be rather than anything else.   (T)

20. I have never been good at games like charades or improvisational acting.   (F)

Table 2-1 *(continued)*

21. I have trouble changing my behavior to suit different people and different situations.   (F)

22. At a party I let others keep the jokes and stories going.   (F)

23. I feel a bit awkward in company and do not show up quite so well as I should.   (F)

24. I can look anyone in the eye and tell a lie with a straight face (if for a right end).   (T)

25. I may deceive people by being friendly when I really dislike them.   (T)

For information on administration and scoring, see Snyder (1974). Items are keyed in the direction of high self-monitoring (T = true; F = false).

lected over 10 years later, the distribution had a mean of 12.48, a median of 12, a standard deviation of 3.90, and a range of 2 to 24 (Gangestad and Snyder, 1985). Moreover, the distribution of Self-Monitoring Scale scores has been stable across geographical regions. The first sample was collected in the state of California; the second was from the state of Minnesota.[1]

---

[1]There may exist small differences between the sexes in their scores on the Self-Monitoring Scale. For example, in one sample of college students, the average score for males was 12.78; for females, 12.08 (Snyder, 1972). This difference, as small as it may be, is in the same direction as other reports of sex differences (e.g., Frazier and Fatis, 1980). In addition, higher scores on the masculinity scale of the Bem Sex Role Inventory (Bem, 1974) tend to be associated with higher Self-Monitoring Scale scores (Lee and Scheurer, 1983). Typically, these differences between the sexes are very modest indeed. In fact, Rosenthal and DePaulo (1979) have reported that, across eight independent samples, the median difference between males and females was only 0.25, or one quarter of a scale point on the 25-item Self-Monitoring Scale.

These small but consistent differences in Self-Monitoring Scale scores notwithstanding the actual phenomena of self-monitoring (as they are revealed by investigations of relevant behaviors) seem *not* to reveal differences between the sexes. Typically, when comparisons are made, the same behavioral phenomena that are strongly linked to self-monitoring are not meaningfully associated with sex (e.g., Snyder, Gangestad, and Simpson, 1983; Snyder and Simpson, 1984a).

Validating the Self-Monitoring Scale

Are the claims that people make about themselves in their responses to the items of the Self-Monitoring Scale valid? Are those who purport to be high or low self-monitors actually so? A variety of different methods for assessing the validity of the scale provides affirmative answers to these questions.[2]

Peer Ratings   The use of peer ratings to verify the validity of the Self-Monitoring Scale is based on the assumption that people who can control their expressive self-presentation and who are sensitive to social-appropriateness cues should be seen as such by those who know them well. And indeed, studies have shown that people can recognize the high and low self-monitors around them.

In one study, members of a fraternity living together (all of whom had previously completed the Self-Monitoring Scale) participated in a sociometric task in which they rated each other on a variety of attributes thought to characterize either high self-monitors (e.g., "Has good self-control of behavior. Can play many roles") or low self-monitors (e.g., "Openly expresses true feelings, attitudes, and beliefs"). People with high scores on the Self-Monitoring Scale are identified as high self-monitors by their peers. They are seen as being skilled at learning what is socially appropriate in new situations, well able to control their emotional expression, and capable of using these abilities effectively to create impressions (Snyder, 1974). However, those high in self-monitoring are *not* seen by their peers as particularly ingratiating, nor are they any better liked by their peers than low self-monitors.

Knowing who is low and who is high in self-monitoring may be of considerable value. With this knowledge, people may be able to recognize if someone is expressing true attitudes and values or is playing a role. And, should they care to, they can take self-monitoring into

---

[2]Investigators have adopted a variety of criteria for operationally defining high self-monitoring and low self-monitoring groups. Some have used a median partition of the distribution of Self-Monitoring Scale scores. Others have sampled from the upper and lower thirds or from the upper and lower quartiles of the distribution. In reporting the results of any specific study, the terms high self-monitoring and low self-monitoring will reflect the particular operational definition employed by the investigator.

account when choosing friends. As we shall see in Chapter 5, the particularly close friends of high self-monitors are themselves high in self-monitoring; those of low self-monitors are relatively low in self-monitoring.

Criterion Groups   Another means of establishing the validity of an instrument is by predicting how predetermined groups will score. Groups known to be particularly skilled at controlling their expressive behavior should have high scores on the Self-Monitoring Scale. By the same token, groups thought to exercise little expressive self-control should have low scores on the Self-Monitoring Scale.

In point of fact, professional stage actors, for whom expressive self-control is a meal ticket, have substantially higher scores on the Self-Monitoring Scale than comparison samples of university students (Snyder, 1974; see also Wilkinson, 1982). Successful courtroom attorneys, diplomats, public relations agents, politicians, and salespeople are probably high in self-monitoring, although they have yet to be studied. Certainly, successful members of professions that call for high degrees of social and communicative skills (for example, managers and mediators) often are high self-monitors (see Caldwell and O'Reilly, 1982; Giacalone and Falvo, 1985; Sypher and Sypher, 1981, 1983). Leaders are frequently high in self-monitoring (see Garland and Beard, 1979; Whitmore and Klimoski, 1984). Finally, it appears that obese people may be higher in self-monitoring than their nonobese counterparts (Younger and Pliner, 1976), possibly a reflection of a hypersensitivity to external cues thought to be characteristic of the obese (see Schachter, 1971). Alternatively, a deviant or stigmatizing status may motivate obese people to monitor their social behavior more carefully to secure social acceptance (Krantz, 1978).

By contrast, the behavior of hospitalized psychiatric patients is known to be less variable in different situations than that of the average person (Moos, 1968). One interpretation is that patients on a psychiatric ward are unable or unwilling to fit their behavior to specifications of situational appropriateness. The average Self-Monitoring Scale scores of hospitalized psychiatric patients are markedly lower than those of comparison samples of college students or of other middle-aged adults (Snyder, 1974; see also Furnham and Capon, 1983). In addition shy people, who may feel inhibited about practicing impression management, are as a group lower in self-monitoring than the nonshy (Pilkonis, 1977; but see also Briggs, Cheek, and Buss, 1980).

Expressive Self-Control   A valid Self-Monitoring Scale ought to measure the extent to which people can exercise intentional control over their nonverbal expressive behaviors. Those with high scores on the Self-Monitoring Scale are particularly talented in this regard. Researchers have had them communicate arbitrary emotions through tone of voice and facial expressions. Thus in one investigation participants read aloud an emotionally neutral paragraph (e.g., "I am going out now. I won't be back all afternoon. If anyone calls, just tell them I'm not here") in ways that conveyed as accurately and naturally as possible each of seven different emotions, for example, happiness, sadness, anger, fear, surprise, disgust, or remorse. Naive judges later indicated, after watching films or listening to tapes, which emotion the person expressed. High self-monitors were much better able than low self-monitors to communicate accurately the intended emotion, in both the vocal and facial channels of expression (Snyder, 1974). They could, with little apparent difficulty, look and sound in quick succession happy and then sad, fearful and then angry, and so on through the long list of emotions.

Moreover, some people high in self-monitoring are such polished actors that they can appear reserved, withdrawn, and introverted and then, with seemingly chameleonlike skill, shift self-presentational colors and act friendly, outgoing, and extraverted (Lippa, 1976b). They can also exploit their self-presentational skills to successfully deceive others in a variety of interpersonal contexts, including face-to-face interviews (Krauss, Geller, and Olson, 1976; Miller, de Turch, and Kalbfleisch, 1983; Turner, 1979; see also Siegman and Reynolds, 1983).

So important is expressive self-control to self-monitoring that the item in the Self-Monitoring Scale that best separates high self-monitors from low self-monitors is "I would probably make a good actor." In fact, studies of impression management (to be discussed in Chapter 3) suggest that high self-monitors are social chameleons who can fashion public images tailored to the dictates of a wide variety of situations.

Attention to Others   A key element of self-monitoring is sensitivity to situational cues to behavioral appropriateness. Therefore, to further validate the Self-Monitoring Scale, researchers have sought evidence that high self-monitors are particularly attentive to any information that might guide their expressive self-presentation. Indeed, when given the opportunity to do so, they consult information about the typical self-presentations of their peers more often and for longer periods of time than their low self-monitoring counterparts (Snyder, 1974; Rhodewalt and Comer, 1981). This tendency has been found in children as young as seven years old. In one study, third graders were asked their opinions on a variety of topics, such as whether *Star Wars* or *E.T.* was the better movie (Leone, Musser, Graziano, and Lautenschlager, 1984). Before stating their opinions, the children were given a chance to see how others had answered the same questions. Those with high scores on a children's version of the Self-Monitoring Scale turned to the data on their peers and studied it long and hard before offering their own opinions.

High self-monitors are also likely to turn to others for guidance in deciding how to cope with unfamiliar and potentially embarrassing social situations (Rarick, Soldow, and Geizer, 1976). So important is such *social comparison* information to high self-monitors that, at times, they may even go so far as to "purchase," at some cost to themselves, information that may help them choose appropriate self-presentations (Elliott, 1977, 1979).

Another set of cues for guiding self-presentation is the nonverbal expressive behavior of other people. Accordingly, those with high scores on the Self-Monitoring Scale ought to be particularly skilled at "reading" others to infer their emotional states. Several investigations have confirmed this "sensitivity" hypothesis (Brandt, Miller, and Hocking, 1980*a*, *b*; Geizer, Rarick, and Soldow, 1977; Krauss, Geller, and Olson, 1976). One study (Geizer, Rarick, and Soldow, 1977) used excerpts from the television program "To Tell The Truth." On this program, one of three guest contestants is the "real" Mr. X. However, all three *claim* to be Mr. X. Participants in this study watched each excerpt and then tried to identify the real Mr. X. High self-monitors were much more accurate than low self-monitors at spotting the truthful contestant and seeing through the deceptions of the other two. Quite possibly, their own ability to look someone in the eye and tell a lie with a straight face (e.g., Krauss, Geller, and Olson, 1976; something which, according to their responses to the Self-Monitoring Scale, they only do "if for a right end") helped them to recognize the deceptions attempted by others.

The Matter of Discriminant Validity

According to the strategy of construct validation, "numerous success-ful predictions dealing with ... diverse 'criteria' give greater weight to the claim of construct validity than do ... predictions involving similar behavior" (Cronbach and Meehl, 1955, p. 295). The different methods of assessing the validity of the Self-Monitoring Scale all con-verge on an image of two distinct types of people—the high self-moni-tor and the low self-monitor.

Might not these two types be identified equally well by existing measures of related psychological constructs? Is there any difference between people thought to be high and low in self-monitoring and those with high and low needs for approval (Crowne and Marlowe, 1964)? Is the high self-monitor simply a Machiavellian (Christie and Geis, 1970) in disguise, and the low self-monitor a non-Machiavel-lian? Or, perhaps, are people high and low in self-monitoring best characterized as extraverts and introverts (Eysenck and Eysenck, 1968)?

To demonstrate *discriminant validity* (Campbell and Fiske, 1959), researchers have compared the ability of self-monitoring with need for approval, extraversion, and Machiavellianism to predict a wide vari-ety of behaviors relevant to self-monitoring. In each case, there was a strong and reliable relation between self-monitoring and the predicted criterion behaviors; however, the effects of need for approval, Machi-avellianism, and extraversion on these behaviors usually have been trivial and statistically insignificant (e.g., Jones and Baumeister, 1976; Krauss, Geller, and Olson, 1976; Lippa, 1976a, b; Snyder, 1972, 1974; Snyder and Gangestad, 1982; Snyder and Monson, 1975). These dis-criminant validation efforts have helped to draw the boundary lines that separate these concepts and give them unique identities.

Not Simply Need for Approval There is much in the research litera-ture that suggests similarities between need for approval (as measured by the Marlowe-Crowne Social Desirability Scale, Crowne and Mar-lowe, 1964) and self-monitoring. People with a high need for approval give socially desirable responses in a wide variety of situations. For example, they conform more than those low in need for approval do, and they do not show overt hostility toward someone who has insulted and double-crossed them (Crowne and Marlowe, 1964). All of this suggests that people with a high need for approval modify their behavior from situation to situation.

However, this does not seem to be the case. In one study, there was no difference in whether or not those high and low in need for approval imitated the behavior of a peer they had watched perform a task appropriately (Crowne and Marlowe, 1964, pp. 61–72). Furthermore, people with high need for approval actually are less able than those with low need to communicate feelings in either the facial or vocal channels of expression (Zaidel and Mehrabian, 1969). Finally, those high in need for social approval may be severely limited in their ability to secure that approval. In a sociometric study involving members of a fraternity, those high in need for approval were described by their peers as loners who spent most of their time by themselves, did not go out of their way to make friends, were not very conversational, and were not friendly toward other fraternity members (Bank, reported by Crowne and Marlowe, 1964, pp. 162–163).

Thus, although people with high scores on the Marlowe-Crowne measure may be motivated to gain social approval, they may lack the necessary expressive self-presentational abilities and skills. This conclusion is bolstered by the fact that scores on the c scale of the Performance Style Test (Ring and Wallston, 1968) are not significantly related to self-monitoring. The c scale was designed to identify a person who seeks social approval by becoming whatever kind of person the situation requires. This suggests that seeking social approval need not be accompanied by the ability to control one's expressive behavior and self-presentations.

As in all discriminant validation efforts, the bottom line is, of course, an empirical one. And in the case of self-monitoring and need for approval, the empirical evidence shows a substantial relation between self-monitoring and relevant criterion behaviors and a negligible relation between need for approval and these behaviors. Moreover, the independence of self-monitoring and need for approval as measured by the Marlowe-Crowne Social Desirability Scale takes on added significance. People have a general tendency to describe themselves in a favorable manner and a close relation does exist between the social desirability of personality statements and the likelihood that people will endorse them (Edwards, 1966). For these reasons, Campbell (1960) has recommended that all tests of the voluntary self-descriptive sort (which the Self-Monitoring Scale is) should predict their criterion behaviors substantially better than a measure of the general social desirability factor (which the Self-Monitoring Scale does).

Not Simply Machiavellianism   The independence of self-monitoring and Machiavellianism is of particular significance in understanding the links between these two concepts. Although both types may be motivated, at times, to get their own way, the tools of their trades differ. The high self-monitor relies on techniques of impression management, and the Machiavellian on more exploitative tactics of manipulation. Moreover, the high self-monitor may use his or her skills in the service of soothing and smoothing the rough edges of social life— to ensure a fluid, pleasing flow of interaction, something that may be out of character for the Machiavellian (Barnes and Ickes, 1979).

The differences between self-monitoring and Machiavellianism can be characterized in terms of a distinction (first suggested by Ickes and Barnes, 1979) between *assimilative* and *accommodative* interpersonal styles. The assimilative style is *self-oriented,* involving use of controlling tactics to manipulate others to suit one's purposes and goals. The accommodative style is *other-oriented,* involving getting along with others by bringing one's own behavior into line with the expectations of others. Ickes, Reidhead, and Patterson (1985) have suggested that the interpersonal orientation of the Machiavellian is self-oriented and assimilative, whereas that of the high self-monitor is other-oriented and accommodative.

In support of these characterizations, the investigators have observed that, in unstructured conversations, Machiavellianism is associated with the use of first-person singular pronouns (I, me, mine), which emphasize the self rather than others, and that self-monitoring is associated with the use of second- and third-person pronouns (you, yours, he, she), which emphasize others rather than the self. The difference between Machiavellianism and self-monitoring is that "high Machs are likely to talk about themselves at the expense of others whereas high self-monitors are likely to talk about others at the expense of themselves" (1985, p. 14).

Not Simply Extraversion   When researchers have directly pitted extraversion and self-monitoring as predictors of behaviors relevant to self-monitoring, self-monitoring typically has outperformed extraversion (e.g., Lippa, 1976*a*, *b*; Snyder and Gangestad, 1982; Snyder and Monson, 1975; Snyder, Gangestad, and Simpson, 1983). However, despite this evidence of discriminant validity, there are some areas of overlap between the concepts of self-monitoring and extraversion. After all, the impression-managing, high self-monitoring orientation occurs, almost by definition, in social situations (it is rather difficult to imagine someone high in self-monitoring engaging in the techniques of impression management when all alone in his or her room). And many of these situations are rather extraverted ones (parties and other social gatherings). For these reasons, we should expect to often find the high self-monitor in the extravert's natural habitat, employing the sociable and gregarious tools of the extravert's trade. It should not be surprising, therefore, to learn that some researchers have detected slight statistical associations between extraversion and self-monitoring (e.g., Lippa, 1978*a*).

Where, then, do the differences between self-monitoring and extraversion lie? One interpretation is that, although self-monitoring and extraversion may involve some of the same well-developed social skills (the kind of skills that might make someone the life of a party), only those high in self-monitoring employ their self-presentational abilities to play different roles with different people in different situations. Extraverts, by contrast, may present the same sociable, gregarious, and outgoing self across a wide range of social situations, including many that call for more reserved demeanors.

A Unique Psychological Construct?

Evidently, self-monitoring is not simply need for approval, Machiavellianism, or extraversion in disguise. The list of other measures with which self-monitoring is *not* meaningfully correlated is a long one: locus of control,[3] inner-directed versus other-directed social character,

---

[3]The independence of self-monitoring and locus of control may reflect the fact that locus of control (as defined by Rotter, 1966) refers to differences in whether people perceive events as being consequences of their own actions and hence under personal control ("internal") or as being unrelated to their own behavior and hence beyond personal control ("external"). Self-monitoring, by contrast, refers not to perceptions of controllability of events but to whether people use information from dispositional (low self-monitors) or situational (high self-monitors) sources as guidelines for their own behavior.

field dependence, self-esteem, hypnotic susceptibility, neuroticism, trait anxiety, repression-sensitization, achievement anxiety, need for cognition, intelligence,[4] academic achievement, religion, public self-consciousness, private self-consciousness, social anxiety, the clinical scales of the Minnesota Multiphasic Personality Inventory (MMPI), socioeconomic status, and birth order, among others.

Although the Self-Monitoring Scale is virtually unrelated to measures of seemingly related psychological concepts, it is nonetheless possible that *component* portions of the Self-Monitoring Scale are substantially correlated with some of these measures. For example, one component of the Self-Monitoring Scale may correspond to extraversion, another to manipulativeness, and a third to need for approval. These intriguing possibilities have been raised by those who have conducted factor analytic studies of the Self-Monitoring Scale (e.g., Briggs, Cheek, and Buss, 1980). However, before we even consider dissecting self-monitoring into components and portions, we ought to learn more about self-monitoring as a whole. (Discussion of the internal structure of the Self-Monitoring Scale is found in Chapters 12 and 13.)

The evidence for discriminant validity notwithstanding, there are—at least in the abstract—meaningful family resemblances between self-monitoring and other concepts concerned with generalized interpersonal orientations. One area of conceptual overlap is with Riesman's (1950) distinction between other-directed and inner-directed *social characters.* Inner-directed people turn to personal values and standards for guidance; other-directed people seem to be particularly adept at molding their behavior to fit the expectations and preferences of reference groups. As a mechanical analogy, Riesman (1950) has suggested that inner-directed people are controlled by an internal gyroscope; other-directed people are guided by a psychological radar set tuned to signs from others. Clearly, there are similarities between someone with an inner-directed social character and a low self-monitor and between someone with an other-directed social character and a high self-monitor.

---

[4]Although there are no overall associations between self-monitoring and intelligence (e.g., Arnold, 1976), there are indications that, at least among males, low self-monitors perform better on measures of verbal ability, but high self-monitors have higher scores on measures of spatial ability (Rim, 1982).

There is, however, a fundamental difference between social character and self-monitoring. Riesman's (1950) types are defined at the level of social characters characteristic of entire nations, societies, cultures, and historical periods. Self-monitoring, in contrast, is conceptualized at the level of the individual. These different levels of analysis may account for the lack of any meaningful association between the Self-Monitoring Scale and a measure of inner-directed versus other-directed social character (that of Kassarjian, 1962).

Nevertheless, it is intriguing to speculate about self-monitoring defined at the same level as social characters. Are there entire nations, societies, cultures, and historical periods that are high or low in self-monitoring, ones for which the most typical personality, and perhaps even the most valued one, is that of the high self-monitor or the low self-monitor? Certainly, Ruth Benedict's anthropological characterizations of Japan in terms more than faintly resembling self-monitoring (see Chapter 1) would suggest that there are.

Just as there may be some conceptual overlap between self-monitoring and the concept of social character, there may also be areas of overlap with other psychological constructs. Nevertheless, as with social character, features of conceptual similarity may not be translated into empirical linkages. In fact, as the overall pattern of validity evidence suggests, self-monitoring is a psychological construct that can be measured with particular effectiveness by the Self-Monitoring Scale.

PART II

The Consequences of Self-Monitoring

THE DEVELOPMENT OF the Self-Monitoring Scale opened the door to understanding the role of control over expressive behavior, self-presentation, and nonverbal displays of emotion in people's lives. Armed with the Self-Monitoring Scale, researchers have been able to explore what self-monitoring can tell us about what goes on in social situations and interpersonal relationships.

Although I began my study of self-monitoring alone, I was soon joined by many other investigators also concerned with the self and social life. Collectively, our studies—conducted in a wide variety of research settings and with a wide variety of research methods—have taught us that the propensities identified by the Self-Monitoring Scale are not just idle beliefs that exist in a vacuum. To the contrary, they have a profound impact: Self-monitoring meaningfully influences people's images of themselves and the world around them, their behavior in social situations, and the dynamics of their relationships with other people.

As we shall see in Chapter 3, high self-monitors typically strive for images particularly appropriate to the social forces operating in their situations. It is as if they ask "Who does this situation want me to be and how can I be that person?" Low self-monitors, by contrast, charac-teristically seek words and deeds that faithfully express their attitudes, feelings, and personalities. It is as if they want to know "Who am I and how can I be me in this situation?"

Moreover, researchers have found that these two characteristic in-terpersonal orientations are accompanied by differing conceptions of self—a pragmatic sense of self for high self-monitors and a principled sense of self for low self-monitors (Chapter 4). In addition, they have discovered how people structure the circumstances of their lives to maximize the fit between their self-conceptions and their social behav-ior. These structuring activities have considerable implications for the social worlds within which people live, particularly relationships with friends (Chapter 5) and romantic partners (Chapter 6).

self-presentations in any ensuing social interaction. "Those who are so motivated" are, of course, those with high scores on the Self-Monitoring Scale.

High self-monitors' investment in "reading" others is also apparent in their studious attention to information useful for inferring a person's intentions (Geizer, Rarick, and Soldow, 1977; Jones and Baumeister, 1976; Krauss, Geller, and Olson, 1976) and predicting his or her behavior (Kulik and Taylor, 1981). In their research, Jones and Baumeister (1976) had college students watch a videotaped discussion between two men who either agreed or disagreed with each other. The students knew that one man had been instructed either to gain the affection of the other man or to win his respect. Low self-monitors tended to accept the behavior of the men at face value. They were attracted to the agreeable person, whether he was seeking the affection or the respect of the other man. By contrast, high self-monitors were acutely sensitive to the motivational context within which the men operated. They liked the man who sought affection better when he was autonomous than when he was agreeable. However, when the same man sought respect, they were more attracted to him when he chose an agreeable rather than an autonomous self-presentation.

Clearly, high self-monitors are keenly attentive to the interplay between actions and motivations. Given their choice, they prefer to acquire information about others in situations where behavior is relatively unconstrained by formal role requirements, and hence likely to reflect personal dispositions (Berger and Douglas, 1981). This careful attention paid to the actions of others may also account for the substantial relation between self-monitoring and eyewitness accuracy—high self-monitoring "witnesses" outperform those low in self-monitoring on incidental learning and facial recognition tasks (e.g., Hosch and Cooper, 1981; Hosch, Leippe, and Marchioni, 1984; Hosch and Platz, 1984).

Specificity and Consistency in Expressive Self-Presentation

High self-monitors usually use their harvest of information to tailor their public images to fit their social circumstances by using techniques of impression management—words and deeds chosen not so much for what they say about private attitudes and feelings, but rather for their tactical value in setting up appearances. And, in fact, studies have confirmed time and again that high self-monitors are skilled impression managers.

In one experiment, students joined discussion groups designed to make them aware that different norms operate in different reference groups (Snyder and Monson, 1975). In some discussion groups, the experimenter led the members to a room furnished with two videotape cameras, a microphone, a videotape monitor, a table, and chairs. Group members then signed release forms to allow their discussions to be videotaped for possible viewing by other students in their undergraduate psychology class. The videotape cameras, the feedback on the monitor, and the explicit consent form all highlighted the *public* nature of the group members' behavior and emphasized their membership in the larger reference group of undergraduates, which favors *autonomy* in the face of social pressure.

In other discussion groups, the meetings took place in a room furnished only with a table and chairs. In these groups, the most salient norms and cues were provided by the group members themselves. Accordingly, in this relatively *private* situation, *conformity* and consensus within the group (in which members would go along to get along) would seem to be the most situationally appropriate behavior.

High self-monitoring group members were acutely sensitive to the differences between the contexts in which the discussions occurred (see Figure 3-1). They were conformist in the private discussions, where conformity was the most appropriate interpersonal orientation, and were nonconformist in the public discussions, where reference group norms favored autonomy as a reaction to social pressure. Low self-monitoring group members were virtually unaffected by their social settings (see Figure 3-1). They did not seem to employ impression management activities and, presumably, their self-presentations were more accurate reflections of personal attitudes and dispositions than were those of the high self-monitors.

Readers should note that, in thinking about this experiment, it would be incorrect to characterize the high self-monitoring orientation as a simple conformist one. Although they respond to interpersonal cues to situational appropriateness, high self-monitors conform *only* when they operate in environments that specify conformity as situationally appropriate. In circumstances with normative climates

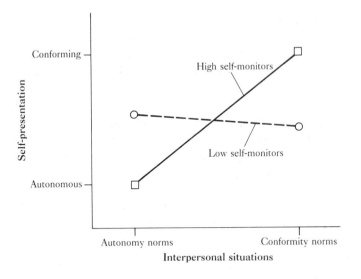

Figure 3-1   Normative climates and self-presentation (Snyder and Monson, 1975).

favoring autonomy, these same people can and do act in independent, autonomous, and nonconforming ways. Thus, studies of personality and conformity have found *no* general associations between self-monitoring and conformity to social pressure (e.g., Santee and Maslach, 1982).

Although flexibility and adaptability are the hallmarks of the high self-monitoring orientation, they are not the only features of this self-presentational style. As researchers, most notably Lippa (1976*a, b*), have conducted more refined analyses of expressive self-presentation, they have discovered that these chameleonlike shifts are acted out against a consistent background of expressive behaviors common to a wide variety of situations. It is not unreasonable to assume that, in most situations, people would prefer to appear "friendly, outgoing, and extraverted" rather than "aloof, distant, and introverted." Similarly, in most contexts, people would prefer to appear "calm and relaxed" rather than "worried and anxious." Therefore, a consistently friendly and nonanxious image may provide the preferred common *ground* against which each specifically edited self-presentation is projected as a shifting *figure*. According to these notions, people high in self-monitoring should give outside observers the general appearance of being *more* "friendly, outgoing, and extraverted" but *less* "worried, anxious, and nervous" than their low self-monitoring counterparts. Exactly this pattern of results has been reported by Lippa (1976*a*, *b*; see also, Cappella, 1985).

For other evidence of the responsiveness to situational consider-ations in the high self-monitoring orientation, see Caldwell and O'Reilly (1982); Danheiser and Graziano (1982); Davis and Lennon (1985); Ferguson (1984); Giacalone and Falvo (1985); Hamilton and Baumeister (1984); Lippa (1976*a*, *b*; 1978*a*); Ludwig, Franco, and Malloy (in press); McCann and Hancock (1983); Rarick, Soldow, and Geizer (1976); Schlenker, Miller, and Leary (1983); Schneider-man, Webb, Davis, and Thomas (1981); Shaffer, Ogden, and Wu (1985); Shaffer, Smith, and Tomarelli (1982); Snyder and Gangestad (1982); Tardy and Hasman (1982); and Tybout and Scott (1983).

Although the vast majority of studies have documented the greater situational specificity of the behavior of high self-monitoring people (for a review, see Snyder, 1979*a*, *b*), there have been a few exceptions to this rule (e.g., Arkin, Gabrenya, Appelman, and Cochran, 1979; Gerstein, Ginter, and Graziano, 1985). These exceptions are a re-minder that, although being high in self-monitoring may entail being quite flexible in self-presentation, situation-to-situation shifts in public appearances are not the only products of impression management.

Indeed, in any given situation characterized by a common impres-sion-management goal, high self-monitoring types ought to be very *consistent* in their presentations of self. The high self-monitoring poli-tician who is desperately trying to appear equally attentive, involved, and statesperson-like in over a dozen different campaign stops sched-uled back-to-back in the same day should be able to consistently project the same vote-getting image by using his or her well-developed impression-management skills. By contrast, low self-monitoring candi-dates might fall victim to shifts in, among other things, their moods and their fatigue levels as the long gruelling day wears on. Lippa's research (1976*a*, *b*; 1978*a*, *b*) on the origins of consistencies in ex-pressive behavior and that of Ickes, Layden, and Barnes (1978) on sensitivity to transitory fluctuations in states of awareness together provide supporting evidence for precisely these forms of consistency and variability.

The Links Between Attitudes and Behavior

Although the high self-monitoring orientation may give people the flexibility and adaptability to cope with a diversity of social roles, there may be costs associated with this way of life. The high self-monitoring orientation may communicate very little about one's private beliefs, feelings, and intentions. By habitually choosing behaviors to fit their current surroundings, high self-monitors may create gaps and contradictions between their attitudes and their actions.

Low self-monitors, on the other hand, excel in the domain of correspondence between private attitudes and public behaviors. They are the ones who claim to value congruence between what they believe and what they do. It follows that consistency between attitudes and behavior should be related to self-monitoring. And, findings indicate that it is.

In one investigation into the links between attitudes and behavior, students served as jurors in a mock court case involving allegations of sex discrimination in employment (Snyder and Swann, 1976). In this simulated court case, jurors read summary curricula vitae of two biologists, Ms. C. A. Harrison and Mr. G. C. Sullivan. Both had applied for the position of assistant professor of biology at the University of Maine. The university chose Mr. Sullivan for the position. Ms. Harrison subsequently filed suit, alleging that the university's decision reflected a bias against women. The jurors then considered the arguments advanced in court on behalf of the plaintiff (Ms. Harrison) and on behalf of the defendant (University of Maine). After reaching their verdicts, they wrote essays explaining their decisions. A panel of raters read the essays and assessed the attitudes expressed toward Ms. Harrison.

Overall, the relation between general attitudes toward affirmative action and judicial decision-making behavior was, at best, modest. However, when this relation was considered separately for low and high self-monitoring jurors, the results were quite different. The verdicts of low self-monitoring jurors were very much related to their attitudes. Those who favored affirmative action rendered verdicts favorable to Ms. Harrison; those who opposed it reached verdicts unsympathetic to Ms. Harrison's complaint. The verdicts of high self-monitoring jurors, however, simply could not be predicted from their attitudes.

Not only is it possible to predict the future behavior of people low in self-monitoring from measures of their present attitudes (Snyder and Swann, 1976), it is also possible to forecast their future attitudes based on their current actions (Snyder and Tanke, 1976). These two kinds of studies make it possible to construct a composite index of the proportions of high and low self-monitors with consistent or inconsistent attitudes and behaviors. This index (presented in Table 3-1) reveals that, for low self-monitors, consistency was over three times as prevalent as inconsistency. By contrast, high self-monitors were about equally likely to act in accord with their attitudes as to contradict them. For other demonstrations of the substantial links between private attitudes and public behaviors typical of the low self-monitoring orientation, see Ajzen, Timko, and White (1982); Becherer and Richard (1978); Kendzierski (1982a); Lutsky, Woodworth, and Clayton (1980); Olson, Zanna, and Fazio (1978); Paulhus (1982); Ross, McFarland, and Fletcher (1981); Snyder (1982); Snyder and Kendzierski (1982a); Zanna and Olson (1982); Zanna, Olson, and Fazio (1980); and Zuckerman and Reis (1978).

Just as there may be costs associated with the high self-monitoring orientation, there may be costs associated with the low self-monitoring concern that behaviors accurately reflect personal attitudes. Sometimes, when low self-monitors engage in behaviors that deviate from their attitudes, their old attitudes will shift to fall into line with their new behavior (Snyder and Tanke, 1976). This practice of changing attitudes to fit behavior may represent what Goffman (1959) has referred to as "role embracement." High self-monitors, who do not regard what they do and what they believe as necessarily equivalent, are relatively unaffected by attitude-discrepant behaviors. Their private attitudes tend to remain stable despite changes in their public behavior—an orientation that may perhaps correspond to what Goffman (1959) has referred to as "role distancing."

Beyond the domain of social attitudes, the low self-monitoring orientation is also marked by substantial correspondence between mood states and self-presentation (e.g., Ickes, Layden, and Barnes, 1978), between personality attributes and corresponding expressive behaviors (e.g., Clark and Lippa, 1980; Lippa, 1978a, b; Lippa, Valdez, and Jolly, 1979), between self-ratings on personality dimensions and ratings by acquaintances (e.g., Tunnell, 1980; but see Cheek, 1982), and between personal conceptions of leadership and actual leadership

Table 3-1   Attitudes and Behavior

Type of Person	Inconsistent (%)	Consistent (%)
High self-monitoring	56.2	43.8
Low self-monitoring	24.5	75.5

Snyder and Swann, 1976; Snyder and Tanke, 1976.

styles (Chemers and Ayman, 1985). In addition, it is characterized by much situation-to-situation consistency in reports of altruism, honesty, and self-restraint (e.g., Snyder and Monson, 1975), as well as in nonverbal behaviors expressive of sociability, anxiety, and sex-role identity (e.g., Lippa, 1976a, b, 1978a, b; Lippa and Mash, 1981). Finally, the low self-monitoring orientation entails considerable stability over time in social behavior (e.g., Lutsky, Woodworth, and Clayton, 1980).

The Dynamics of Social Interaction

The consequences of self-monitoring are also captured in the events of social interaction. To study the interactional dynamics of self-monitoring, Ickes and Barnes (1977) arranged for pairs of strangers to spend time together in a waiting room, ostensibly waiting for an experiment to begin. The researchers then surreptitiously made audio and video recordings of the behavior of both people over a five-minute period. For a schematic representation of this situation, see Figure 3-2.

Ickes and Barnes then had research assistants code and analyse the behavior recorded on the tapes for evidence of the impact of self-monitoring on these spontaneous encounters between strangers. What they found was very revealing. The higher self-monitoring members of the dyads took an active role in the conversations, being inclined to talk first and to initiate subsequent conversation. They also felt, and were seen by their partners to have, a greater need to talk. In addition, the lower self-monitoring members felt that their partners had more control over the direction of the conversations. By adopting this active role, high self-monitoring members of these dyads may have enhanced their ability to influence the course of the interaction and to promote the desired images. Low self-monitoring members, by not becoming

a   Top view

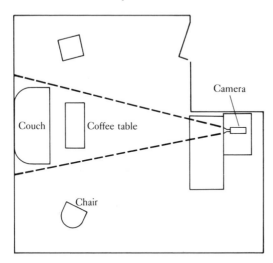

b   Side view

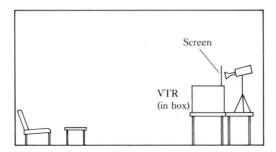

Figure 3-2   Studying the interactional dynamics of self-monitoring (Ickes and Barnes, 1977).

so involved in the pragmatics of these conversations, may have had a greater opportunity to "be themselves," expressing their attitudes and feelings and displaying their traits and dispositions.

The high self-monitoring participants in these conversations seemed particularly concerned with creating and maintaining a smooth and pleasing flow of conversation. Among the "lubricating" techniques they employed is one that would have warmed the heart of Dale Carnegie, author of *How to Win Friends and Influence People* (1936).

The high self-monitors talked about the other person (and other people, as well) instead of talking about themselves. Indeed, as Ickes, Reidhead, and Patterson (1985) have pointed out, first-person singular pronouns (e.g., I, me, my, mine, myself) occur with relatively low frequency in the conversations of high self-monitors. They do not, however, shun the first-person plural pronouns (e.g., we, us, our, ours, ourselves), which suggests that they use these pronouns in an impression-management attempt to, perhaps, ingratiate their partners by implying bonds of quick-and-easy acquaintance.

There are no doubt additional techniques used by high self-monitors in these interactions, including conveying an immediate sense of intimacy (Riggio, Friedman, and DiMatteo, 1981), pacing the conversations (Dabbs, Evans, Hopper, and Purvis, 1980), using humor (Turner, 1980), reciprocating self-disclosures (Shaffer, Smith, and Tomarelli, 1982), and employing "social skills" techniques (Furnham and Capon, 1983; Riggio and Friedman, 1982). For other studies of the interactional dynamics of self-monitoring, see Cappella (1985); Dabbs, Evans, Hopper, and Purvis (1980); Davis (1978); Ickes (1982); Ickes and Barnes (1977, 1978); Ickes, Reidhead, and Patterson (1985); and Miell and LeVoi (1985).

Detecting Self-Monitoring in Others

Often people find themselves wondering whether another person's behaviors truly reflect underlying attitudes and feelings or whether they are impression-management tactics designed to create an image. When a job candidate recites a long list of impressive qualifications, should the personnel manager be impressed or skeptical? When a salesperson says "What good taste you have," should the customer take it as a sincere compliment or as a trick of the sales trade? When the defendant takes the witness stand and pleads innocence, should the jurors believe the testimony and vote to acquit or should they discount it and vote to convict? In order to react appropriately to another person's messages, people must be able to tell truth from deception, accurate self-presentation from strategic (and possibly self-serving) impression management.

One way to read through the masks of impression management encountered in social relationships is to be aware of the self-monitoring status of other people. As it happens, people are able to recognize the self-monitoring propensities of those with whom they are well acquainted (Snyder, 1974). Presumably, they can use this knowledge to interpret and react appropriately to the messages other people send and the overtures they make. With this knowledge, they can look for the attitudes and feelings behind the words and deeds of their low self-monitoring friends and the situational considerations that prompt the public postures of their high self-monitoring associates.

But how is a person to tell when strangers and casual acquaintances engage in self-monitoring? Are there some channels of expression and communication that reveal more than others about a person's true inner self, even when he or she is practicing the art of impression management? Perhaps it would be easier to "read" others (both strangers and friends) if the one managing impressions controls various channels of expression with varying degrees of success. If so, what is communicated by one channel (e.g., the face) might differ from what is communicated by another (e.g., the body). Thus, someone might mask feelings of sadness by putting on a happy face, but might forget—so to speak—to put on a happy body.

Sigmund Freud once observed, "He that has eyes to see and ears to hear may convince himself that no mortal can keep a secret. If his lips are silent, he chatters with his fingertips, betrayal oozes out him at every pore" (Freud, [1905] 1959, p. 94). It is, in fact, possible to rate channels of expression and communication according to how amenable they are to self-monitoring: Some channels of expression are less likely to be controlled and hence reveal more about feelings and dispositions than others. Facial expression is much more easily controlled than are body movements. This point is best demonstrated by the research of Ekman and Friesen (1969, 1974).

In one of their studies, student nurses participated in two interviews (Ekman and Friesen, 1974). In one interview, they frankly and honestly described their reactions to a pleasant film. In the other, they did their best to express positive feelings toward a distinctly unpleasant film. Observers then watched two sets of videotapes of these interviews, one showing only the faces of the nurses, the other showing only their bodies from the neck down. The observers' task was to decide whether each tape segment reflected honesty or deception. The observers, of course, knew nothing about which film the nurses had actually been watching when the tape was made. Thus, they could rely only on nonverbal information to make their judgments.

The results revealed striking differences in the information conveyed by face and body. Observers were considerably more accurate in detecting deceptive self-monitoring when they viewed the body than when they viewed the face. In another study, Ekman and Friesen (1969) showed that it is much easier to tell when psychiatric patients are faking improvement by scrutinizing bodily rather than facial cues. Clearly, then, people ought to focus their attention on the body and other low self-monitoring channels when trying to infer true attitudes, feelings, and dispositions.

In addition, the consistency of people's self-presentations varies across channels of expression: some people manifest greater consistency in some expressive behaviors than others. In search of such differences, Lippa (1976a) collected rich samples of expressive behavior by videotaping people as they taught simple geometric triangles to an imaginary class by drawing the triangles on a large pad of paper on an easel. He then assessed patterns of consistency and inconsistency in the vocal, facial, and bodily channels of expressive behavior. High and low self-monitoring "teachers" differed in the extent to which their cross-channel expressive behavior was consistent. High self-monitoring teachers showed less expressive consistency among voice, face, and body channels when displaying extraversion than did low self-monitoring teachers. The inconsistencies of the high self-monitoring teachers seem to be a result of differential self-monitoring of the various channels. Lippa's high self-monitoring teachers were more likely, as were Ekman and Friesen's nurses (1974) and psychiatric patients (1969), to monitor their facial and vocal expressive behaviors than to monitor their bodily expressive behaviors.

When various channels of communication are monitored differentially, what is expressed and communicated in one channel may contradict what is communicated by another. At times, such differential self-monitoring across channels may be the product of differential ability: Some people may be able to put on a happy face but be unable to put on a happy body. At other times, differential self-monitoring may be the product of neglect: A person may remember to put on a happy face but forget to put on a happy body. And at still other times, inconsistent messages may be the product of deliberate and conscious intent: People may speak pleasantly and congenially to those they dislike but purposely do so in tones of voice that make their true negative feelings perfectly clear.

Orientations to Interpersonal Situations

What we have, then, are two characteristic interpersonal orientations. The high self-monitoring social style, it seems, is one that chronically strives to present the appropriate type of person called for in every situation. People with this orientation are sensitive and responsive to interpersonal cues to situational appropriateness. It is as if they direct their social behavior by answering the question, *"Who does this situation want me to be and how can I be that person?"*

In marked contrast, the low self-monitoring orientation is geared toward displaying a person's true dispositions and attitudes in every situation. People of this type usually are less responsive to situational specifications of behavioral appropriateness. Their social style seems to be predicated on the answer to the question, *"Who am I and how can I be me in this situation?"*

CHAPTER 4

The Self in Action

■

WHAT ACCOUNTS FOR the interpersonal styles of self-monitoring? Why do some people adjust their behavior to fit their social circumstances and others act according to their attitudes, feelings, and dispositions? As researchers have addressed these questions, they have discovered that the motivations behind the self-monitoring orientations are to be found, in large measure, in the *conceptions of self* associated with self-monitoring propensities.

What, then, are the selves of self-monitoring? High self-monitors act as if they possess a repertoire of selves from which they strategically choose the one that best fits their current surroundings, like Lauren of the Calvin Klein ad, who owned a closet full of attitudes from which to choose, and like those about whom William James theorized when he proposed, in 1890, that people display different social selves to different reference groups. Almost a century later, we now have some evidence to back up James' proposition. He was correct, but only for some people—it is only the high self-monitors of the world who, properly speaking, may be said to have not one, but many social selves. For low self-monitors, the public appearances and private realities of the self seem to be one and the same.

Strikingly different ideas about what constitutes a self seem to be closely associated with differences in self-monitoring propensities. It appears that people reveal some fundamental truths about their sense of self and identity in their responses to the items of the Self-Monitoring Scale. They are disclosing their personal "theories" of their natures as individuals and as social beings.

The Pragmatic Self

People high in self-monitoring regard themselves as rather adaptive creatures who shrewdly choose selves that fit their situations. They seem to endorse a rather *pragmatic* conception of self that defines identity in terms of specific social situations and corresponding roles. That is, their sense of self is a flexible "me for this situation." As one person put it in describing his "self": "I am me, the me I am right here and right now." Moreover, high self-monitors often sketch their self-portraits in terms of the roles they play. Another person, when asked the question "Who are you?" answered with this recital of roles: "I am a student, I am a post office employee, I am first violin in a chamber music group, I am quarterback of my fraternity's football team."

These anecdotal descriptions are corroborated by more systematic studies of self and identity. When Ickes, Layden, and Barnes (1978) had students answer the question "Who am I?" they found that high self-monitoring answers were particularly likely to indicate role relationships. In a related investigation, Sampson (1978) presented people with a set of "identity characteristics." Half of them were *externally located* features of a person's surroundings (e.g., "memberships that I have in various groups"). The other half were *internally located* features of identity (e.g., "emotions and feelings"). When people judged the importance of each feature for their "sense of who I am," a clear pattern emerged. High self-monitors considered externally located identity characteristics particularly important and internally located identity features less important to their personal identities.[1] In addition,

---

[1]There is some uncertainty about whether these findings should be interpreted as differences in two separate underlying variables of externally-located features of identity and internally-located features of identity, or whether they should be regarded primarily as relative differences in the importance of social aspects of identity (Cheek and Briggs, 1981; Cheek and Busch, 1982).

they usually explained their actions with reference to situational considerations (e.g., Brockner and Eckenrode, 1978; Furnham, 1981; Gutkin and Suls, 1979; Schneiderman, Webb, Davis, and Thomas, 1981; Snyder, 1976; Snyder and Tanke, 1976).

The high self-monitors are also knowledgeable about the pragmatics of self-presentation. When asked to do so, they can readily report all the behaviors that would convey specific social images and all the situations that would provide opportunities to play particular roles (Snyder and Cantor, 1980). Thus, for instance, even if they don't necessarily regard themselves as adventurous types by nature, they can nonetheless readily report what they could do to create the appearance of possessing the very spirit of adventure.

If the self they know consists of the repertoire of roles they play, and the how and why of playing these roles, how do high self-monitors use this knowledge to plan and guide their actions in social situations? Conceivably, they draw on this library of information to choose self-presentations that fit the dictates of their situations. In a research seminar they could bring to mind an image of the "intellectual" role to help them enact just the right combination of serious, thoughtful, and reserved behaviors. At a cocktail party following the seminar, they could borrow from their understanding of the "extraverted" role to create a mix of friendly, sociable, and outgoing behaviors blended to the requirements of that situation.

Precisely how high self-monitors use such social knowledge is not yet known. One speculation is that, when confronted with the task of choosing actions in social situations, high self-monitors construct a mental image of the ideal person (either a specific example—perhaps a friend or acquaintance—or a generalized image) for the situation at hand. This image, and the information it offers, may provide a "script" (Schank and Abelson, 1977) or a "plan" (Miller, Galanter, and Pribram, 1960) to follow. It is, so to speak, as if the high self-monitor puts himself or herself "into the picture," becoming the imagined person.

The Principled Self

Some strikingly different ideas about the self are harbored by people low in self-monitoring. They (the ones who claim that "I would not change my opinions [or the way I do things] in order to please someone or win their favor") seem to cherish images of themselves as rather principled beings who value congruence between "who they think they are" and "what they try to do." They seem to be endorsing a rather *principled* conception of self that defines identity in terms of inner characteristics and personal attributes. Theirs is a single, unified, coherent identity expressed in consistent fashion from situation to situation. They feel that they must not compromise their identities for other people and should not bend to the will of circumstance. Their sense of self seems to be an enduring and a continuing "me for all times and places" that does not vary from role to role and from situation to situation.

Indeed, the sense of self conveyed by low self-monitors typically is cast in terms of stable traits, enduring dispositions, and other identity characteristics thought to reside within people (e.g., Sampson, 1978). For example, as one person said of her "self": "I am friendly, I am even-tempered, I am reliable, I am a liberal." Moreover, they also tend to explain their behavior as internally motivated (Brockner and Eckenrode, 1978; Furnham, 1981; Gutkin and Suls, 1979; Schneiderman, Webb, Davis, and Thomas, 1981; Snyder, 1976; Snyder and Tanke, 1976).

People low in self-monitoring also possess very rich and accessible knowledge of themselves. They are particularly adept at conveying detailed reports of their characteristic dispositions in a wide variety of domains of identity (Snyder and Cantor, 1980). Those who regard themselves as, say, creative types can readily list all the ways they are creative and all the situations in which they display their creative natures. The precise form of their knowledge remains to be identified, perhaps with techniques useful in other studies of cognitive aspects of the self (e.g., Greenwald, 1981; Markus, 1980; Rogers, 1981).

This self-knowledge may be of considerable utility to low self-monitors in their continuing efforts to choose words and deeds that accurately reflect their underlying beliefs, attitudes, and dispositions. Thus, at parties low self-monitors may guide their behavior by their self-images in the domain of sociability. A low self-monitor who is typically shy may engage in quiet conversations at a party. One who is characteristically gregarious may be the life of the party.

The precise mechanics of how low self-monitors use these images of their characteristic selves are yet to be specified. Perhaps, like their high self-monitoring counterparts, they work within the guidelines of scenarios. However, rather than turning to an image of how someone else would handle the situation, they may draw on an enduring self-image of how they would characteristically cope with such a situation. These self-images may be what allow them to "be themselves" in the situation at hand.

The Pragmatic Self and the Principled Self in Action

These conceptions of self are ones that fit well with the self-monitoring propensities associated with them. High self-monitors conceive of themselves as rather flexible and pragmatic types; indeed, they do much in the way of situation-to-situation fashioning of the selves they present to others. Low self-monitors conceive of themselves as rather consistent and principled; their actions, in fact, typically do reflect their attitudes, feelings, and dispositions. Both types seem to live up to the dictates of their own particular conceptions of self.

Clearly, the self experienced by those low in self-monitoring is much more in keeping with traditional assumptions about the self—a coherent, enduring, unified, and traitlike sense of "me for all times and places and relationships." But, is it really a "principled" self? If we take them at their word, low self-monitors regard themselves as committed by their beliefs to act in certain ways ("I can only argue for ideas which I already believe") and averse to saying or doing anything for self-serving or strategic reasons ("At parties and social gatherings, I do not attempt to do or say things that others will like"). That is, as their reactions to the items of the Self-Monitoring Scale suggest, they seem to regard themselves as people of principle who would never contradict their attitudes or abandon their values for the sake of expediency or social gain. And, in some sense, the behavioral consistencies they display suggest that their attitudes and personalities actually do operate as guiding principles, exerting a directive influence on their actions. Nevertheless, to characterize the low self-monitoring sense of self as principled is not to confer on it any special ethical or moral status. Indeed, as we shall see in Chapter 14, there are no reasons to regard either self-monitoring type as inherently better or worse than the other.

In the context of traditional assumptions about the self, the high self-monitor must seem almost to lack a "self." However, when evaluated against the standards of their own definitions of the self, they are very much in possession of selves. However, the selves they possess seem to be rather pragmatic and flexible ones, bound up in the network of social circumstances and interpersonal roles that define their lives.

It is not that the low self-monitoring self is completely unknown to high self-monitors. There are times when, in keeping with the pragmatic dictates of their current situations, they can and do display some of the self-relevant phenomena typically seen in low self-monitors. For example, they are quite able to attribute responsibility to the self (e.g., Schneiderman, Webb, Davis, and Thomas, 1981) and to display pronounced consistency between attitudes and behaviors (e.g., Snyder and Kendzierski, 1982a) when such typically low self-monitoring habits happen to be situationally appropriate. Evidently, there are times when a pragmatic conception of self calls for adopting a low self-monitoring posture.

It is apparent that the intimate bonds between self-monitoring and conceptions of self are not accidental ones. To the contrary, these links seem to be products of motivated and strategic activities. High self-monitors are directly involved in designing social worlds in which it is easy for them to act appropriately. Low self-monitors, too, are actively involved in constructing worlds in which it is easy for them to act in accord with their attitudes, feelings, and dispositions.

Prominent among the strategies people use for structuring their social worlds is the act of choosing the situations, surroundings, and circumstances in which they live. People, it seems, systematically and purposely choose to enter and spend time in social situations particularly conducive to their self-monitoring propensities. What, then, are the features of these social situations? The high self-monitoring orientation ought to be facilitated in settings that offer clearly defined cues for people to use in fitting their self-presentations to their situations. To use a theatrical metaphor, high self-monitors ought to choose situations that have good scripts with explicit stage directions. By contrast, the low self-monitoring orientation ought to be facilitated in settings that permit people to "be themselves." Low self-monitors ought to choose, whenever possible, to spend time in situations where it will be appropriate to express their own attitudes, feelings, and dispositions.

How do people gravitate toward social situations conducive to their self-monitoring propensities? One way to find out is to look at what people do when faced with two competing social situations, only one of which they can choose. For instance, when someone arrives at a party and discovers two distinct groups of people already involved in conversation, unless this partygoer prefers to stand alone, he or she must decide which conversational group to join. That is, the two conversations constitute two social situations between which the partygoer must choose.

The partygoer's dilemma can be represented by maps, such as the one in Figure 4-1 which depicts two groups of three people each engaged in conversation at a cocktail party. One conversation has a high clarity of definition (three similar people; here, a theater lover, a music lover, an art lover). The other conversation has low clarity of definition (three people of divergent type; here, a pacifist, a militarist, a shy person). When people "join" one of these two conversational situations by placing themselves on the map, their self-monitoring propensities come into action.

When faced with such choices of situations in an experiment (Snyder and Harkness, 1984), high self-monitors were clearly drawn toward the conversation with high clarity of definition. Here, the common interests of the other members provided a clear definition of the situation and how to handle it. For example, with the theater lover, the art lover, and the music lover, someone high in self-monitoring could affect a highly cultured attitude. High self-monitors stayed away from the conversation with low clarity of definition. There, the diverging interests of the other members provided conflicting specifications of how to be an effective participant in the conversation. Should they side with the pacifist and risk offending the militarist? Should they try to draw the shy person out of his or her shell, perhaps ending up with a stiff, awkward, and unsatisfying conversation? By avoiding situations that might pull them in more than one self-presentational direction, high self-monitors escape the horns of such dilemmas.

The preference for highly structured situations may, at times, prompt high self-monitors to try to restructure and transform their situations. Thus, when asked what would make a prospective job situation more appealing to them, high self-monitors in one experiment indicated that they would like their role to be more clearly defined (Snyder and Gangestad, 1982). This preference for clearly defined behavioral guidelines may also reflect a general preference for the systematic rather than the spontaneous, the scheduled rather than the unplanned, and for decision rather than impulse (Mill, 1984).

By contrast, low self-monitors confronted with the same choices of conversational situations were quite insensitive to the clarity of defini-

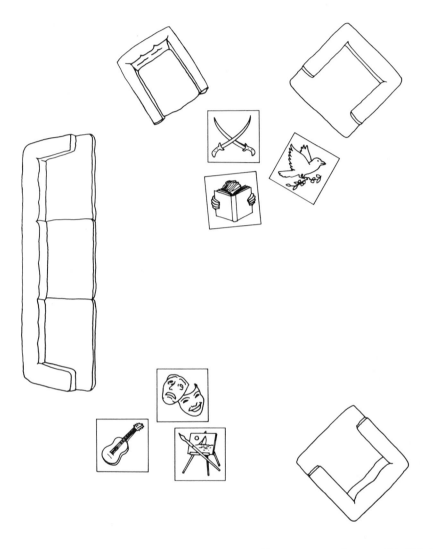

Figure 4-1   Choosing between situations: Two conversations, only one of which the person can join (Snyder and Harkness, 1984).

tion of the conversations. Instead, they entered the situation where there was someone with whom they identified. Thus, for instance, those who regarded themselves as pacifists were drawn to the group containing another pacifist, even though that situation might occasion some conflict with the militarist. Presumably, choices that put them in touch with a kindred spirit make it easy for them to say and do things that reflect their own attitudes and values.

The importance of such choices for low self-monitors is highlighted in another study, in which students joined groups devoted to discussions of issues of current concern (Snyder and Kendzierski, 1982*b*). Low self-monitoring students accepted these invitations if the topic for discussion was in line with their own attitudes. Thus, they were eager to join a group devoted to discussing the benefits of affirmative action for women and minorities if they personally favored affirmative action. If they were opposed to such policies, they had little interest in a group with that topic on its agenda. These choices may also shed some light on the origins of the consistency between attitudes and actions typical of the low self-monitoring orientation. If people habitually gravitate toward situations that encourage them to act on their attitudes, and studiously avoid situations that dispose them to betray these attitudes, they may come to live in worlds that help them turn private attitudes into public behavior.

But what about the high self-monitoring students? What were they doing while their low self-monitoring peers were approaching attitude-congruent and avoiding attitude-incongruent situations? Whether high self-monitoring students accepted or declined the invitations in no way reflected their general attitudes toward the issue on the agenda for discussion. Rather, they were most sensitive to the role appropriateness of their membership in the groups. For whatever reasons, high self-monitoring women regarded membership in a group devoted to the benefits of affirmative action as more appropriate for their gender role than did high self-monitoring men. One consequence of choosing a situation on the basis of role-related considerations may be that high self-monitors display substantial amounts of role-appropriateness in their social behavior. Gender roles, demographic roles, occupational roles, familial roles, and status roles may perform the same function for high self-monitors as attitudes and dispositions do for low self-monitors—serving as sources of regularities and consistencies in social behavior.

Consequences of the Self in Action

The consequences of people's choices of situations may be considerable and profound. To the extent that high self-monitors gravitate toward situations with clearly defined roles for them to play, they provide themselves with settings ideally suited for acting out their pragmatic conceptions of self and for maintaining their chameleonlike behavioral orientation. To the extent that low self-monitors gravitate toward situations that call for their attitudes and personalities, they will provide themselves with settings that allow them to act on their principled conceptions of self and to maintain their consistency-seeking behavioral orientation.

That people choose to operate in conducive settings may suggest that the manifestations of self-monitoring are, to some extent, specific to particular life domains. Thus, as an example, some people high in self-monitoring may structure their lives so that they can exercise their considerable self-presentational skills in their professional dealings. But, these same people may organize their personal affairs so that the roles they take on with family and friends are ones that entail expressions of their own attitudes, preferences, and values. Similarly, some people low in self-monitoring may at times enter situations that call for the playing of roles. However, they may only enter those situations that call on them to play roles that happen to fit their own dispositions. Clearly, then, a full understanding of people's choices of situations must include specifications of when and why they are motivated to enter not only situations conducive to their own self-monitoring propensity, but also those conducive to the other self-monitoring style.

Some readers may sense that this analysis of motivated activities constitutes a shift in emphasis within self-monitoring theory. Some may have thought strategic activities to be the exclusive province of the high self-monitoring orientation. Yet, it now appears that people of both types are actively engaged in choosing their situations. What is different is the motivation behind these strategic activities. High self-monitors choose their social situations in the service of a pragmatic sense of self. Low self-monitors select their situations in the service of a principled sense of self.

What this means is that although the behavior of low self-monitors typically reflects their personal attributes, they are not amotivational. To the contrary, the consistency between their attitudes and actions seems to be as much the product of motivated activities as is the high self-monitoring orientation. Indeed, just as it may take a considerable amount of "stage work" to convey just the right image, it may take a considerable amount of careful choosing of situations to display true inner beliefs and feelings.

When considering the motivational nature of the low self-monitoring orientation, it may be worth considering the possibility that much of their quest for consistency has a self-presentational element to it. Greenwald and Breckler (1985) have suggested that there may be more than one target for self-presentation. There is, of course, an outer audience composed of other people. But, there also may be an inner audience for self-presentation (namely, oneself) that evaluates presentations with reference to personal standards. In this regard, Greenwald and Breckler (1985) have suggested that, just as the impression-management activities of high self-monitors may be regarded as presentations to outer audiences, the consistency-seeking behavior of low self-monitors may be regarded as presentations to this inner audience.

If these proposals are correct, then some new insights into the low self-monitoring orientation may be forthcoming. Much as it may seem, at an intuitive level, that there is something automatic, unreflective, and unconscious about expressing one's attitudes and "just being oneself," it really may be that these features of the low self-monitoring orientation demand as much deliberate, intentional, and motivational planning as the impression-managing activities of the high self-monitoring orientation.

Does this emphasis on motivated activities necessitate an alteration in self-monitoring theory? Typically, the social behavior of low self-monitors is highly responsive to dispositional influences and only minimally responsive to situational considerations. Nevertheless, the fact that they actively structure their social situations suggests that low self-monitors are not totally unconcerned with situational considerations. Rather, they are attentive to those situational considerations that permit them to size up the potential of social situations to allow them to "be themselves." Once in social situations, they then respond to their own dispositions.

Self-monitoring may not be the only domain in which conceptions of self guide and direct people's choices of situations. Consider, as just one example, the case of self-conceptions associated with Machiavellianism (Christie and Geis, 1970). What kinds of situations would be particularly conducive for people who conceive of themselves as

Machiavellians? Machiavellians are most successful at manipulation in face-to-face situations where they have some latitude for improvising tactics to suit their targets and goals and where they can use emotional arousal to distract their targets and make them more susceptible to control (Christie and Geis, 1970). Perhaps Machiavellians systematically choose situations with these features and attempt to inject these features into situations that lack them. As a consequence of acting on their situations, Machiavellians may come to live in settings conducive to Machiavellian conceptions of self.

Indeed, choosing situations may be one of the primary vehicles by which conceptions of self become embodied in social behavior. There will be much more said on this topic in Chapters 15 and 16. Moreover, choices of situations may be reinforced by tendencies to look at social situations through spectacles tinted by one's self-conceptions (e.g., Battistich, Assor, Messé, and Aronoff, 1985). For example, when people expect to interact with another person, those who think of themselves as dominant tend to focus on assertiveness-related characteristics in the other person; those who see themselves as dependent, however, tend to focus on affiliativeness-related behaviors in the other person (Battistich and Aronoff, 1985). As a result, people may see primarily those features of their social worlds that support their self-conceptions. Working together, these cognitive-perceptual activities and choices of situations may defend and preserve people's conceptions of self and the social orientations associated with them.

Thus, returning to self-monitoring, people actually may create worlds through the use of strategic activities that support and perpetuate their self-monitoring propensities. They may come to live in worlds that allow high self-monitors to continue to be high in self-monitoring and low self-monitors to continue to be low in self-monitoring. In fact, as we shall see in the next two chapters, these structuring activities may even go so far as to influence the social networks of their friends, acquaintances, and romantic partners.

CHAPTER 5

The Social Worlds
of Self-Monitoring

IT'S A SUNNY summer afternoon. You're trying to decide whether to play tennis—one of your favorite pastimes—with your friend Paul or with your friend Mike. You know that you like Paul more than Mike, but you also know that Mike is a better tennis player than Paul. What do you do? How you solve this dilemma may reflect your approach to friendship.

If you choose Paul, chances are that you choose your friends on the basis of your feelings for them and that you keep the same friends for most of your social activities. If, in addition to playing tennis, some of your favorite leisure pursuits were discussing politics, listening to music, and going to art museums, you probably would prefer the same well-liked friend as a partner for each of these activities. Overall, you probably strive to spend your time with friends who closely resemble you and each other in their general attitudes, values, and personalities.

On the other hand, if you choose Mike, you probably choose your friends on the basis of their skills in particular areas and you are likely to have different partners for different activities. Not only will you choose to play tennis with a particularly good tennis player, but you will choose to discuss politics with a different friend who is an expert on politics, listen to music with another friend who happens to be a music buff, and go to art museums with yet another friend who really knows art. In general, you probably tend to match your friends to activities for which they are well suited as partners for you.

Researchers have discovered that a person's self-monitoring orientation accounts for which approach to choosing friends is adopted. Low self-monitors, who choose to spend time with well-liked friends, tend to live in fairly homogenized social worlds in which contact between friends is made easy by the fact that their friends all tend to be alike. On the other hand, high self-monitors, who choose to spend time with friends who are highly skilled activity partners, tend to live in rather compartmentalized social worlds, choosing certain friends only for certain activities and rarely allowing the different friendships to overlap.

Choosing Friends and Activity Partners

These characterizations are supported by a study in which people made "maps" of their social worlds (Snyder, Gangestad, and Simpson, 1983). To draw these maps, participants made lists of people with whom they regularly spent time and engaged in social activities. They then nominated the one specific activity most typical of their social life in each of several categories. For example, one person specified "going to a fancy French restaurant" for the category "going out to dinner," "playing tennis" for the category "competitive recreational activity," and "going to the ballet" for the category "attending live entertainment."

With the matrix defined by the people and activities they had nominated, these people then drew maps of their social worlds. Specifically, they indicated how likely they would be to choose each person in the matrix as a partner for each activity, and how much they would enjoy each activity with each person. Statistical analyses of these maps revealed considerably more partitioning and segmentation (see Figure 5-1) in the social worlds of high self-monitors and considerably more uniformity and homogeneity in those of low self-monitors.

Typically, high self-monitors chose specific friends for particular activities, and usually only for those activities; clear activity boundaries defined and separated their friendships. In addition, the social lives of high self-monitors often are characterized by great spatial separation and geographical segregation of the actual physical settings

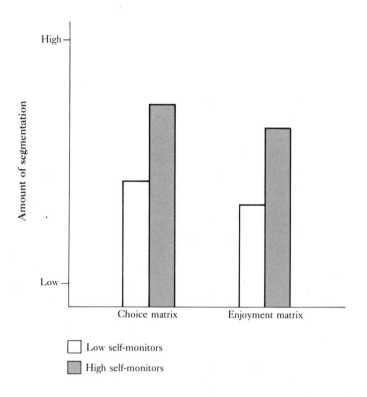

Figure 5-1   Segmentation of social worlds (Snyder, Gangestad, and Simpson, 1983).

in which they interact with their friends and acquaintances (e.g., Zaidman and Snyder, 1983).

The maps of the social worlds of low self-monitors indicated that they were much more likely to retain the same friends for many, and sometimes for most, of their activities. Some of the low self-monitors clearly had a best friend with whom they engaged in many leisure pursuits. Others seemed to belong to a group that did almost everything together. This pattern of segmentation for high self-monitors and homogeneity for low self-monitors was true for both women and men.

How do these social worlds come about? How do people actually structure their social lives? The considerations people invoke when deciding who they like and when choosing friends as activity partners help answer these questions. High self-monitors appear to like those with similar activity preferences, whereas low self-monitors seem to like those with similar attitudes (Jamieson, Lydon, and Zanna, 1984). Moreover, when it comes to choosing between competing leisure-time activities, high self-monitors choose to spend time with people who are "specialists" in the activity at hand, and low self-monitors give their time to people they like a lot.

One way to watch these choices being made is to present people with choices in the form, "playing tennis with _____" (someone who is a particularly good tennis player but only average in general likability) or "going sailing with _____" (someone else who is very high in general likability but only average in sailing ability). In one study, college students made a series of choices of leisure-time activities that directly pitted the partner's specific expertise against his or her general likability (Snyder, Gangestad, and Simpson, 1983). Fully 80 percent of high self-monitoring students chose friends as activity partners on the basis of their skill in the activity at hand (choosing, for example, to play tennis with the expert tennis player). In contrast, only 33 percent of low self-monitoring students used this strategy. Within the same set of choices, as many as 67 percent of the low self-monitoring students chose activity partners on the basis of their global likability (choosing, for example, to go sailing with the well-liked friend); as few as 20 percent of those high in self-monitoring did so. Finally, there were no differences in the choices of women and men.

Structuring a Social World

Although choices of friends contribute substantially to compartmentalization and homogeneity in friendship networks, there are no doubt additional tactics involved in the creation of social worlds. Several sets of tactics are suggested by Goffman's (1959) analysis of *audience segregation* and *front*.

Audience Segregation   Audience segregation refers to efforts to insure that those to whom people have presented one image will not see them presenting an incongruent image to others. The situation-to-situation fashioning of images typical of high self-monitors may require a considerable amount of audience segregation. High self-monitors simply may be unwilling to let one set of acquaintances see them as they are with other acquaintances. For instance, students who present very different images to their co-workers and their schoolmates might avoid seeing members of both groups together, when they might be called upon to act out two incompatible roles. This form of audience segregation may require geographical separation of the different sets of audiences. In fact, there is some evidence that high self-monitors are particularly concerned with maintaining a wider spatial realm as a context for their friendships (Zaidman and Snyder, 1983).

Low self-monitors, on the other hand, might initiate and encourage contact between members from different areas of their lives. They may have little resistance to mixing their audiences. They may, for example, be perfectly willing to invite their employees into their homes where these employees will see the usually authoritative and domineering boss being kind and submissive in family matters.

Front   Front consists of aspects of the interaction setting (e.g., scenery, stage props) and features of personal appearance (e.g., clothing, jewelry, cosmetics). Such items may function as symbols of the self and convey images of the self to other people (cf. Schlenker, 1980). Carefully selected items of front may help convey just the right image for any social occasion. As it happens, high self-monitors are often seen as being particularly concerned with their outer appearances (e.g., Glick, 1983). They are very aware of the messages projected by clothing and personal effects, and they choose these items of front according to their strategic value in controlling the images they project in social situations (e.g., Davis and Lennon, 1985). They also may be avid readers of magazines (e.g., *Gentlemen's Quarterly*) and books (e.g., *Dress for Success*) geared to these concerns. Low self-monitors may make their choices of front, instead, on the basis of abiding tastes and preferences. Thus, when deciding whether to wear the suit or the sportcoat, a high self-monitoring man might wonder which outfit would better suit the occasion, whereas one low in self-monitoring might think about which outfit he happens to like better.

In addition, when furnishing and decorating their living and working spaces, high self-monitors might be expected to choose items on the basis of the messages they convey. High self-monitoring doctors, lawyers, and professors may equip their offices with all of the symbols, trappings, and icons of their professions (to make them look the way doctors' offices or lawyers' offices or professors' offices should look).

Low self-monitoring members of these same professions may decorate their offices with items that reflect their own, more idiosyncratic likes and desires.

As a result of these choices, the sets of clothing, books, records, magazines, and artifacts owned by high self-monitors may be rather eclectic and heterogeneous. After all, the quest to forever present "correct" images requires a rather large and diverse set of costumes, props, and other accessories. Relatively speaking, the collections of such items possessed by low self-monitors may be rather homogeneous and internally coherent. There is some evidence that this is so, at least within the domain of clothing. The wardrobes of high self-monitoring men contain more different items of clothing in more different styles than those of low self-monitoring men (for whatever reason, this phenomenon appears to be restricted to the wardrobes of men; Zaidman and Snyder, 1983).

Styles of Friendship

What we are seeing is that the high self-monitoring social world is one of considerable partitioning, differentiation, and segmentation in which friends are chosen on the basis of special qualifications for the roles they play. What this means can perhaps be stated best by those who live in this kind of social world. As one high self-monitoring man explained, after choosing one friend over another as an activity partner: "Bob may be a better friend, but he's a lousy basketball player" (Snyder, Gangestad, and Simpson, 1983). In a more general observation about structuring a social world, a high self-monitoring woman explained: "I guess I'm fairly aware of matching certain people with certain activities. Now that I think of it, I've rarely engaged in some of my favorite activities with some of my best friends" (Snyder, Gangestad, and Simpson, 1983).

No doubt segmentation makes it easier to maintain the high self-monitoring interpersonal style and to take on different identities with different social partners. A pattern of segregation will also minimize the overlapping of friendships, effectively guaranteeing that those who have seen one image (e.g., the jock) will not be exposed to a contrary image (e.g., the intellectual). In this way, segregation preserves the credibility of the social performances of high self-monitors.

In addition, if friends are chosen for their unique qualifications as activity partners, leisure-time activities will provide added opportunities to act out the high self-monitoring orientation. A highly skilled activity partner will help someone appear to be the "ideal" performer. After all, it is much easier for someone to play a good game of tennis with a skilled partner who can provide opportunities to excel on the tennis court. As one high self-monitoring tennis player observed: "When I want to play tennis, I select a partner who can challenge me. There's nothing worse than having to play with someone who hits the ball everywhere except over the net" (Snyder, Gangestad, and Simpson, 1983).

In such carefully segmented social worlds, are there no particularly *close* friends? Does the term "close friend" even have meaning for people who choose to live this way? It is said that the pianist Liberace once claimed to have sent party invitations to 5000 of his closest and dearest friends (Duck, 1983). Without presuming to question the closeness of Liberace's 5000 friends (and without presuming to diagnose his self-monitoring status), one wonders whether high self-monitors apply the term "close friend" so inclusively as to embrace very large numbers of acquaintances.

Based on studies of their friendship worlds, high self-monitors do seem to have close friends who span diverse activity domains and who perform multiple social roles. Moreover, these close friends are themselves relatively high in self-monitoring and appreciably higher in self-monitoring than casual friends are (see Figure 5-2; Snyder, Simpson, and Smith, 1984). Perhaps those high in self-monitoring are only willing to be seen in all their diversity by others who share an appreciation of diversity and the functions it serves.

The homogeneous nature of the low self-monitoring social world can also be conveyed by firsthand accounts. As one low self-monitoring woman explained, when reflecting on her choice of a friend as an activity partner: "Jan's my best friend. Besides, she's the most fun to be around, whatever the activity" (Snyder, Gangestad, and Simpson, 1983). As a more general observation, a low self-monitoring man commented, after being interviewed about the structure of his social world: "When you kept asking me those questions comparing people and activities, I kept thinking 'Why does he keep giving me the activity with the person? I can make my decision by knowing only the people'" (Snyder, Gangestad, and Simpson, 1983).

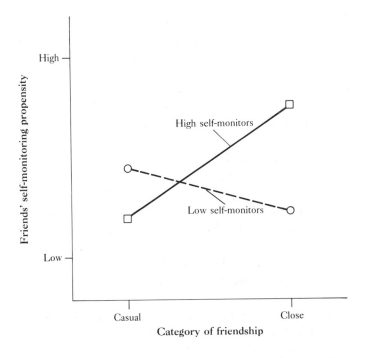

Figure 5-2   Choosing close and casual friends (Snyder, Simpson, and Smith, 1984).

One consequence of such a basis for choosing friends may be a social world particularly conducive to the low self-monitoring social style. In worlds where friends are chosen for their global similarity and their general likability, people will find a receptive and supportive climate for "being themselves," for revealing their attitudes and dispositions in the company of others of like attitudes and dispositions. One low self-monitoring person put it this way: "When I engage in an activity, I want to be with someone I feel comfortable with. Usually, my closest friends fill this role. Besides, it's the people who define the activity, I mean whether it's fun or boring, memorable or forgettable, isn't it?" (Snyder, Gangestad, and Simpson, 1983). Perhaps for these reasons the close friends of low self-monitors also tend to be low in self-monitoring, much more so than their casual friends (see Figure 5-2; Snyder, Simpson, and Smith, 1984).

How people choose their friends may influence the emotional reactions that occur when friendships end. If low self-monitors spend large portions of their time with the same few people, their lives should be more disrupted, and they should be more distressed, by the departure of a member of their social worlds (cf. Berscheid, 1983; Cairns, 1966). At the same time, by confining their interactions with any one person to a relatively small range of activities, high self-monitors may not develop particularly strong attachments to members of their social worlds. Thus, they may not be so vulnerable to the departure of any one activity partner.

Furthermore, it ought to be easier for high self-monitors to find replacement partners (they need only find partners for limited activity-specific purposes) than for low self-monitors (who need to find partners who can function across diverse domains). Conceivably, each pattern of choice should serve the motivational concerns of those who adopt it. Hence, people of either self-monitoring type may be equally satisfied with their friendships, even though the cost of the low self-monitoring orientation may be more disruptive distress and the price of the high self-monitoring orientation may be a lack of close attachment in their social lives.

The Meaning of Friendship

Knowing about the social worlds of self-monitoring may also tell us something about the nature of friendship itself. Clearly, to be a friend of someone high in self-monitoring is an experience considerably different from being a friend of someone low in self-monitoring. A friend in a high self-monitoring world is "on call" for certain activities and, often, only for those activities. To be such a friend is to be valued for your skilled performance in the activity at hand, not the mere pleasure of your company. Presumably, were your skills to diminish, you would no longer be invited to be an activity partner.

On the other hand, a friend in a low self-monitoring social world shares in a wide variety of activities. To be such a friend is to have your presence as an activity partner matter more than your performance of the activity itself. Here, it is the overall similarity and compatibility of your personality that makes you generally well liked. Presumably, as long as you continue to be generally similar and hence well liked, you will be sought out for the pleasure of your company.

In fact, people high and low in self-monitoring operate with rather different *conceptions* of the meaning of friendship. For high self-monitors, friendship is defined in terms of properties of the activities they engage in with others; friends are evaluated in terms of their suitability as partners for specific activities. For them, friendship is a relatively activity-based phenomenon: A friend is someone with whom you do this or that. But, for low self-monitors, friendship seems to be defined in terms of properties of the people with whom they spend time; friends are evaluated on the basis of their similarity to the self and the affection they inspire. For them, friendship is a relatively affect-based phenomenon: A friend is someone who likes you and whom you like.

Research has confirmed these contrasting conceptions of friendship. In one study, people wrote essays characterizing a relationship with a person they considered to be a friend (Snyder and Smith, 1984; in press). High self-monitoring essay writers conceptualized friendship in terms of an *activity-based* orientation, an animated and emphatic tone to the interactions, a somewhat shallow sense of friendship, little conception of compatibility beyond the present context, and little conception of nurturance. Low self-monitoring essay writers conceptualized friendship in terms of an *affect-based* orientation, a definite sense of depth of friendship, considerable conception of compatibility and endurance beyond the present context, and much evidence of a conception of nurturance and sympathy within friendship. Moreover, for them, true friendship seems to be more important as an intrinsic value (DeBono and Omoto, 1984).

The reader may sense something of a paradox here. The high self-monitoring social style is particularly oriented toward others; witness the pronounced tendency to look to the behavior of others for cues to the situational appropriateness of their behavior. Yet, within their friendship worlds these people seem to have relatively little investment in others. Rather than reaching out to others, they seem to build barriers by segmenting and compartmentalizing their friendships. Similarly, the low self-monitoring orientation emphasizes looking inward to attitudes and dispositions as guides for behavior, rather than turning to others for cues. Yet, these people practice a friendship orientation characterized by a great investment of both time and emotion in other people.

As with so many paradoxes, this one may be only apparent. Why do some people who are otherwise so "social" in their orientation avoid close bonds of friendship? Perhaps their responsiveness to interpersonal considerations and their compartmentalization of friendships both operate in the service of the same goal, that of being able to act like a different person in different situations and with different partners. And other people who are generally so attuned to themselves in guiding their behavior but who invest so much in specific friendships may do so in the service of a common goal. Both a dispositionally-guided behavioral orientation and the formation of close attachments to friends may maximize opportunities for these people to "be themselves," to display their own attitudes, traits, and dispositions.

These contrasting orientations toward friendship—activity-based and affect-based—suggest taking a new look at an old assumption, the assumption that *who approaches whom* is intimately related to *who likes whom* (cf. Berscheid, 1985). As intuitively plausible as it may be to assume that people associate with others whom they like, this assumption may be made much more appropriately for low self-monitors (who do choose friends on the basis of general feelings of liking) than for high self-monitors (who, instead, choose friends on the basis of specific skills and expertise). This is not to say that high self-monitors don't like the people they spend time with. Even though liking is not their primary consideration in choosing their friends, they nonetheless may genuinely like those who serve as skilled activity partners, those who help them play their preferred roles, and those who help them live the way they seek to live. Whether this liking is of the same order as that experienced by low self-monitors remains to be seen.

Finally, these differing orientations toward friends and friendships just may substantiate a typology proposed by Aristotle in the Nichomachean ethics. Among the types of friendships he described was one entered into because of the sheer pleasure derived from being with someone of that overall character. Another type of friendship he described was one entered into because of the resources and skills of the other person. The first of these friendships, referred to by Aristotle as *friendships of pleasure,* seems to have much in common with those of people low in self-monitoring. The second of these friendships, which Aristotle referred to as *friendships of utility,* seems to have much in common with those of people high in self-monitoring. If so, Aristotle was only partially correct when he asserted that "some people are called good in respect to a state of character, others in respect to an activity, so too in the case of friendship" (1968, p. 1063).

Knowing what we do about self-monitoring, we can now say that it is low self-monitors for whom issues of "character," and high self-monitors for whom matters of "activity," are paramount when contracting and maintaining friendships.

CHAPTER 6

The World of
Romantic Relationships

■

WHAT IS IT that makes your life meaningful? For most people, romantic partners figure prominently in their answers to this question (Klinger, 1977). Romantic relationships have—to say the very least— enormous impact on the lives of most people (Bachman and Johnston, 1979). Think of how much time people spend in romantic relationships and how many activities they share with romantic partners. Think of the wide range of roles played by romantic partners and the many essential functions they serve.

Researchers who have explored the world of romantic relationships have discovered two different and contrasting orientations toward romantic relationships. Low self-monitors tend to prefer to establish relatively close and exclusive romantic relationships; high self-monitors tend to prefer to maintain less close and relatively nonexclusive ones.

The strategies that people adopt toward "investing" themselves in romantic relationships reveal these differing orientations. They include: the considerations that people invoke when initiating dating relationships; whether people take a "committed" or an "uncommitted" stance in their dating relationships; and whether people adopt a "restricted" or an "unrestricted" approach toward sexual relations with different partners.

Dating Relationships

Any romantic relationship must have a starting point. Typically, one person asks another out on a "first date." As common as that experience may be, people differ greatly in how they decide who to ask out. High self-monitors place relatively great emphasis on, and therefore pay considerable attention to, exterior appearances when choosing whether or not to date someone. On the other hand, low self-monitors place relatively great emphasis on, and are therefore sensitive to, the interior qualities of their prospective dating partners.

The Initiation of Dating Relationships   In one study of dating relationships, college-aged men who were not committed to a steady dating partner studied file folders that contained photographs and personality sketches of potential dating partners. Each of these potential partners was within a generally acceptable range of physical attractiveness and desirability of personality. As the men worked their way through the file folders, the researchers recorded how much time each man spent examining the information about physical appearances and how much time he spent studying information about personalities, attitudes, and preferences. (For details on this experiment, see Snyder, Berscheid, and Glick, 1985.)

The high self-monitoring men allocated their attention to physical appearances (see Figure 6-1). They spent proportionately more time than low self-monitoring men inspecting the photographs of their potential partners. Low self-monitoring men devoted their attention to the psychological characteristics of their potential partners. They spent proportionately more time than high self-monitoring men studying the personality sketches.

In a related experiment, other college-aged men chose between two prospective dating partners (Snyder and Simpson, 1984a). One had a physically attractive exterior but, as revealed in the file, a rather moody, withdrawn, and self-centered personality. The other was much less attractive on the outside (and, in fact, was of below average physical attractiveness) but had, as revealed in the file, a highly desirable (sociable, outgoing, and open) personality. Here, when forced to sacrifice one feature for another, 69 percent of the high self-monitoring men chose the physically more attractive date even though she possessed a relatively undesirable personality. In contrast, 81 percent of

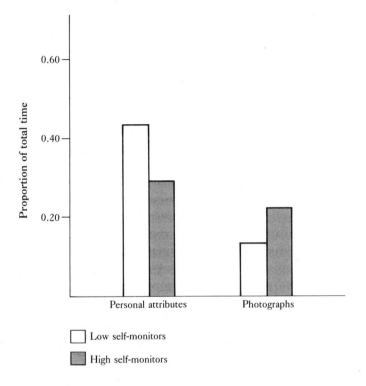

Figure 6-1   Attention to information about potential dating partners (Snyder, Berscheid, and Glick, 1985).

the low self-monitoring men preferred the partner with the sterling inner qualities, even though this desirable personality was housed in an unattractive exterior.

Taken together, these two studies suggest that people initiate romantic relationships on very different bases—exterior appearances for high self-monitors and interior qualities for low self-monitors. Incidentally, these studies were conducted with men because, at least at the time of the studies, males still predominantly initiated dates in our society. It remains to be seen what would happen if the roles were reversed and women were allowed to scrutinize information about looks and personality of prospective dates. Just about all of the other studies described in this chapter have involved both men and women and have yielded virtually identical findings about the role of self-monitoring in the romantic relationships of men and women.

How people initiate romantic relationships is revealed further in the ways people "advertise" for romantic partners. In recent years, our society has witnessed the growth and development of a new social phenomenon—personal advertisements. In ever increasing numbers, people in search of companionship and love are taking out advertisements in magazines and newspapers that make explicit their wants and needs in romantic partners. So widespread are personals that, in some urban areas with large concentrations of young professionals, there are even agencies that, for a fee, offer help in writing, placing, and answering personal advertisements. Advice and counsel on the phenomenon is also available in self-help books (e.g., Block, 1983).

Who are the people behind the personals? What do they want from them? Answers to questionnaires sent to advertisers (both men and women) in the personals section of a local weekly newspaper point to the role of self-monitoring in advertising for love and companionship (Omoto, DeBono, and Snyder, 1985). In keeping with their concerns with physical attractiveness, high self-monitoring advertisers are most likely to request a photograph of potential partners and to write ads with a heavy emphasis on considerations of physical appearance. They also tend to advertise for short-term and casual relationships. By contrast, low self-monitoring advertisers are most likely to write ads that focus on the personalities they desire in prospective partners. They tend to advertise for long-term relationships of a rather serious nature. Moreover, the same considerations are invoked in deciding to *answer* the personals. Advertisements focusing on appearance are particularly likely to arouse the desires of high self-monitoring readers, whereas those devoted to matters of personality are most likely to spark the interests of low self-monitoring readers (Omoto, DeBono, and Snyder, 1985).

These orientations toward romantic relationships are not limited to the initial choice of partner. They also determine the choice of the situation in which the relationship is conducted. High self-monitors choose situations with romantic connotations when their partners have physically attractive exterior appearances; low self-monitors choose romantic situations when their partners possess personally desirable inner attributes (Glick, 1984). In either case, as Glick has suggested, people may be seeking to steer their relationships on the course toward romance. The romantic relationships that ensue may be ones that provide different rewards, including perhaps the pleasure of being associated with an attractive partner (and the esteem it may bring from others; Sigall and Landy, 1973) for high self-monitors and the satisfaction of being involved with someone with a compatible personality for low self-monitors.

The bases on which relationships are founded may have implications for the degrees of closeness of the relationships. That is, if someone desires a close relationship, it is important to know what the other person is like, what his or her inner qualities are, and how well these personal characteristics will mesh with one's own. If, however, a close relationship is not so important, then it is only necessary to find out if the potential partner possesses the few characteristics necessary for satisfactory interaction in the limited, restricted situations in which interaction is anticipated.

Structural Features of Dating Relationships   It would seem that the dating relationships initiated by low self-monitors would have greater potential for closeness than those of high self-monitors. And, in fact, this speculation is borne out by investigations of the dating lives of college-aged men and women (Snyder and Simpson, 1984a). High self-monitoring men and women tend to adopt an "uncommitted" orientation toward dating relationships. They say they are quite willing to engage in social activities with other dating partners. When given the chance to terminate a current relation and form a new one, they indicate that they are quite willing to do that, too. Indeed, their recent dating histories (see Table 6-1) reflect this uncommitted orientation. These high self-monitoring students usually have dated steady, exclusive partners for rather short periods of time (on average, barely 12 months) and, if not involved in a steady relationship, they have dated a relatively large number of different partners (on average, about six) in the preceding 12 months (see also, Leone, 1979). Moreover, when queried about their dating relationships, high self-monitors acknowledge that their partners invest more time and emotion in the relationship than they themselves do and that their partners would characterize the relationship as closer than they would (Snyder and Simpson, 1984b). Finally, their uncommitted orientation is revealed by a relatively slow rate of growth of intimacy in their dating relationships.

Low self-monitoring men and women, by contrast, tend to adopt a "committed" orientation in their dating relationships. They express little willingness to spend time with people other than their current

Table 6-1   Dating Histories of College Students

	Type of person	
Type of dating relationship	High self-monitoring	Low self-monitoring
Multiple daters Number of different partners dated within preceding 12 months	5.81	3.59
Single daters Number of months having dated current partner	10.85	20.22

Snyder and Simpson, 1984*a*.

dating partners, even if the other people are highly skilled in the social activities under consideration. And, when given the opportunity to terminate their current dating relationship for a new one, they overwhelmingly reject it. Furthermore, their recent dating histories (see Table 6-1) clearly reflect this committed orientation. They typically have dated steady, exclusive partners for relatively long periods of time (an average of about 20 months), and, if not involved in an exclusive dating relationship, they have dated a fairly small number of different partners (an average of fewer than four) in the preceding year. Moreover, when asked to characterize their investment in their dating relationships, low self-monitoring men and women admit that they have made a greater investment of time and emotion in the relationship than their partners and that they would describe the relationship as closer than their partners would (Snyder and Simpson, 1984*b*). Finally, their committed orientation is revealed by the fact that in the long term they reach relatively high levels of personal intimacy.

Sexual Relations

One of the most intimate forms of personal relationships is, of course, the sexual one. Here, too, self-monitoring affects both attitudes and behaviors. Orientations toward sexual relations are revealed by the "Social and Sexual Behavior Survey" (Snyder, Simpson, and Gange-

Table 6-2   Patterns of Sexual Behavior

| | Type of person | | | |
| | High self-monitoring | | Low self-monitoring | |
Behavioral index	Male	Female	Male	Female
Number of different partners in the past year	2.30	1.67	1.55	1.17
Number of different partners foreseen in the next five years	7.02	3.74	4.30	2.21
Percentage of people having experienced a "one-night stand"	75	75	62	36

Snyder, Simpson, and Gangestad, in press.

stad, in press), an extensive questionnaire dealing with previous and anticipated, overt and covert, sexual behavior. It includes items to assess, among other things, frequency of sex in the past month, oral-genital sexual experience, number of lifetime sexual partners, number of sexual partners in the past year, number of sexual partners foreseen in the next five years, number of "one-night stands," frequency of sexual thoughts, and frequency of fantasizing about having sex with different partners. It also includes measures of attitudes toward sex with someone to whom one is not committed and feelings of comfort with engaging in sex with different partners.

High self-monitors report that they have engaged in sex with a large number of different partners in the preceding year and foresee themselves having sex with many different people over the next five years (see Table 6-2). They also are more likely to have engaged in sex with partners on one and only one occasion. Low self-monitors indicate that they would be rather reluctant to have sex with someone to whom they were not exclusively committed. They also claim that they would be relatively uncomfortable with, and therefore less likely to enjoy, engaging in casual sex with different partners. That is, the high self-monitoring orientation toward sexual relations is relatively unrestricted; the low self-monitoring one, a relatively restricted orientation.

Closeness in Romantic Relationships

What accounts for these contrasting orientations to romantic relationships? What might lead low self-monitoring men and women to maintain close and quite exclusive romantic relationships and, at the same time, lead those high in self-monitoring to establish less close and nonexclusive ones? Perhaps systematic differences in conceptions of love, in the number of alternative partners available, and in inclination to avoid tempting feelings about alternative partners contribute to these contrasting orientations (Snyder and Simpson, in press).

When it comes to conceptions of love, not everyone subscribes to the traditional ideal that for each person there is one and only one true love. Although people low in self-monitoring usually agree with the statement "There is only one real love for a person," those high in self-monitoring typically believe that "It is possible to love two people at the same time" (Snyder and Simpson, 1984b). Clearly, if people adhere to the philosophy of one love for one person, they will be highly invested in forming relatively committed and restricted romantic relationships. But, if they subscribe to the principle of more than one lover for one person, they will be more likely to strive for relatively uncommitted and unrestricted romantic relationships.

With respect to alternative partners, at least four sources of evidence suggest that high self-monitors have (at least in their perception) a large number of potential romantic partners available to them. First, high self-monitors not involved in an exclusive relationship report nearly twice as many different partners in the preceding year as low self-monitors (Snyder and Simpson, 1984a). Second, they claim that they spend more time socializing with someone other than their dating partner (Snyder and Simpson, 1984a). Third, among people with sexual experience, those high in self-monitoring report having engaged in sexual activities with nearly twice as many different partners within the preceding year (Snyder, Simpson, and Gangestad, in press). And finally, they foresee themselves as having sex with nearly twice as many different partners in the next five years (Snyder, Simpson, and Gangestad, in press). Clearly, people with a large number of alternative partners (real or imagined) might be less committed and attached to any current relationship. Perhaps the high self-monitors' preference for less close and nonexclusive relationships is, to some extent, related to their rather large number of (actual or planned) alternative partners.

Contrasting romantic orientations may be tied also to the inclination or the ability to avoid or resist the temptation of attractive alternative partners (Kelley, 1980, 1983; Rosenblatt, 1977). In fact, self-monitoring seems to be linked to such self-control processes. When asked to indicate how frequently they fantasize about having sex with someone other than their most steady dating partner and how often they fantasize about having sex with someone other than their most steady dating partner *while actually engaging in sex with their most steady partner,* low self-monitors report that they fantasize about such activities much *less* often than do high self-monitors (Snyder, Simpson, and Gangestad, in press). No doubt, people who are willing and able to resist tempting thoughts and feelings will be less likely to stray from their current partners. For this reason, low self-monitoring romantic relationships may be more stable than high self-monitoring ones.

Differing orientations toward romantic closeness also may help explain the stages through which relationships pass as they evolve over time. Typically, relationships are thought to proceed from relatively superficial to progressively more intimate stages (see Berscheid, 1985). The differing orientations of people low and high in self-monitoring suggest not only that their relationships move through the stages at different rates, but also that they actually begin and end at different stages. Murstein, for one, has proposed (in his stimulus-value-role theory, 1970) that relationships begin at a "stimulus" stage, in which a person is concerned with the exterior attributes of the partner, and then proceed to a "value" stage. Only then does the person become concerned with compatibility of values.

Glick (1984) has suggested that low self-monitoring romances *start* at the value stage. After all, low self-monitors invoke such considerations even before beginning dating relationships. High self-monitors, in contrast, initiate dates on the basis of physical appearance. They often maintain multiple dating relationships of relatively short duration, and they are quite willing at least to consider "shopping around" for new partners. For these reasons, some high self-monitoring romances may not even make it to the value stage.

The final stage of relationships is often thought to be one of deep mutual investment and commitment (Altman and Taylor, 1973; Levinger, 1974; Secord and Backman, 1974). Low self-monitors, because of the time and effort they devote to developing bonds of closeness and intimacy, may be more likely than high self-monitors to reach this final stage.

Marriages and Other Long-Term Relationships

Since most research has centered on college students in dating relationships, little is known about self-monitoring and the romantic orientations of people at other life stages and in other varieties of romantic relationships. But dating relationships often serve as important first steps toward more involved, intricate, and permanent unions. Since orientations present in the early stages of a relationship can have a direct bearing on what occurs in its later stages (Snyder, Tanke, and Berscheid, 1977), people's dating lives may have implications for their later relationships, including their marriages. After all, according to the U.S. Bureau of the Census, some 90 percent to 95 percent of adults will, at some time, enter into marriages (1976; see also, Kelley et al., 1983).

What, then, are the implications of orientations toward romantic relationships for understanding marriages and marriage-like partnerships? First of all, with respect to self-monitoring, there is no evidence of "assortative mating"—with people gravitating toward mates of like self-monitoring propensities. Among dating couples, there is no association at all between the self-monitoring scores of the two partners; the same holds true for couples who have been married long enough to have children of college age (Snyder and Simpson, 1983). Moreover, in an experimental simulation of dating encounters, Tomarelli and Graziano (1981), who had predicted that complementary self-monitoring propensities would enhance attraction between dating partners, found no evidence of a complementarity effect or, for that matter, of a similarity effect. Why a match in self-monitoring orientation should be involved in choosing friends (see Chapter 5) but not in selecting romantic partners, curious as that state of affairs may seem, remains to be seen.

But, if there is no indication that who marries whom is a function of self-monitoring, there are clear indications that why a person marries may be so. Those high in self-monitoring, being sensitive to the fit between partners and social activities, may view marriage as a partnership built around the mutual enjoyment of shared activities. In fact, at least among dating couples who regard themselves as close (many of whom presumably will be married), high self-monitors admit that they often wish their partners were more skilled in leisure activities (Snyder and Simpson, 1984*b*). Low self-monitors, who strive to maximize the fit between themselves and their partners, may view marriage instead as a partnership centered on each other. For them, marital satisfaction would be derived from the pleasure and enjoyment of simply being with each other.

What are the consequences of viewing marriage as an activity-centered phenomenon or a partner-centered phenomenon? High self-monitoring spouses might have more activity partners outside the marriage than would those low in self-monitoring. Thus, for example, if you are high in self-monitoring and your spouse does not share your enjoyment of golf, you might seek other golfing partners. But, if you are low in self-monitoring, you might put your golf clubs in the attic and concentrate on some other activity, perhaps tennis, that both of you can enjoy. Moreover, high self-monitors, with their unrestricted orientation toward sexual relations, may be more likely than low self-monitors to have extramarital sex and, possibly, to accept their spouses doing the same.

When it comes to long-term consequences, people with a partner-centered orientation may display great commitment to their marriages. If so, low self-monitoring partnerships ought to be relatively long-lasting and stable ones. This is not, of course, to say that these partnerships are invulnerable to breakups. Relationships based on similarity between the partners may be threatened by substantial and undeniable changes in the attitudes, values, and personality of either partner (or the revelation of previously unknown and undesirable characteristics in the partner). In addition, because of their orientation toward sexual relations, low self-monitors may regard sexual infidelity on the part of either spouse as sufficient, and perhaps even necessary, grounds for terminating the relationship.

Relationships contracted on the basis of exterior appearances (including, but not necessarily limited to, physical attractiveness and sexual desirability) and maintained as activity-centered partnerships may be vulnerable to threats of their own kind. When time and gravity take their inevitable toll on face and body, or when the partner is no longer available for certain activities, high self-monitors may find themselves looking elsewhere for new partners. Too, the availability of other partners of more desirable exterior appearances or greater resources as an activity partner may be grounds for ending relationships of this type.

These differing threats may provide some perspective on the accounts people offer about relationships in jeopardy. Thus, for instance, when the marriage counselor hears the complaint "My spouse is just not the same person I married," the message may have very different meanings, depending on the speaker. When it comes from a low self-monitor, he or she may be lamenting changes in the spouse's personality, attitudes, and values. But, when the same message comes from a high self-monitor, that person may be bemoaning the spouse's faded good looks and diminished skills as an activity partner.

Finally, if low self-monitors adopt a committed, partner-centered orientation in their relationships, their lives should be greatly disrupted and they should be very distressed if and when their partners leave them or die. This distress and disruption may be accompanied by long gaps between relationships as they seek a new partner with the potential for developing another committed, partner-centered relationship. High self-monitors, on the contrary, should adjust more readily to their partners' departures, quickly seek out replacements, and develop new relationships fairly soon. Nevertheless, these new relationships, like the previous ones, also may be somewhat lacking in closeness, emotional involvement, and psychological investment. It is relevant that when asked to project their reactions to a breakup, people high in self-monitoring predict that they could more easily make an emotional adjustment and find a replacement partner more quickly than do those low in self-monitoring (Snyder and Simpson, 1984b).

Many of these suggestions are, of course, conjectures. Nevertheless, if there are differing orientations to marriages and marriage-like partnerships, theorists and practitioners alike can bring fresh perspectives to understanding these relationships. Knowing the different bases on which such partnerships are founded and maintained, and the different types of events that may threaten and eventually dissolve them, they may be able to develop two psychologies of romantic relationships— one applicable to the personally committed, emotionally invested, and sexually restricted orientation of low self-monitors; the other applicable to the relatively uncommitted, activity-based, and sexually unrestricted orientation of high self-monitors.

PART III

Explorations in Applying Self-Monitoring

THERE IS NOTHING SO practical as a good theory. This credo is a fundamental part of Kurt Lewin's legacy to psychology (Marrow, 1969). It holds, on the one hand, that practical problems are best tackled with the guiding hand of theory and, on the other hand, that one measure of theory is its ability to speak meaningfully to practical concerns. In keeping with these beliefs, researchers have devoted more and more attention to the implications of self-monitoring for understanding practical problems. Among the items that have claimed their place on the applied agenda for self-monitoring are applications to industrial psychology, consumer psychology, and clinical psychology.

Why these domains of application? Some of the most important and consequential decisions in people's lives are those concerning the jobs they seek and the careers they pursue. Accordingly, this section begins with a look at what self-monitoring can say about jobs, careers, and professions (Chapter 7). In addition, advertising, in its attempts to mold and shape the attitudes, preferences, and behavior of consumers, represents one of the most intensive applications of principles of attitude change, persuasion, and social influence (Chapter 8). And, among the most pressing personal problems people must deal with in their lives are those of adjustment and readjustment, stress and coping, and conflict and its resolution—the problems that motivate people to seek the advice and counsel of practitioners of the counseling arts. Hence, we examine (in Chapter 9) applications of self-monitoring to personal problems, counseling, and therapy.

CHAPTER 7

Jobs, Careers, and Professions

■

IT WOULD BE something of an understatement to say that the impact of jobs and careers is widespread and long-lasting. Jobs and careers determine what people do, as well as the satisfactions (both economic and personal) that they receive from their work. Less obvious, perhaps, but no less important are some of the more far-reaching consequences of jobs and careers. Jobs affect where people live. Often, as they follow job openings and pursue career opportunities, people move from region to region of the country and, in some cases, to far-flung corners of the globe. Jobs and careers even influence who people's friends are; after all, the people they meet at work are prime candidates to become their friends and intimates.

Consider the case of someone who chooses to pursue a career as a university professor. Obviously, this choice allows this person to work at the noble tasks of uncovering new knowledge and educating the youth of the country. Less obvious, though, are the other consequences of this career choice for our professor's geographical and social worlds. The odds are that he or she will not be living in a large city; most universities—at least those in the United States—are located in "college towns." And the odds are that he or she will be forming friendships with a somewhat different class of people than will, say, someone climbing the corporate ladder to the executive suite.

Choosing Jobs and Careers

What role does self-monitoring play in the choice of occupations and professions? We know (from Chapter 4) that self-monitoring is often involved in choosing social situations. People, it appears, gravitate toward situations conducive to their self-monitoring propensities. Perhaps these same motivations determine choices of jobs and careers. Some people (those low in self-monitoring) may choose occupations and professions that support their own attitudes and personalities. Thus, those low self-monitors who consider themselves to be warm and compassionate beings with much sympathy for the needy would choose careers in the social service or "helping" professions. But those who consider themselves rather assertive and aggressive types who value material possessions would choose careers in business, law, real estate, or other entrepreneurial professions.

High self-monitors may choose occupations and professions that call on them to portray one or more clearly defined roles. For example, people of this type may be attracted to careers in theater, public relations, law, politics, sales, or diplomacy precisely because these fields allow them to exercise their self-presentational and expressive skills. Whatever their career choices, the potential success of high self-monitors may be much less dependent on a good match between the personality required by the job and their own traits and dispositions than typically would be true for low self-monitors.

Evidence for these propositions comes from a variety of sources. From the psychological laboratory comes an experimental simulation of applying for a job (Snyder and Gangestad, 1982). In that simulation, researchers announced that they were about to hire a student to work for them as a confederate in one of their experiments. They informed prospective job candidates that they needed someone to play the role of an *extravert* in a group discussion. They then noted who was interested in applying for the job and their reasons for being interested.

High self-monitoring candidates, it turned out (see Table 7-1), wanted the job if and only if it had been defined for them in very great

Table 7-1   Willingness to Apply for Jobs: The Influence of Personality of the Applicant and Definition of the Job

Type of applicant	Job definition	
	Vague	Detailed
High self-monitoring	27.40	31.99
Low self-monitoring	26.60	25.59

Type of applicant	Applicant's personality	
	Introvert	Extravert
High self-monitoring	28.69	30.70
Low self-monitoring	23.44	28.76

Higher numbers indicate greater willingness to apply for the job. Snyder and Gangestad, 1982.

detail, right down to the specifics of what they would say and do (including the nonverbal gestures required) to play the role of the extraverted group member. They showed little inclination to pursue the job if the role of the confederate had been defined only in vague terms. Low self-monitoring candidates reacted quite differently to this job opening (see Table 7-1). They wanted the job only if they were natural extraverts (as revealed by their scores on a personality test) and could fulfill the requirements of the job just by being themselves in the group discussions. Low self-monitoring introverts were distinctly unwilling even to consider a job that would require them to earn a living by behaving contrary to their own introverted natures.

To some extent, the considerations that determine whether a certain type of person applies for a job have their counterparts in the strategies that person uses to seek employment. When Latham (1985) surveyed college students about to enter the work force, he found that high self-monitoring students were more likely to view activities such as setting a precise job goal, locating job openings, taking job interview training, and using reference groups to gain organizational access as helpful in gaining employment than were those low in self-monitoring. Moreover, high self-monitoring job seekers were particularly likely to have engaged in these activities during their last job search.

Performance in the Workplace

The role of self-monitoring is further revealed by studies actually conducted in the workplace. In one, Caldwell and O'Reilly (1982) examined "boundary-spanning" jobs in a corporate setting. Boundary-spanning jobs require people to function effectively in "go between" roles. Holders of these jobs have to interact and communicate effectively with people or groups who are so different that they often cannot deal directly with each other (for example, management and labor, or production and marketing). Such boundary-spanning jobs seem particularly well suited to the interpersonal styles of high self-monitors.

In their research, Caldwell and O'Reilly (1982) identified, by means of an analysis of job duties, the job of field representative for a large franchise organization as a boundary-spanning position. In a typical workweek, field representatives spend at least three days "contacting franchisees and presenting corporate positions, mediating franchisee-corporate differences of opinion, and referring franchisees to information sources and suppliers" (Caldwell and O'Reilly, 1982, p. 125).

When Caldwell and O'Reilly examined the company's performance evaluation forms, they found that success on the job was a function of self-monitoring. High self-monitoring field representatives performed more effectively than low self-monitoring ones. Perhaps these representatives were able to draw on the persuasive abilities and communication skills that are often seen in high self-monitoring job holders (Sypher and Sypher, 1981, 1983). Indeed, there are indications that interpersonal competence plays a considerable role in vocational achievement (Holland, 1973).

Presumably (although Caldwell and O'Reilly did not actually measure this), the high self-monitoring field representatives were experiencing greater satisfaction with their jobs than low self-monitoring field representatives. Perhaps, too, workers terminated from boundary-spanning positions for poor performance were more likely to be low rather than high in self-monitoring. Indeed, Caldwell and O'Reilly

(1982) did find that low self-monitoring franchise representatives had held their jobs for shorter periods of time than their high self-monitoring counterparts.

Furthermore, if job performance is rewarded with opportunities for advancement, then employees promoted out of their boundary-spanning jobs and invited to assume greater responsibilities in the upper reaches of the corporate structure will tend to be high in self-monitoring. In fact, in one study of a large insurance company, there was an association between self-monitoring and job level: Employees with higher level jobs (e.g., managers and supervisors) typically were high self-monitors; employees with lower level jobs (e.g., clerical, technical, and support staff) usually were low self-monitors (Sypher and Sypher, 1981, 1983). Moreover, in another study, employees in the managerial ranks of supermarkets were higher in self-monitoring than supermarket employees drawn from the nonmanagerial ranks (Giacalone and Falvo, 1985). The prevalence of high self-monitoring managers and supervisors may reflect the high self-monitor's preference for occupations with status, prestige, and desirable images (Matwychuk and Snyder, 1982).

In addition, this prevalence may reflect the high self-monitor's ability to emerge as a leader in groups and organizations (e.g., Garland and Beard, 1979; Miller, 1984; Schubot and Kurecka, 1980, 1981; Whitmore and Klimoski, 1984). The same social style that prompts high self-monitors to initiate conversations in one-to-one situations (Ickes and Barnes, 1977) may, in group situations, lead them to provide rewarding interactions for other group members, which would in turn facilitate their emergence as leaders.

Are leaders high in self-monitoring? In studies of groups involved in brainstorming tasks, group members who emerged as leaders often were high in self-monitoring (Garland and Beard, 1979). In addition, Whitmore and Klimoski (1984) have documented the emergence of high self-monitoring leaders in groups devoted to problem-solving tasks. Finally, Miller (1984) has examined some of the tactics employed by high self-monitoring leaders. These include motivating others by showing them that their efforts will be rewarded, encouraging others to cooperate when necessary, setting clear goals and emphasizing deadlines, being supportive and making others feel at ease, and listening to others' suggestions and letting them use their own judgment where appropriate.

The reader should resist the temptation to conclude that being a success in the workplace and being high in self-monitoring go hand in hand. Much of the research on job performance and leader emergence has focused on jobs (such as the boundary-spanner) that call for high self-monitoring skills. In addition, high self-monitors do not have a universal tendency to become leaders. They emerge as leaders only in situations involving high levels of verbal interaction (Garland and Beard, 1979) and normative climates that encourage leadership strivings (Whitmore and Klimoski, 1984). These situations are all but custom-made for high self-monitoring leaders.

There very well may be other circumstances more conducive to the low self-monitoring interpersonal style. In these situations, when leaders emerge, they may be low in self-monitoring. Moreover, in jobs that call for the low self-monitoring social style, the low self-monitoring employees would perform better, be more satisfied with their jobs, and earn the raises, bonuses, and promotions. And, in such job categories, it would be high self-monitoring employees who perform less well, derive less satisfaction from their work, and find pink slips in their pay envelopes. There are indications that being low in self-monitoring enhances the job performance of managers who must work effectively with relatively homogeneous work groups (Anderson, 1981). Moreover, the low self-monitoring leader is typically one whose actual leadership style reflects his or her personal views of leadership (Chemers and Ayman, 1985). A low self-monitor who believes that a good leader is decisive and directs others typically is a task-oriented leader, whereas one who believes that a good leader is tolerant and understanding usually adopts a relationship-oriented style of leadership. Finally, studies of leadership style and managerial performance suggest that low self-monitoring managers perform best in situations that match their personal leadership styles: "task-oriented" and "relationship-oriented" leaders perform best in situations conducive to their own particular natural styles (Chemers and Ayman, 1985).

Career Counseling

Every year, legions of students trying to choose a career seek advice and guidance from high school and college counselors. They ask: What am I suited to do? Will I succeed? Will I be happy? A little knowledge about self-monitoring may take career counselors a long way in answering these questions. If self-monitoring affects the "fit" between people and jobs, as the research we have just examined suggests, then techniques for measuring self-monitoring should be incorporated into the tools of the counseling trade.

This incorporation could be helped along by some ideas from Holland's (1966, 1973, 1976) theory of vocational choice. This theory, in addition to being a mainstay of counseling services, focuses explicitly on the fit between people and their jobs. According to this theory, people seek occupations that allow them to use "their skills and abilities, express their attitudes and values, and take on agreeable problems and roles" (Holland, 1973, p. 4). Also, according to this theory, people will be most satisfied, most productive, and hold their jobs the longest when their values and abilities match those called for by their jobs (for another discussion of the fit between self and occupation, see Super, Starishesky, Matlin, and Jordann, 1963).

Holland (1966, 1973) has developed an inventory to describe people in terms of six themes: Realistic, Investigative, Artistic, Social, Enterprising, and Conventional. The inventory can be used in vocational counseling to steer people into jobs that match their type, for example, science careers for investigative types and business for enterprising types.

What correspondences might the career counselor find between the Holland themes and self-monitoring orientations? The thematic profiles of high and low self-monitors may have differently located "high points"—perhaps Enterprising and Social themes in the high self-monitoring profile but Conventional and Realistic in the low self-monitoring profile. In addition, the consistency between measured dispositions and actual behavior typical of low self-monitors (see Chapter 3) may mean that the Holland themes function particularly well as predictors of their occupational choices.

If counselors apply self-monitoring to these themes, people who take their counselors' advice will find themselves in occupations and careers well suited to their sense of self and to their particular social styles. As just one indicator of the importance of fitting job situations to self-monitoring propensities, consider the possibility suggested by the research of Sparacino, Ronchi, Bigley, Flesch, and Kuhn (1983; see also, Ronchi and Sparacino, 1982): High blood pressure may be one consequence of being "trapped" in a job that calls for an interpersonal style contrary to one's own self-monitoring orientation.

If vocational counseling based on an integration of self-monitoring and the Holland themes is successful, its success may come from its broadly defined, global themes. Holland's theory embodies elements of concern to high self-monitoring job holders (the opportunity to "take on . . . agreeable roles") and to low self-monitoring job holders (the opportunity to "express their attitudes and values"). For this reason, this approach may be more universally productive than one that takes the more narrow focus of matching job seekers' attitudes, values, and preferences with those of people already in particular jobs (a strategy relatively well suited for low self-monitoring job seekers). And it may be more effective than a strategy dealing primarily with the match between job seekers' repertoires of roles and those required in particular jobs (an approach relatively well suited for high self-monitoring job seekers).

Personnel Selection

There are two sides to every story, and finding a job is no exception. There are those who look for jobs and those who offer jobs. Self-monitoring affects not only a person's choice of a job and his or her performance; it may also affect the decision about which job seeker receives the offer and which one gets the "Don't call us, we'll call you" message (e.g., Smith and Davidson, 1983; Snyder, Berscheid, and Matwychuk, 1985).

What criteria do people invoke when they choose among job candidates? In an experimental simulation of personnel selection, college students examined personnel folders of two candidates for particular jobs (Snyder, Berscheid, and Matwychuk, 1985). Some of them were "hiring" a salesclerk; others were choosing a camp counselor. Each folder contained information that characterized the applicant as either particularly well suited or less well suited in terms of personality and temperament for the job. Each folder also contained a photograph that portrayed the applicant as having a relatively appropriate or relatively inappropriate appearance for the job under consideration.

Faced with this information, these students then decided which applicant should receive the job offer. The impact of self-monitoring on these choices was substantial, as Figure 7-1 reveals. High self-monitors were particularly likely to select an applicant who *looked the part* for the job. For example, they wanted to hire the attractive, well-

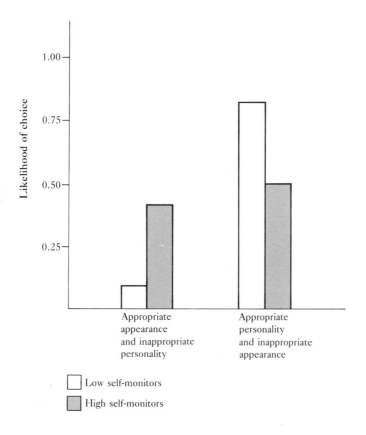

Figure 7-1   Selection of job candidates (Snyder, Berscheid, and Matwychuk, 1985).

dressed applicant who appeared to be concerned with her appearance for the position of salesclerk in a sophisticated women's clothing store, even though she was rather unsociable and lacked organizational ability. Low self-monitors were more inclined to choose an applicant who *was the part* for the job by virtue of job-linked inner dispositions. They preferred, for instance, to give the camp counselor job to the applicant with a very gregarious and empathic personality, even though he looked and dressed more like a junior account executive then a camp counselor.

Of course, a job-appropriate appearance is not necessarily a physically attractive appearance, although it may be. For example, stereotypes about receptionists are more likely than stereotypes about day-care workers to include physical attractiveness. By contrast, day-care workers are more likely to be stereotyped as having "parental looks." In fact, high self-monitors are responsive both to the sheer physical attractiveness of job candidates and to the fit between candidates' appearances and stereotyped conceptions of looks appropriate to the job under consideration (Snyder, Berscheid, and Matwychuk, 1985).

Does what happens in these experimental simulations also go on in actual personnel selection contexts? If it does, high self-monitoring personnel selectors will be swayed by the appearance, demeanor, and mannerisms of those they evaluate for jobs. Also, low self-monitoring personnel selectors will be moved by evidence of experience, training, aptitude, and other job qualifications. Moreover, high self-monitoring personnel selectors may profess great confidence in the interview with its high potential for face-to-face observation of the candidate's appearance and expressive style. Those who are low self-monitors, however, may place their faith and trust in objective procedures such as tests of job-related aptitudes, experiences, and dispositions.

When the time comes to make decisions about who gets to keep their jobs and who is to be rewarded with raises and promotions, similar considerations may come into play. When high self-monitoring evaluators make these decisions, matters of style on the job may be paramount. But when the same determinations are made by low self-monitoring decision makers, issues of job performance may be critical.

Needless to say, some restraint must be exercised before leaping from the results of experiments with untrained college students to conclusions about trained professionals engaged in personnel selection. However, this restraint ought to be tempered by the fact that "recent research suggests that the threat to generalizability by using students as interviewers seems minimal" (Arvey and Campion, 1982, p. 294). Nevertheless, if the reader is concerned that trained professionals would never do what some college students did in our experiments, then he or she need only turn to a vast and extensive literature that documents the powerful impact of considerations that have little objective relevance for job performance (physical appearance is one such consideration) on hiring decisions, including those made by trained professional interviewers (Arvey, 1979; Arvey and Campion, 1982; Beehr and Gilmore, 1982; Cann, Siegfried, and Pearce, 1981; Cash, Gillen, and Burns, 1977; Dipboye, 1982; Dipboye, Arvey, and Terpstra, 1977; Dipboye, Fromkin, and Wiback, 1975; Dunnette and Borman, 1979; Heilman and Saruwatari, 1979; Zedeck and Cascio, 1984).

The question, therefore, is not whether trained professionals would allow one source of information to outweigh another—the answer to that question is unequivocally "yes!" The question, instead, is whether high and low self-monitoring professionals will invoke the same judgmental considerations as high and low self-monitoring college students. Although appropriate field investigations will be needed before this question can be answered, the fact that both subjective and objective considerations influence the judgments of practicing interviewers does not preclude a "yes" answer.

If self-monitoring does influence personnel selection, people may be best qualified to select candidates for jobs that match their own self-monitoring propensities. Thus, when selecting among applicants for jobs with much public contact, in which appearance, style, and manner are central to the makeup of the job, the high self-monitoring strategy of personnel selection may be particularly effective. But when choosing candidates for jobs that involve specialized aptitudes, experiences, and dispositional properties, the low self-monitoring approach to personnel selection may be most useful.

That self-monitoring may be involved in how people function as occupational gatekeepers—determining whether exterior appearances or interior attributes will get people into jobs and then help them get ahead—may take on added significance in the light of changing career patterns. *Newsweek* magazine has noted "the change in the nature and function of the American face, which in addition to its traditional ornamental role increasingly is being pressed into service as an essential business accessory, a mobile billboard for the owner's brilliance, energy and savvy" (May 27, 1985, p. 65). In part, according to *Newsweek,* "this reflects the decline in occupations for which appearance is pretty much irrelevant, such as farming, and a corresponding rise in the number of jobs for which the primary qualification is *to be able to look as if one knows what one is doing*—management consulting, say" (p. 65, emphasis added). If *Newsweek* has correctly sized up the situation, then the attitudes and values of high self-monitors are what those who set the standards for job qualifications have in mind. Whether this is in fact the occupational state of affairs, and whether that state of affairs will persist, only time (and data) can tell.

The Fit Between People and Occupations

At this point, applications of self-monitoring theory and research to jobs, careers, and professions have only just begun. Although these applications may still, at this time, be somewhat sketchy, there is a common theme that defines and unifies them. That theme is the fit between people and their work situations. It is a theme that surfaces in considering how people choose jobs and careers, in examining how people perform on the job, and in thinking about career counseling and personnel selection. It recognizes the interactive influences of people's characteristic social styles and their work situations. And, it is a theme that recognizes the active role people take in choosing and influencing their occupational situations.

This theme, too, is one that characterizes the theory of work adjustment, which emphasizes correspondence between the person and the environment (Dawis and Lofquist, 1984). This theory proposes that "work represents a major environment to which most individuals must relate" (p. 54) and that "correspondence can be described as the individual fulfilling the requirements of the work environment and the work environment fulfilling the requirements of the individual" (p. 54). When the correspondence between the person and the work environment is achieved, workers are satisfied with their jobs, perform satisfactorily, and remain in their jobs. Clearly, correspondence can be enhanced by applying any principles that predict the fit between people and occupations. Self-monitoring is the basis of just such an application.

The importance of these applications may be considerable. Of all the life choices made *by* people, few are more consequential than the choice of profession and career. Similarly, of all the decisions made *about* people, few may have more far-reaching implications than the job opportunities and career paths made available to them. Accordingly, an understanding of the issues of job and career has the potential to help people as they make some of the most important plans of their lives.

CHAPTER 8

Advertising, Persuasion, and Consumer Behavior

■

MANY YEARS AGO, President Coolidge called it "the most potent influence in adapting and changing [our] habits and modes of life, affecting what we eat, what we wear, and the work and play of the whole nation." More recently, social historian David Potter compared it with "such long-standing institutions as the school and the church in the magnitude of its social influence," suggesting that it "dominates the media, it has vast power in the shaping of popular standards, and it is really one of the very limited groups of institutions which exercise social control" (1954). "It" is advertising, whose messages reach out and try to touch us—not only to encourage us to buy this or that consumer product, but also to influence our attitudes and behavior in social, cultural, and even political realms.

Like it or not, advertising is virtually impossible to avoid or ignore. Television viewers are exposed to tens of thousands of commercial messages every year (Hacker, 1984). Not surprisingly, advertising is big business. In 1980 alone, $54.6 billion went into advertising. How are these billions spent? One might say that they are being invested in applying psychological principles of persuasion. In fact, a giant of the advertising industry once said, "Advertising is persuasion, and persuasion is . . . an art. Advertising is the art of persuasion" (Bernbach, cited in Fox, 1984, p. 251). As persuasion artists, advertisers seem to belong to one of two schools, known within the industry as the "soft sell" and the "hard sell" (Fox, 1984).

The Psychology of Advertising: The "Soft Sell" and the "Hard Sell"

Members of the "soft-sell" school typically create advertisements that appeal to the *images* consumers may project by using a product. Adherents of this image-based tradition believe that how a product is presented by its advertising is as important as the product itself. Therefore, they create advertisements that are visually striking, paying attention to the finer details of color and form. Typically, the written copy conveys, explicitly or implicitly, the images associated with the product. Rarely, if ever, does image-oriented advertising actually mention the quality of the product.

A landmark case of image-oriented advertising was the campaign for the Arrow shirt collar, which focused not on the product itself but on the image of the man who used it. Here, the advertisers "created a campaign stressing the accessories and background of the man who wore the product. Instead of picturing the collar by itself, [they] put it around the neck of a stylish young man, impossibly clear of eye, clean of jowl and square of jaw and surrounded with opulent possessions and women" (Fox, p. 44). Perhaps the best known contemporary instance of image-oriented advertising is that for Marlboro cigarettes, revolving as it does around the rugged, masculine image of the man who smokes Marlboros. As is typical of image-oriented advertising, neither of these campaigns provides any explicit information about the product itself, but only allusions to the images identified with it.

Members of the "hard-sell" school typically create advertisements based on claims about the inherent *quality,* intrinsic merit, and functional value of the product. Their advertising informs consumers about how good the product is, how well it works, or, in the case of things to eat and drink, how good it tastes. Here, it's the "matter, not the manner" that counts. Early practitioners of this approach applied their techniques to advertising patent medicines and cure-alls, one of which was Lydia E. Pinkham's Vegetable Compound. Its ads featured the hard-sell claim that it was "a sure cure for all female weaknesses, . . . efficacious and immediate in its effects" (cited in Fox, p. 141). Recent advertisements for Total cereal, which emphasize the nutritional benefits of the cereal, and those featuring the "Pepsi challenge" taste tests, dramatizing the supposedly superior taste quality of Pepsi, clearly are members of the same category of advertising.

These two schools have flourished throughout the history of the industry. Both have produced their "great masterpieces" (for a review see Fox, 1984). The fundamental questions, though, concern the basis of the effectiveness of either type of advertising: What is it that makes appeals to images and claims about quality succeed in engaging, motivating, and persuading consumers? What psychological mechanisms render each of these strategies effective?

Some understanding of these psychological mechanisms is provided by the fact that susceptibility to one or the other type of advertising is another feature of the social orientations associated with self-monitoring. High self-monitors are particularly responsive to image-oriented advertising; low self-monitors are most sensitive to quality-oriented advertising (Snyder and DeBono, 1985*b*).

Appeals to Image and Claims about Quality

In our research, we have created advertisements that, in pictures and words, represent image-based and product-quality-based messages. We have advertised products as diverse as coffee and cars, whiskies and shampoos, and cigarettes (in ads whose message is "smoke this brand" as well as those which say, "be a nonsmoker"). In some studies, we used sets of magazine advertisements, each containing two ads for a particular product that were identical in all respects save one—the written message or slogan associated with the picture. One message highlighted the *image* associated with the product whereas the other stressed the product's *quality*. For example, in a set of advertisements for Canadian Club whisky, the picture prominently displayed a bottle of Canadian Club resting on a set of house blueprints. The written copy for the image-oriented ad stated, "You're not just moving in, you're moving up." The product-quality-oriented ad claimed, "When it comes to great taste, everyone draws the same conclusion."

Reactions to these advertisements (see Figure 8-1) revealed that high self-monitors thought the image-oriented ads were better, more appealing, and more effective. Moreover, they were willing to pay more for a product if its advertising appealed to considerations of image, and they were more likely to try a product if it was marketed

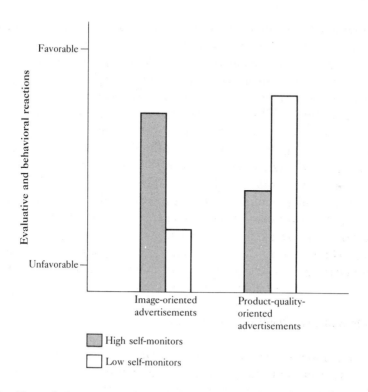

Figure 8-1   Reactions to advertising messages (Snyder and DeBono, 1985*b*).

with an image orientation. By contrast, low self-monitors reacted more favorably to product-quality-oriented ads. They were willing to pay more for a product if its advertising stressed the product's quality and willing to try a product if claims were made about its quality.

The differential appeal of image-oriented and quality-oriented messages is, it should be noted, not limited to the domain of consumer products. We have also created a series of ads for the purpose of encouraging people *not* to consume a product—in this case not to smoke (Snyder, Nettle, and DeBono, 1985). We developed three sets of "be a nonsmoker" advertisements, each containing two ads with the same pictorial content but different verbal messages. One made an appeal to considerations of images and exterior appearances; the other spoke to matters of health quality and inner well-being.

For example, one set featured a picture of a rather pensive-looking young man, about the right age to be an older brother to the students who served in the study, with a cigarette in his hand. In the image-oriented message, his thoughts were devoted to his appearance: "Bad breath, yellow teeth, smelly clothes . . . Is smoking really worth it?" In the health-quality-oriented message, he was thinking of the physical consequences of smoking: "Coughing, shortness of breath, sore throat . . . Is smoking really worth it?"

When college students indicated which advertisement in each set was, in their judgment, better (that is, more appealing, more effective, more successful, and so on), high self-monitoring students chose the image-oriented pieces and low self-monitoring students favored the health-quality-oriented ones. Moreover, when other students chose which ads to use to persuade a fellow student to be a nonsmoker, high self-monitors featured the image-oriented messages; low self-monitors used the health-quality-oriented messages.

Before considering further the psychology of advertising and consumer behavior, it is necessary to examine more carefully the distinction between image-oriented and quality-oriented advertising. What are the characteristics that define and separate the two kinds of advertisements? For example, is an advertisement that speaks of "people of good taste" or one that speaks of "quality-conscious people" an appeal to image or a claim about quality? To answer these questions, consider these rules of thumb. If the advertisement appeals to the image of having good taste or the image of quality consciousness that comes with using the product (and, at the same time, does not claim the product tastes good or has high quality), then it should be regarded as image-oriented. As such, it ought to appeal mostly to high self-monitoring consumers. By contrast, if the ad makes actual claims about the product's good taste or its high quality (by claiming or hinting that by buying the product consumers are expressing intrinsic desires for things that taste good or an inherent appreciation of things high in quality), then it should be classified as quality-oriented. As such, its claims ought to be most effective with low self-monitoring consumers.

It is also necessary to specify when *attitudes* will be translated into actual consumer *behaviors*. Will high self-monitoring consumers buy every product that promises an image? Will low self-monitors buy every product of high quality? Clearly not. It is possible to specify (at least tentatively) which specific products will actually be used by particular types of consumers. High self-monitors typically choose their public images on the basis of the appropriateness of particular images to specific situations (see Chapter 3). Such considerations ought to affect their reactions to advertising. Imagine a high self-monitoring smoker who seeks to project an image of rugged masculinity on his weekend forays with his hunting buddies. In addition to choosing appropriate words, deeds, and mannerisms, he may also choose to smoke the cigarettes (and perhaps prominently display their package) that are associated with a ruggedly masculine image. Moreover, he probably would not, in these same circumstances, smoke the brand whose advertising appeals to an image of cultural sophistication (even though, if asked, he might grant that it's a good ad). That is, although high self-monitoring consumers may be generally favorable toward appeals to images, their actual purchases reflect the images they project at particular times in their social lives.

The social behavior of low self-monitors typically reflects their own general attitudes and dispositions (see Chapter 3). Such personal considerations also ought to affect their reactions to advertising. Consider a low self-monitor who enjoys the taste of gin but not that of bourbon. He or she ought to purchase the brand of gin advertised as having a fine taste but not the bourbon that advertises its fine taste, even though he or she might regard both advertisements as particularly appealing, engaging, and effective. That is, low self-monitoring consumers ought to be generally favorable toward advertising that makes claims about product quality, but they choose among products advertised in this way on the basis of the fit between these products and their attitudes and preferences.

Understanding the Effectiveness of Advertising

How, then, are we to understand the effectiveness of advertising? Reactions to advertising may be features of the high and low self-monitoring social orientations. Responding favorably to image-based advertising may reflect chronic strivings to be a pragmatic creature of one's situations and to project images appropriate to one's circumstances. Responding favorably to quality-oriented advertising may reflect a continuing quest to be a principled being, displaying congruence between one's actions and underlying attitudes, values, and dispositions.

It is also possible to offer some thoughts about the kinds of persuasion involved in advertising. Consider the distinction made by Kelman (1961) who proposed three processes that can produce agreement with a message: compliance, identification, and internalization. When it comes to advertising, the most meaningful of these processes are identification and internalization. Identification, Kelman claimed, occurs when people agree with a message because it allows them to project a desirable image and to fit into important social situations and peer groups. This agreement may be rather ephemeral because it can easily change when the image projected is no longer desirable. Accordingly, identification may be involved in the favorable reactions of high self-monitoring consumers to image-based advertising appeals. Internalization, said Kelman, takes place when people accept a message because it is congruent with their personal value system. As such, internalization may be implicated in the impact of product-quality-oriented ads on low self-monitoring consumers.[1]

Because Kelman's theory is concerned primarily with reactions to the *source* of a persuasive message (expert sources, he thought, produced agreement by means of internalization; attractive sources, by means of identification), its applicability may be greatest for advertising that involves endorsements and testimonials. For example, the race car driver who lends his expertise about things automotive to this or that brand of motor oil may persuade through internalization. But the movie star who lends her aura to this or that brand of coffee may persuade by way of identification. Sources of high credibility who offer testimonials may be most influential with low self-monitoring consumers; the very same messages, offered by sources of high personal attractiveness may be most impressive to high self-monitoring consumers.

Choosing Consumer Products: Form and Function

Aside from helping us understand the psychology behind advertising, self-monitoring can be of practical use to the advertiser. To attract

---

[1]Some readers may wonder about the links between the image-quality distinction in advertising and the "central versus peripheral" routes to persuasion (Petty and Cacioppo, 1981) and "systematic versus heuristic" processing of persuasive messages (Chaiken, 1980) distinctions. There are reasons to believe that reactions to both types of advertising are instances of central routes to persuasion and the outcomes of systematic processing, for both high and low self-monitoring consumers (see Snyder and DeBono, 1985*b*).

high self-monitors, a potent image-oriented campaign should create images that fit into important life situations. And the most effective quality-oriented advertising will appeal to low self-monitors by implying that the products will give people the opportunity to be true to their attitudes and values. Interpreting advertising in terms of self-monitoring may explain why the image-oriented "soft sell" and the claim-oriented "hard sell" approaches to advertising have succeeded, survived, and flourished: Each appeals to a distinct type of consumer.

Perhaps, too, advertisements that feature elements of both strategies—information about image and about quality—work because they draw both types of consumers. However, a word of caution ought to be associated with this suggestion. We do not yet know whether preferences for either image-oriented or quality-oriented advertising are accompanied by an actual aversion to the other type of advertising. For example, are people who prefer quality-oriented messages simply indifferent to image-oriented ones (so that a hybrid ad would appeal to them as much as a quality-only ad) or are they perhaps actively opposed to image-oriented messages (so that a hybrid might appeal to them *less* than a quality-only ad)?

Closely related to the "hybrid" is the "ambiguous" advertisement, which may be interpreted either in terms of image or in terms of quality. Think, for a moment, of an advertisement for a health club featuring a picture of a person—one whose appearance is both physically attractive and physically fit—surrounded by a gym full of exercise equipment. Imagine, further, that this picture is accompanied by the simple message, "Shape Up." To some extent, this advertisement constitutes a "projective test": Its interpretation can be guided by the motivational orientations of its viewers. Some people may identify with the physical attractiveness of the person featured and interpret the written message as an appeal to the more attractive and alluring shape their own body will take on as a result of exercise. Other people may focus on the physical fitness of the person in the picture and see the message as a claim about the health benefits of getting in shape by embarking on an exercise program. The first type may be high in self-monitoring. They may be motivated to engage in exercise in search of a more attractive exterior appearance. They also may be attracted to forms of exercise (such as working out on Nautilus-type machines) that concentrate on sculpting the musculature to produce appealing looks. The second type may be low in self-monitoring. They may be drawn to exercise in search of the health benefits of physical fitness and may be attracted to the type of exercise (such as aerobic workouts) that is directed primarily at conditioning the cardiovascular system and other inner workings of the body.

Advertising campaigns that have successfully shifted their strategy—from quality to image or vice versa—may provide some perspective on advertising as a process of persuasion. The advertising campaign for Clark's Teaberry Gum, for example, moved from quality to image. It abandoned an emphasis on the flavor of the gum for the catchy "Teaberry Shuffle" image and the slogan "Have a little fun . . . try Clark's Teaberry gum" (Engle, Wales, and Warshaw, 1975). In the early 1900s, advertising for Pepsodent toothpaste switched from a "claim" orientation to focus on beauty and the "pretty teeth available to customers" (Fox, 1984, p. 55). Similarly, in the 1920s, automobile advertisers, who once emphasized the reliability and soundness of their products, began to stress the styling and aesthetic aspects of the automobile (Fox, 1984).

Not all switches have been from claim to image. Force cereal, for one, was first advertised in the image tradition, but after disappointing sales, the strategy "gave way to harder selling . . . copy about the nutritional benefits of Force" (Fox, 1984, p. 48). And Alka-Seltzer, which once relied on appeals to images (remember the "I can't believe I ate the whole thing" commercials), switched after a sharp decline in sales. Said Mary Wells of the advertising firm of Wells, Rich, and Greene: "We will be more product-oriented and try to explain more clearly what Alka-Seltzer does" (Fox, 1984, p. 314).

There are, of course, many explanations of why these switches have worked. One of the more intriguing is that some products (such as chewing gum that can help you look fun-loving) may contribute primarily to exterior appearances and public images. As such, the natural target population of advertising for such products may be high self-monitoring consumers, who may look to advertising when choosing products for image-making purposes. By contrast, other products (such as a nutritious breakfast cereal) may contribute primarily to interior well being. For these products, the natural target population may be low self-monitoring consumers, who may look to advertising when choosing products for the intrinsic functions they perform. Thus, advertisers of both kinds of products ought to gear their advertising to the concerns of their natural audiences.

Thus, high self-monitoring consumers may be the ones who purchase the sleek, flashy, sporty-looking car (even if its performance and handling characteristics are far from sports car caliber), the ones who use the toothpaste that makes their teeth look the whitest (even if there is some suggestion that, over a long enough period of time, its abrasive content may threaten the enamel of their teeth), and the ones who pour the "super premium" beer, that special imported beer that says something more about its drinker's status (even if it tastes no different than the less expensive domestic brands). Such consumers may be choosing *form* over *function.*

By contrast, low self-monitoring consumers may be the ones who purchase the nutritious breakfast cereal (even if it isn't the one endorsed by the Olympic gold medal winner), the ones who use the mouthwash that is purported to kill the most bacteria (even if it does leave their breath with that faint medicinal odor), and the ones who choose the energy-efficient refrigerator (even though it's not available in the most trendy platinum-toned, designer-styled finish). They may be choosing *function* at the expense of *form.*

As tests of these speculations, surveys of buying habits and inventories of consumer products would be most informative. Such surveys and inventories would tell us, for instance, if Close Up brand toothpaste (which promises a better smile) is found in the medicine cabinets of high self-monitors and Crest brand (which promises fewer cavities) in those of low self-monitors. In addition, magazines devoted to images, fashions, and appearances (e.g., *Gentlemen's Quarterly, M, Glamour, Vogue*) should be found in the homes of high self-monitors; those that feature product evaluations and test reports (e.g., *Popular Photography* for camera buffs, *Car and Driver* for car enthusiasts, *Personal Computing* for computer lovers, *Audio* for audiophiles), in the homes of low self-monitors (cf. Snyder and DeBono, in press). Such surveys and inventories also might tell us something about another feature of consumers' attitudes and behaviors. Low self-monitors may be particularly likely to endorse the use of *generic* products, whereas high self-monitors may harbor some reluctance in this regard. Indeed, in one survey, 59 percent of low self-monitoring consumers agreed with the statement "I think generic products are just as good as name-brand products." Only 42 percent of high self-monitors agreed (Snyder & DeBono, 1984).

Different orientations toward form and function have implications for the ways people evaluate consumer products. How do people gather and interpret information relevant to such evaluations? When forming impressions of products and judging their merits, at least two kinds of information are available to consumers. First, and most easily accessible, is the physical appearance of the product—its look, color, feel, and other exterior aspects. Second, is the performance of the product. The product's dependability, reliability, and other intrinsic features of quality may be difficult to determine, but they are very important when evaluating consumer products.

How, then, do consumers use these two kinds of information? In one study, people studied a test report of a car (Snyder and DeBono, 1985a). Although the report (identified as coming from *Consumer Reports*) always described a car of average performance, some readers believed that the car was the rather attractive, quite sporty-looking Pontiac Fiero. Others believed that it was the somewhat less attractive, rather boxy-looking Volkswagen Rabbit (color photographs of these cars accompanied the test reports). After studying the reports, all readers offered their judgments about the car and, one week later, they reported their conclusions about the quality of the car.

Despite the fact that the test reports said that the two cars were functionally equivalent in performance and handling, people were swayed by the appearance of the cars. High self-monitoring readers evaluated the sporty-looking Fiero more favorably and judged it to be of higher quality. Low self-monitoring readers evaluated the Rabbit more favorably and judged it to be of higher quality.

One interpretation of these findings is that people have very different assumptions about the links between attractiveness and quality of consumer products. High self-monitors may believe in a positive association between attractiveness and quality, thinking that a good-looking product is a high quality product. Thus, when they see an attractive product, they may assume (often without much further consideration) that it is also of high quality. Low self-monitors, however, may think that attractiveness and quality are inversely related, believing that things either look good or work well—but not both. They may believe that products packaged in attractive exteriors may be masking flawed interiors and that some manufacturers may try to substitute good looks for good performance.

The Functional Bases of Consumer Attitudes and Behavior

Studies of self-monitoring and the psychology of advertising also may have implications for understanding the nature of attitudes. These studies suggest that attitudes serve different *functions* for different people. High self-monitoring participants in these studies seem to have formed more favorable attitudes toward products that help them create images appropriate to social situations. That is, their attitudes may have been serving a *social adjustive* function and may have been formed on the basis of how the products help them to behave appropriately in their various reference groups (Katz, 1960; Smith, Bruner, and White, 1956).

By contrast, low self-monitoring participants in these same studies reacted positively to products that allowed them to express underlying attitudes and values. These attitudes may serve a *value expressive* function and may have been formed on the basis of how well the products reflect, express, and communicate more fundamental underlying values (Katz, 1960; Smith, Bruner, and White, 1956). This possibility is consistent with the repeated finding that the attitudes, expectations, and personal attributes of low self-monitoring consumers are good predictors of their consumer behavior, especially in their choice of brands (e.g., Becherer and Richard, 1978) and their satisfaction with and complaints about products they have purchased (e.g., Bearden, Teel, and Beno, 1982).

That reactions to advertising may reflect differing functional bases of consumers' attitudes is intriguing. The Achilles' heel of most functional interpretations of attitudes has been the lack of a way to systematically test them (cf. Insko, 1967; Kiesler, Collins, and Miller, 1969) although there have been some attempts to test hypotheses from functional theories (e.g., Culbertson, 1957; Elms, 1976; Herek, 1984; Katz, McClintock, and Sarnoff, 1957; Katz, Sarnoff, and McClintock, 1956; McClintock, 1958; Stotland, Katz, and Patchen, 1959; Wagman, 1955). Theories about the links between self-monitoring and the functional bases of attitudes may solve this long-standing problem.

Of critical necessity in testing the validity of any functional approach is the ability to identify *in advance* the functions being served by a specific attitude for a particular person. In the past, this identification has proved very difficult to achieve and may, in part, explain why the functional theories went into hibernation several decades ago. However, studies of self-monitoring suggest one way of overcoming this hurdle. Just as it is possible to identify categories of people who are especially responsive to image-oriented versus quality-oriented advertising, it may be possible to identify categories of people who are especially likely to hold attitudes serving particular functions.

Thus, if researchers were seeking candidates to study the social adjustive function of attitudes, they might seek out high self-monitors. Similarly, if they wished to probe the dynamics of the value expressive function, they might focus on low self-monitors. In fact, DeBono (1985) has employed precisely this strategy to investigate the functions of attitudes toward mental illness. In his study, college students learned that the psychology department was sponsoring a "Mental Health Week," during which speakers from all over the country would visit the campus to present lectures and lead discussions on various aspects of mental illness. As preparation for these visits, these students listened to a tape of (the fictitious) Professor Gregory Stevenson from the University of Nebraska.

Some students heard Professor Stevenson talk (in the "social adjustive" condition) about a survey he had conducted which revealed that 70 percent of college students favored treating the mentally ill in state hospitals and institutions, 23 percent favored treatment at the community level in halfway houses, and 7 percent had no opinion. Other students heard Professor Stevenson talk (in the "value expressive" condition) about research he had conducted that indicated that the values of loving and responsibility (values that *all* students in the study rated highly on the Rokeach [1968] measure of values) underlie favorable attitudes toward institutionalization and that the values of imaginativeness and courageousness (values that all students rated as unimportant) underlie favorable attitudes toward deinstitutionalization.

After hearing the tape, the students reported their personal attitudes toward the care, housing, and treatment of the mentally ill. The extent to which the messages influenced the students' attitudes were, as Figure 8-2 reveals, very much a reflection of their self-monitoring propensities. High self-monitoring students reported more favorable attitudes toward institutionalization after hearing the message that played on social adjustive concerns than after hearing the value expressive message. Low self-monitoring students were most influenced

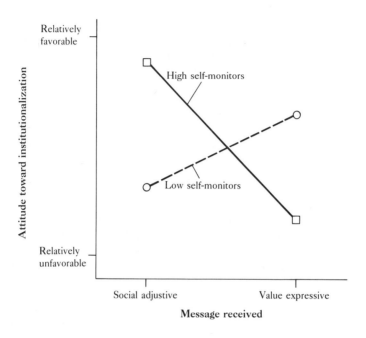

Figure 8-2   The functional bases of attitudes and persuasion (DeBono, 1985).

by the message that addressed itself to value expressive concerns, stating attitudes more favorable to institutionalization after hearing that message than after hearing the social adjustive message.

Researchers could use DeBono's (1985) method to study the functions of other attitudes. They might study high self-monitors to explore political attitudes and party preferences that reflect the normative climates of people's social networks. Similarly, they might examine low self-monitors to investigate political attitudes and candidate preferences that stem from deeply rooted, long-standing value orientations. Whatever the specific attitude of concern to the particular investigator, the strategy of inquiry would remain the same. Identifying categories of people for whom one or the other function is characteristic would not serve as an end in itself, but as a vehicle for understanding the functional underpinnings of attitudes. Applications of this strategy may have the potential to awaken the functional approach to attitudes, persuasion, and social influence—with all of its promise of theoretical utility and potential for practical significance—from its long winter of hibernation.

CHAPTER 9

Personal Problems, Counseling, and Therapy

SOME OF THE problems people experience are of the everyday garden variety, causing momentary stress and distress. Others are more persistent, such as the years-long struggle to lose those extra 10 pounds or to kick that nasty cigarette habit. The more pressing problems are those that interfere with a person's ability to lead a satisfying and effective life. These are the problems of adjustment and readjustment, stress and coping, and conflict and its resolution that motivate some people to seek professional help.

Of what relevance is theory and research on self-monitoring to understanding the concerns of clinical and counseling psychology? Is self-monitoring implicated in the frequency with which people experience problems adjusting to and coping with events in their lives? Are the events that lead to problems a reflection of self-monitoring propensities? Are the coping strategies that people adopt associated with self-monitoring? Are different types of professional counseling and therapy effective depending on whether someone is high or low in self-monitoring?

And what about the professionals who deal with those who experience personal problems? Do high and low self-monitors differ in their interest in entering the counseling and therapeutic professions or in their suitability for these professions? Are different types of counseling and therapy used more effectively by high and low self-monitoring practitioners? Research and theory can speak to these and other questions about personal problems, counseling, and therapy.

Problems of Adjustment and Psychopathological Conditions

First of all, there is no indication that personal problems are more common among people high or low in self-monitoring or that one type is more susceptible to psychopathological conditions. There are no meaningful relations between self-monitoring and measures of neuroticism (Snyder and Monson, 1975), anxiety (Snyder, 1974), depression (White-Phelan, 1983), or any of the clinical scales of the MMPI (Arnold, 1976). In addition, there are no substantial associations between self-monitoring and level of psychopathology. Among adults seeking treatment, either as psychiatric outpatients at a mental health center or as clients at a private therapy organization, those diagnosed as normal, sociopathic, neurotic, or psychotic (using the Goldberg formulas, 1972) typically do not differ in self-monitoring orientations (Arnold, 1976).

Nevertheless, hospitalized psychiatric ward patients do tend to have relatively low scores on the Self-Monitoring Scale (Snyder, 1974). These low scores, however, may be as much a reflection of their status as ward patients as of their psychiatric diagnoses. The frequently demonstrated links between impression-management skills and quality of life in institutions (e.g., Braginsky and Braginsky, 1971; Braginsky, Braginsky, and Ring, 1969) suggest that low self-monitoring patients (with their lesser impression-management skills) may be consigned to the (presumably) less desirable living situations offered by wards.

That self-monitoring is not linked to problems of adjustment or psychopathology no doubt reflects the fact that there is nothing inherently better or worse about either interpersonal orientation. Each self-monitoring style has its assets and liabilities, the assets of one being the liabilities of the other. Although the high self-monitoring orientation may provide the flexibility and adaptability to cope with a wide variety of circumstances, it may be an obstacle to intimacy in close relationships. High self-monitors lack (by design, it would seem) intimacy, closeness, and commitment in their relationships. This may occasion some distress when they enter relationships (such as marriages) in which their partners expect intimacy, closeness, and commitment. The low self-monitoring orientation, on the other hand, is well-suited to close and intimate relationships. It may not serve so well in maintaining a broad range of relationships, especially when different relationships make conflicting demands. Low self-monitors also may be vulnerable to psychological distress and emotional upset triggered by the dissolution of their relationships.

Although neither self-monitoring type is inherently "better" or "worse," each may have its pathological counterpart. In some people predisposed to psychopathology, the chameleonlike, impression-managing, role-enacting, high self-monitoring approach may, in its most exaggerated forms, resemble the histrionic personality.[1] And, in other people predisposed to psychopathology, the consistent "speaking-their-minds" and "sticking-to-their-guns" low self-monitoring orientation may, in its most exaggerated forms, resemble the rigidity of the authoritarian personality.

As Goffman has written in a somewhat different, but clearly related, context:

> Too little perceptiveness, too little *savoir faire,* too little pride and considerateness, and the person ceases to be someone who can be trusted to take a hint about himself or give a hint that will save others embarrassment. Such a person comes to be a real threat to society; there is nothing much that can be done with him. . . . Too much *savoir faire* or too much considerateness, and he becomes someone who is too socialized, who leaves the others with the feeling that they do not know how they really stand with him, nor what they do to make an effective long-term adjustment. (1955, p. 227)

Just as, for Goffman, deficits and excesses in "savoir faire" may pose threats to the social order, gross exaggerations of either self-monitoring orientation may cause difficulties. These difficulties may plant seeds that grow into problems of coping and adjustment or even blos-

---

[1]In its most exaggerated forms, the high self-monitoring orientation also may resemble the "as-if" personality described by Deutsch (1965), which describes a person who, suffering from a fragile sense of self, is constantly attuned to signals from the outer world and forever ready to shift roles in hopes of shoring himself or herself up.

som into psychopathological conditions. In this regard, Block (1961) has proposed that extreme role diffusion ("where an individual is an interpersonal chameleon, with no inner core of identity, fitfully reacting in all ways to all people," p. 392) and extreme role rigidity ("where an individual behaves uniformly in all situations, disregarding the different responsibilities different circumstances may impose," p. 392) may indicate problems of ego identity and psychological adjustment.

In fact, when people do encounter problems, self-monitoring does have an impact on the type of problems they experience, the kinds of events that lead to these problems, and their personal modes of coping. Each of these aspects of personal problems—what they are, what triggers them, and how people cope with them—is illustrated by the specific case of depression.

Depression: Precipitating Events and Coping Strategies

Depression is not a phenomenon confined to an unlucky few. In our lifetimes, some 20 percent of us will suffer bouts of depression, lasting anywhere from a few days to many years (Task Panel Reports Submitted to the President's Commission on Mental Health, Vol. 4, Appendix, 1978). In fact, the National Institute of Mental Health has suggested that depression is second only to schizophrenia as a national mental health problem (Secunda, Friedman, and Schuyler, 1973). Moreover, since depression occurs most frequently during the adult years of family development and career productivity, it is a family and an economic as well as a personal problem (Craighead, 1981).

Incidence and Prevalence   Studies of college students have revealed that depression is a common experience. During their first year of college, three out of four students experience at least mild depression, with four out of 10 experiencing moderate to severe depression (Bosse et al., 1975). Moreover, in one survey of depressive episodes (Snyder and Smith, 1985), college students reported that they got depressed between once a month and a couple of times a month. They also reported that their depressions lasted from a few hours to several days.

However, the self-monitoring orientations of college students do not influence how often they get depressed, how long their depressions last, or how deeply depressed they get (Snyder and Smith, 1985). In addition, studies of clinical populations (e.g., White-Phelan, 1983) have confirmed that people high and low in self-monitoring do not differ in their levels of depression, as measured by scores on the Beck Depression Inventory (Beck, Ward, Mendelson, Mock, and Erbaugh, 1961).[2]

Precipitating Events   Although self-monitoring does not determine the incidence and prevalence of depression, it does figure prominently in the events that *precipitate* depressive episodes (Snyder and Smith, 1985; also see Figure 9-1). When questioned about the events that trigger their experiences of depression, high self-monitoring college students point to events such as trying out for a team or a play and not making it, planning a party that was a failure, having to work with people who are incompetent, being told that they are not good at something they care about, or failing an important job interview. Students low in self-monitoring identify events such as discovering that a best friend has problems with drugs or alcohol, having to work with people they do not like, being dumped by a girlfriend or boyfriend for someone else, being told that they are hypocrites, or discovering that a friend no longer shares their attitudes and values as the sources of their bouts with depression.

The unifying characteristic of each set of events is the person's interpersonal orientation. In so many arenas of their lives, high self-monitors seem to be invested in skilled performances—whether in the careful choice of words and mannerisms to present images appropriate to current situations or the choice of friends with special skills as activity partners. People of this type seem also to be vulnerable to the depressing impact of being frustrated in their efforts to provide skilled performances, being viewed as an unskilled performer, and being forced to deal with others who do not provide skilled performances.

Low self-monitors, on the other hand, show in many domains of their lives an abiding desire to be true to their attitudes and values—

---

[2]Rahaim, Waid, Kennelly, and Stricklin (1980) have reported that, in two small samples, the depressed were *lower* in self-monitoring than the non-depressed. However, this apparent inverse relation is undermined considerably by their finding that a sample of institutionalized depressed psychiatric patients actually had *higher* Self-Monitoring Scale Scores than either depressed or non-depressed non-institutionalized people.

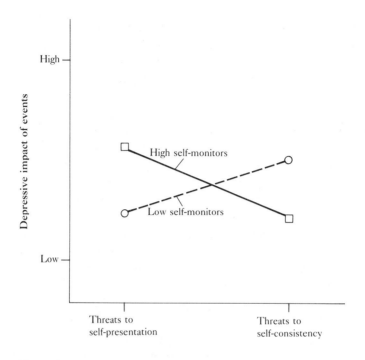

Figure 9-1 Depression in college students: Precipitating events (Snyder and Smith, 1985).

whether in choosing behaviors that reflect inner attributes or in choosing friends of similar attitudes and values. For these people, events that thwart their quests for consistency between self and social behavior and for the company of similar others whom they like and who like them may have depressing consequences.

Coping Strategies   How do people deal with depression? What *coping strategies* do they use? There are indications that, at least for college students, self-monitoring propensities come into play (Snyder and Smith, 1985; also see Figure 9-2). High self-monitoring students report that they adopt an active, self-regulatory approach to their depressions. They try to be alert to signs of depression, try to avoid situations that might depress them, try to know what to do about their depression, and they actively do things (such as acting as if they are in a good mood when really they are depressed) to rid themselves of depression.

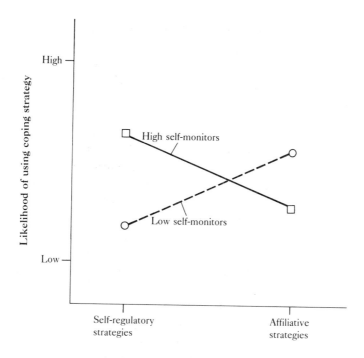

Figure 9-2   Depression in college students: Coping strategies (Snyder and Smith, 1985).

Low self-monitoring students claim that, when they find themselves depressed (which, for them, often happens without warning), their coping strategies focus on affiliation with other people. They prefer to talk to a friend, believing that it helps to "open up" to others who know them well. They approach friends not so much as sources of advice but as sympathetic listeners who let them "get it out of their systems."

Is the self-regulatory or the affiliative approach the more effective strategy for coping with depression? There is probably no difference in effectiveness. After all, both high and low self-monitors seem to be experiencing depressive episodes with equal frequency and of equal duration. Were the two strategies differentially effective, there ought to be differences either in the frequency or duration of the depressions experienced by those who practice either strategy. Since such differences do not exist, each coping strategy seems to effectively serve the needs of those who adopt it.

Effectiveness of Treatment: Modes of Therapeutic Intervention

What happens if and when problems reach a critical point and people abandon self-help strategies to seek the advice and counsel of professionals? Are different therapeutic regimens indicated for people high and low in self-monitoring? It would be an understatement to say that there is more than one approach to therapy. Indeed, an authoritative review for the National Institute of Mental Health (Parloff, Wolfe, Hadley, and Waskow, 1978) lists over 250 different schools of therapy. And, in a survey covering only "well-established systems that have proven their validity through popularity and survival," there are fully 13 categories of psychotherapy alone, each encompassing several variations on a common theme (Corsini, 1979). The list of therapies may be long, but there are some common features. For our purposes, I have categorized therapies in terms of two fundamental distinctions.

Types of Treatment   The first distinction concerns the locus of the problem to be dealt with by the therapy. Some therapies focus on the overt behaviors that are of current concern to the client, regarding them not as symptoms of some underlying disorder but rather as the problems themselves. These therapies seek to replace maladaptive and dysfunctional behaviors with more adaptive and functional ones. Other therapies see the current behaviors as symptoms of a problem in underlying attitudes, values, and motives. These therapies attempt to deal with the underlying problems, treating symptoms only indirectly. The behavioral therapies, such as those based upon principles laid down by Skinner (1953) and Wolpe (1958), are prominent in the first category. In the second category are the insight-oriented therapies, such as psychoanalytic therapies practiced by, among others, the disciples of Freud (1914) and Jung (1909) and the client-centered psychotherapy developed by Rogers (1954).

The second distinction concerns the role of the therapist. The behavioral therapies (e.g., Wolpe, 1958) and the more directive psychotherapies (e.g., Ellis, 1970) prescribe an active, assertive, directive role for the therapist, who structures the therapeutic process, either by providing an explicit explanation of the underlying source of the client's problem or by providing a clearly defined regimen for solving these problems. Other therapies cast the therapist in a relatively nondirective role; he or she provides a supportive and nurturing climate that encourages the client to gain insights into the source of the problem and the means to solve it. The defining example of this category is Rogerian client-centered therapy (e.g., Rogers, 1951), but it also includes the group therapies that came out of the sensitivity training and encounter group movements (e.g., Solomon and Berzon, 1972).

Types of People   Self-monitoring may be a relevant factor when choosing the therapy best suited to a person and his or her problems. For a variety of reasons, therapies that focus on modifying actual behaviors may be most appropriate for high self-monitors. Those aiming to influence underlying thoughts, feelings, and motives may be best suited for low self-monitors.

The behavioral therapies, which focus on modifying problematic behaviors by influencing the situational contingencies and rewards that support them, would seem to be particularly conducive to the situationally guided high self-monitoring orientation. People with this orientation are highly sensitive and responsive to situational considerations (see Chapters 3 and 4). Accordingly, they ought to be at home in therapies that assume, as they themselves do, that their behavior is a product of their situations. Also, they ought to be willing and able to mold their behavior to fit new guidelines provided by behaviorally oriented therapies.

By contrast, insight-oriented therapies, which focus on deeply rooted and firmly implanted beliefs, feelings, and intentions that support maladaptive behaviors, ought to be particularly appropriate for low self-monitors whose behavior typically reflects their attitudes and dispositions (see Chapters 3 and 4). Accordingly, they ought to respond to therapies that probe the underlying bases of their problems. People of this type ought to translate new beliefs, intentions, and motives acquired in therapy into new patterns of behavior.

Moreover, whether the therapist is cast in a directive or nondirective role may influence the client. The frequently demonstrated preference of high self-monitors for highly structured situations with clearly defined guidelines (see Chapter 4) ought to make them receptive to the prescriptions of relatively directive therapists. However, the nondirective therapist who provides a supportive and nurturing context may be most appropriate for low self-monitors. This type of therapeutic approach has much in common with the coping strategy low self-monitors use when they deal with problems on their own

(Snyder and Smith, 1985). A supportive and nurturing therapist may provide a professional version of the services offered by a good friend who listens sympathetically and provides a warm shoulder to cry on.

The Fit Between Person and Treatment   One of the most critical decisions to be made in any therapeutic endeavor is choosing a therapy suitable not only for the problem but also for the person with the problem. Over the years, it has become increasingly clear that no one brand of therapy corners the market on therapeutic effectiveness. Instead, what works for one person may not work for another person with the same problem. Accordingly, successful therapy must involve a careful matching of person and treatment (Garfield, 1978; Liberman, 1981; Luborsky, Singer, and Luborsky, 1975; Shaw, 1981).

Counselors and therapists can apply knowledge about the self-monitoring status of their clients when referring people to treatments. And just as with self-monitoring, other features of personality may be implicated in therapy effectiveness. For example, people who differ in their locus of control (Rotter, 1966) may also respond differently to therapies. Those with an internal locus of control (who believe that the forces determining their behavior are within their control) may perform well in therapies that prescribe an active, involved role for them as administrators of their own therapeutic regimens. But those with an external locus of control (who believe the forces determining their behavior to be beyond their control) may respond best to treatments in which their problems are solved for them, with their therapists providing prescriptions (either behavioral or, in some cases, pharmacological) for eliminating their distress. Similarly, authoritarians may respond well to the highly structured dictates of powerful therapists and Machiavellians may fare poorly in therapies that require them to place great trust in their therapists.

Coping with Personal Problems: Approaches to Self-Management

Of course, not all attempts to deal with problems occur in the offices of professionals. Often people engage in "self-management" activities, frequently relying on their own intuitions about how to solve problems. Sometimes, however, they employ techniques suggested by the authors of self-help books found in the psychology section of bookstores. Or, they may use strategies suggested by media psychologists who appear on the early-morning or late-night talk shows. Typically, the problems people try to deal with on their own are losing weight, quitting smoking, becoming assertive, and the like—problems of sufficient concern to make people try to change themselves but not of sufficient gravity to cause them to seek professional advice and counsel.

What suggestions can be offered to people who are about to embark on such self-help programs? Some of the most effective self-management programs have come out of the cognitive-behavioral tradition, so named because of its blending of principles of cognitive and behavioral approaches to influencing behavior (e.g., Hollon and Beck, 1978, 1979; Rehm and Kornblith, 1979). Consider these two self-management strategies for people who want to quit smoking, one designed for high self-monitoring smokers, the other for low self-monitoring smokers.[3]

An Image-Oriented Approach to Self-Management   If their sensitivity to considerations of public images can be translated into a self-management strategy, high self-monitoring smokers could be encouraged to engage in the following image-oriented activities. When they find themselves reaching for a cigarette, they could rehearse a series of thoughts concerning all the negative features smoking adds to their exterior appearances (e.g., bad breath, stained teeth, yellow fingers, smelly clothes, dirty hair). In addition, they might imagine vivid scenarios in which they suffer unpleasant social consequences of smoking (e.g., others terminating conversations with them when they light up, others refraining to sit next to them because of their habit, others refusing to be intimate with them because they smell and taste of smoke).

---

[3] These self-management programs should be distinguished from "behavioral self-observation" therapies that try to modify behavior by the reactive influence of observing one's behavior (e.g., Gottman and McFall, 1972; McFall, 1970; McFall and Hammen, 1971). These therapies are often labeled "self-monitoring" therapies; nevertheless, the self-monitoring in their label is not the self-monitoring of this book. Instead, it is the simple procedure of observing, counting, and recording one's responses. Based on a review, Kazdin has concluded that the effects of this procedure are inconsistent—the behavior under scrutiny is only sometimes altered, and then the change usually lasts only for a short time (1974).

Perhaps, too, high self-monitoring smokers could imagine themselves improving their exterior appearances and their social lives by becoming nonsmokers. Moreover, they could encourage those around them to help them with reminders (e.g., commenting on how much more attractive and appealing they look when they are not smoking, delivering tokens of social recognition and approval for not smoking). With this little bit of help from others, they may make the transition from being smokers to being nonsmokers.

A Value-Oriented Approach to Self-Management   What about low self-monitoring smokers who seek to rid themselves of the smoking habit? The relatively great value they place on consistency between attitudes and behavior suggests a different self-management strategy for them. They could be encouraged, when struck by the urge to smoke, to rehearse a series of thoughts concerning all the ways smoking creates gaps and contradictions between their attitudes and values (e.g., that their willingness to tolerate coughing, shortness of breath, and sore throats questions the value they place on their health, that wanting to stop smoking and not stopping suggests they may not be all that true to their selves).

Perhaps, too, low self-monitoring smokers could imagine graphic scenarios in which they face personal consequences of the inconsistencies between their values and actions (e.g., being disappointed with themselves for valuing their health but not doing what it takes to maintain it, censuring themselves for committing themselves to quit smoking and not living up to their commitments). Moreover, they might encourage others to create a climate that would provide behavioral supports (e.g., have friends remind them of the ways smoking sets them apart from their nonsmoking friends, point out that smoking may threaten the bonds of closeness they crave in their relationships, provide examples of how others have lived up to their own commitments to rid themselves of unwanted habits). By taking these reminders to heart, low self-monitoring smokers may capitalize on their high investment in relationships to help themselves become nonsmokers.

Further Applications of Self-Management: Health and Wellness   The same image-oriented and value-oriented approaches to self-management may help people deal with nagging problems in other life domains. For example, high self-monitors trying to lose weight might concentrate on instructing themselves about the benefits to their exterior appearances and public images if they were only to succeed in shedding those extra pounds. However, low self-monitors might instruct themselves about the enhanced inner well-being and healthiness that will come from slimming down to their ideal weights.

When it comes to health management, there may be other benefits to considering the role of self-monitoring. High self-monitors may be particularly likely to follow "wellness" regimens if they think of them in terms of their public images. Low self-monitors may be more willing to adopt wellness practices that help the inner workings of the body. As one example, high self-monitoring sufferers of colds or flu may be attracted to remedies that mask superficial symptoms of coughing, runny noses, and sneezing, which make them socially unattractive (even if those remedies do nothing to actually "cure" colds and flu). Perhaps, too, these same people would be willing to use preparations that actually prolong the illness if only their symptoms could be erased for the moment. However, low self-monitors may care less about the effects of particular remedies on exterior symptoms. They may be more concerned with whether a remedy can fight viruses or whatever else is wrong with their inner workings. They may even go so far as to prefer remedies that temporarily exacerbate external symptoms in order to produce a speedier recovery.

Effectiveness of Counselors and Therapists

Are some people better suited, by virtue of their self-monitoring propensities, to enter the professional practice of counseling and therapy, to offer advice and counsel to those who seek help, and to perform therapy when pathological conditions indicate it? Graduate students in training to be counseling and clinical psychologists are neither higher nor lower in self-monitoring than their counterparts in the more research-oriented areas of psychology (e.g., Arnold, 1976). Thus, one probably cannot say, based on self-monitoring status alone, whether or not people should enter the professional practice of psychology. However, there are ways to predict what skills they will bring to the counseling or therapeutic enterprise and what forms of counseling or therapy they will be best suited to practice.

The Role of Empathy in Counseling and Therapy   Mill (1984) has analyzed the role of empathy in counseling and psychotherapy. In doing so, she has drawn on a distinction, first made by Gladstein (1983), between *cognitive* empathy (which "refers to intellectually taking the role or perspective of another person" and "seeing the world as the other person does"; Gladstein, 1983, p. 468) and *affective* empathy (which "refers to responding with the same emotion to another person's emotion" and "feeling the same way as the other person does"; Gladstein, 1983, p. 468). Both types of empathy are, according to Mill, important skills for counselors and therapists. Cognitive empathy may be reflected in the ability to judge a client's emotional reactions accurately; affective empathy determines the ability to genuinely experience and sincerely reflect back a client's feelings.

In her investigations, Mill has found ties between self-monitoring and empathy. High self-monitoring counseling students were particularly skilled in cognitive empathy. They could interpret the nonverbal behavior of other people more accurately than those low in self-monitoring. Low self-monitoring counseling students were particularly skilled in affective empathy. In dyadic interactions they were perceived to genuinely experience more affective empathy than their high self-monitoring counterparts. Perhaps, too, practitioners draw on one or the other form of empathy to assess their confidence in their clinical judgments. Low self-monitoring practitioners may rely on affective empathy and high self-monitors on cognitive empathy as bases for confidence in clinical judgment. If so, low and high self-monitoring practitioners ought *not* to differ in their confidence in clinical judgments. In fact, there is no association between self-monitoring and confidence in clinical judgment (Abston, 1980).

Based on her findings, Mill (1984) has concluded that people of both self-monitoring types possess the necessary skills to practice counseling and psychotherapy. Moreover, she has proposed that the training of counselors and therapists should concentrate on *perfecting* skills that trainees already possess (judging the client's emotional reactions for high self-monitoring trainees, experiencing the client's emotional reactions for low self-monitors) as well as on *acquiring* skills that come less naturally (training high self-monitors to experience more genuine affective empathy, teaching low self-monitors to perform more accurate cognitive assessments of clients).

Interpersonal Orientations of Counselors and Therapists   There may be additional features of self-monitoring relevant to the professional activities of counselors and therapists. The active, initiatory, and directive posture that high self-monitors are disposed to adopt in social interaction (Ickes and Barnes, 1977) and their preferences for highly structured situations with clearly defined behavioral guidelines (Chapter 4) suggest that they will perform most effectively in highly directive counseling and therapeutic roles. Thus, they may be best suited to practice forms of counseling and therapy that require them to provide clients with explicit guidelines, prescriptions, and scripts to follow (e.g., social skills training and systematic desensitization).

Moreover, their acting skills may permit high self-monitoring practitioners to act as effective role models in therapeutic interventions in which the client's modeling of desired behaviors is an essential component (e.g., assertiveness training, social skills training). In addition, their acting skills may help high self-monitors perform well when they must feign greater interest and concern than they really experience. Thus, high self-monitoring counselors may be able to express as much interest in a problem the hundredth time they hear about it as the first time, to convey the same air of professionalism whatever their personal reactions to clients and their problems, to seem as attentive to the last client of the day as to the first, and so on. Indeed, in some professional contexts, there are indications that expressive self-control (as measured by skill in facial deceiving) and performance (as measured by clinical grades of students in training) go together (Ekman and Friesen, 1969, 1974).

Similarly, low self-monitoring practitioners may be better suited to other brands of counseling and therapy. The low self-monitoring propensity to adopt a "listener" role in social interaction (e.g., Ickes and Barnes, 1977), as well as a preference for settings that permit them to express their attitudes and values (see Chapter 4), may serve particularly well in professional roles that call on counselors and therapists to be responsive listeners and to provide feedback based on their own emotional responses to their clients.

Moreover, the special value that low self-monitors place on closeness in relationships (see Chapters 5 and 6) may be useful in any counseling and therapeutic endeavors (such as some of the humanistic ones) that are facilitated by developing bonds of psychological closeness with clients. This value also may be helpful with those clients who respond best to counselors and therapists they regard as friends. It may even make low self-monitors especially suited to practicing in areas (such as relationship counseling and family therapy) specializing in problems arising within the context of close relationships. For these reasons, the criteria of unconditional positive regard, genuineness in the therapeutic endeavor, and accurate emotional empathy—thought to define the ideal practitioner of the Rogerian brand of client-centered nondirective therapy (Rogers, 1942)—may be describing precisely the low self-monitoring therapist or counselor.

Perhaps, too, therapists and counselors will perform most effectively when paired with clients whose self-monitoring orientations are similar to their own (Sparacino, 1981). Quite possibly, the "interactional strain" that often characterizes interactions between people of discrepant self-monitoring orientations (Ickes and Barnes, 1977) may lead to "dead spots" in the therapeutic interchanges of mixed pairings and reduced rapport between therapist and client, eventually undermining the client's motivation to continue in therapy. If so, matchmaking that produces therapists and clients of like self-monitoring status may be in the interest of all concerned.

Counseling and Therapy: Those Who Seek and Those Who Offer

Clearly, when it comes to understanding personal problems, counseling, and therapy, there is an applied message about self-monitoring. Applications of theory and research have proved their usefulness in understanding those who seek *and* those who offer counseling and therapy. These applications suggest which types of people will be most susceptible to what kinds of precipitating events, which types of people will be most responsive to certain forms of counseling and therapy, and which types of people will be best suited to practice different approaches to counseling and therapy. The benefits of this knowledge may be considerable. The training of practitioners may be refined, and the effectiveness of the counseling and therapeutic arts and sciences may be enhanced by applying this knowledge.

PART IV

The Roots of Self-Monitoring

WHY IS IT that some people grow up to be high in self-monitoring and others to be low in self-monitoring? Over the years, I have been asked this question more often than any other. Understanding the origins and development of self-monitoring is undeniably one of the most important challenges facing researchers concerned with self-monitoring. No account of the nature of self-monitoring could possibly be complete, or even close to complete, without some understanding of its emergence and course of development.

In fact, developmentally-oriented researchers are working to trace the roots of self-monitoring. And, although much of their work is still in its beginning stages, they have already provided some provocative clues about the origins and development of self-monitoring. Whether people are high or low in self-monitoring may to some extent be biologically determined (Chapter 10), although socialization processes may play a critical part in the course of development of the self-monitoring orientations (Chapter 11). That is, when it comes to self-monitoring, people are first born, then made.

The Origins of Self-Monitoring

■

WHAT ARE THE roots of self-monitoring? Among the questions about the origins and development of self-monitoring that readily come to my mind: Are people born with a biological or genetic predisposition to become either high or low in self-monitoring? If so, are these predispositions of ability or motivation? Do some life experiences prompt concerns with public impressions and images, whereas others stimulate concerns with private attitudes and values? If so, do these experiences plant seeds that grow into either the high or the low self-monitoring orientation?

Although questions about the origins of self-monitoring may come easily, the answers are much more difficult to find. It is not always clear how researchers should approach such questions. Should they look first to the larger demographic variables and ask whether high and low self-monitoring orientations are products of socialization patterns associated with differences in social class, economic status, religious affiliation, or geographical location? For example, one could advance the hypothesis that the high self-monitoring orientation is an urban phenomenon, drawing on the diversity provided by big cities, and that the low self-monitoring orientation is a rural phenomenon, reflecting the greater homogeneity of small-town living. Or, instead, should investigators focus on particular psychological events known to be important in social development and probe their specific implications for the development of self-monitoring? For instance, one could focus on family relationships and ask about factors (such as identification with a role model, whether a parent or a sibling, who is either high or low in self-monitoring) that might foster the beginnings of either self-monitoring orientation.

The Etiology of Self-Monitoring

It may be most productive to consider the origins of self-monitoring by asking perhaps the most fundamental question of all: *When it comes to self-monitoring, are people born or are they made?* Or, more formally, what are the roles of biological-genetic and environmental-socialization influences in the development of self-monitoring? On first consideration, the answer may seem a forgone conclusion. After all, self-monitoring gives every indication of being a fundamentally social phenomenon. It occurs of necessity in social settings. It invokes the essence of a person's social identity as it is intimately intertwined in the fabric of his or her interpersonal relationships. Why, the reader may wonder, am I being asked to even consider a biological-genetic basis for self-monitoring?

Admittedly, the possibility of biological-genetic origins may confound intuitions. However, a cardinal rule of all good detective work is that no suspects are excluded, even (or especially) the one who at first glance seems least likely to be the culprit. And there are reasons to at least consider the possibility that biological-genetic factors play a meaningful role in *predisposing* people toward one or the other self-monitoring orientation. Foremost among these reasons is the fact that self-monitoring seems *not* to be linked in any meaningful fashion to many indicators of socialization practices, indicators often thought to be critically important in development.

Consider some of the larger demographic variables: social class, economic status, geographical region, religious affiliation, and so on. These variables often serve as "summary" indexes, reflecting a host of social and psychological factors. Therefore, they ought to function as "sponges," soaking up substantial amounts of variance and hence serving as good predictors of the phenomena of personality and social psychology. Thus, it is not at all unreasonable to wonder whether any of the major demographic variables could account for self-monitoring. In fact, my own earliest thoughts about the origins and development of self-monitoring centered on precisely such links between socialization practices associated with major demographic variables and the self-monitoring orientations.

Yet, as plausible as such links may be, repeated efforts, using surveys and questionnaires, to implicate demographic variables as predictors of self-monitoring have come up empty-handed (e.g., Snyder and Tanke, 1974; Snyder and Simpson, 1983, 1984a, b). There is simply no reliable evidence that self-monitoring is meaningfully associated with social class, economic status, regional origins, geographical movement (being high or low is not the product of frequent moves and adjustments to new surroundings or the stability of remaining in the same community from birth through adulthood), or religious affiliation.

Of course, these surveys do not close the book on socialization accounts of the roots of self-monitoring. One way to cope with the frustration of coming up empty-handed is by pointing to the limitations of these surveys (they are largely based, for example, on retrospective reports that may not be accurate). Another coping strategy, in keeping with the "exclude no suspects" rule, is to consider (at least for the sake of argument) the possibility of biological-genetic origins for self-monitoring.

A Biological-Genetic Etiology?   Could self-monitoring have biological-genetic origins? A second cardinal rule of good detective work is to find facts and use them to rule out suspects. Even those who doubt that self-monitoring has a biological-genetic etiology must admit that the genetic hypothesis is highly testable. Monozygotic twins share all of their genetic material. They are, truly, "identical" twins. Dizygotic or "fraternal" twins share, on average, half of their genetic material, the same proportion shared by single-birth siblings. Accordingly, comparisons of the self-monitoring status of monozygotic and dizygotic twins provide a test of the hypothesis that self-monitoring has genetic origins. At the very least, such a test has the potential—should it come up empty-handed—to discredit the genetic hypothesis.

In one test of the genetic hypothesis, Dworkin (1977) studied pairs of twins. He found that the within-pair variability on the Self-Monitoring Scale for identical twins was less than half the within-pair variability for fraternal twins. Perhaps Dworkin's results suggest that self-monitoring propensities can be traced to genetic origins. As intriguing as Dworkin's data are, they are unfortunately based on only a small number of twin pairs—54 pairs of identical twins and 34 pairs of fraternal twins. But Dworkin's data are enhanced by a stronger test of genetic influence conducted by Gangestad (1984).

Gangestad has argued that, under the genetic hypothesis, identical twins (who share all of their genetic material) must *always* be of the same self-monitoring type: Both must be high or both must be low in self-monitoring. That is, for identical twins, the concordance rates for self-monitoring status, at an underlying level of causality, must be perfect, equal to 1.00. The concordance rates for fraternal twins (who share on average half of their genetic material) should be substantially less than 1.00. Since he could not simply look at a pair of twins to "see" whether they actually are of the same self-monitoring type, Gangestad employed a series of mathematical procedures to estimate the true concordance rates on self-monitoring for 149 pairs of identical twins and 76 same-sex fraternal twin pairs (Table 10-1).

In support of the genetic hypothesis, Gangestad's mathematical operations estimated the concordance rate for identical twins to be .95, very near the predicted rate of 1.00. However, he was concerned that some of the twin pairs he thought to be identical actually were not, since the biographical questionnaire method of finding out if twins are identical is accurate only about 95 percent of the time. Therefore, he also estimated the concordance rate only for those pairs known to constitute a pure sample of identical twins. These twin pairs had been identified by blood-typing and fingerprinting, procedures that are virtually error-free. Here, the estimated concordance rate reached a nearly perfect .99. The same mathematical procedures yielded an estimated concordance rate of only .74 for dizygotic twins.

Interpreting Studies of Twins   If we are to believe the twin studies, genetic influences are, if not exclusively, then at least substantially implicated in the origins of self-monitoring. But the twin method has been the target of some criticism (see, for example, Lewontin, Rose, and Kamin, 1984). According to the logic of this method, identical and fraternal twins differ only in how much genetic material they share; thus any differences between the two types of twins must be due to genetic influences. However, the environments of identical twins may be more similar than those of fraternal twins. After all, identi-

Table 10-1   Concordance Rates for Identical and Fraternal Twins

Type of twin pair	Concordance rate
All identical twins	.95
Identical twins, determined by blood type	.99
Fraternal twins	.74
Random pairs	.55

Gangestad, 1984.

cal twins (see Table 10-1) are treated more similarly by their parents and are more likely to share the same friends than nonidentical twins (Loehlin and Nichols, 1976; Scarr, 1968; Smith, 1965).

But do these shared environments create psychological similarity of twins? Apparently not. Twins wrongly thought to be identical and fraternal twins who look very much alike (and who are thus treated more similarly than other fraternal twins) share no more psychological similarity than is typical of fraternal twins (e.g., Matheny, Wilson, and Dolan, 1976; Plomin, Willerman, and Loehlin, 1976; Scarr, 1968; Scarr and Carter-Saltzman, 1979). In addition, if the shared environments of twins account for their psychological similarity, then twins who have been reared together should have greater psychological similarity than those reared apart. But, if anything, identical twins reared together demonstrate more *differences* in personality than identical twins reared apart (e.g., Farber, 1981; Lykken, Tellegen, and Bouchard, 1984). Indeed, the overall pattern of evidence has led at least one expert to conclude that "differential treatment of twins by their social environment does not appear to be responsible for the greater similarity of monozygotic versus same-sex [dizygotic] twins for such characteristics as intelligence, personality, and language and perceptual skills" (Kendler, 1983, p. 1416). Thus, in the case of self-monitoring, there seems to be little reason to attribute the differences between identical and fraternal twins to differences in their environments.

Implications of a Biological-Genetic Etiology   What, then, does it mean to have identified a biological-genetic etiology for self-monitoring? Let me first be explicit about some of what it does *not* mean. A biological-genetic etiology does not mean that the behaviors associated with self-monitoring are rigidly fixed in each person and immune to change through experience or with training (e.g., Meehl, 1972). After all, best estimates tell us that the latent self-monitoring causal variable accounts for about 50 percent of the variation between people in expressive self-control (Gangestad and Snyder, 1985). Thus, even if biological-genetic influences do account for that 50 percent, the person least disposed by those biological-genetic influences to be high in self-monitoring still could learn the skills needed to exercise self-control over his or her expressive behavior and self-presentations.

Moreover, a biological-genetic etiology for self-monitoring is *not* the end of the developmental story. To the contrary, it constitutes, at best, *only the beginnings* of the developmental course of self-monitoring. After all, genes do not have psychological or behavioral characteristics themselves. They can only influence psychological or behavioral characteristics through a course of development that requires an appropriate environmental context (e.g., Lehrman, 1970; Scarr and Kidd, 1983). And a biological-genetic etiology is hardly a complete beginning. No one knows (at least not yet) the precise form of the biological-genetic factor that disposes people to be high or low in self-monitoring. It might operate through a *specific* biochemical pathway, or it might be implicated in a number of *non-specific* and independent biochemical pathways. (For some informed speculation about one possible candidate for a specific biochemical pathway, see Gangestad, 1984.)

But beyond matters of beginnings, we must still trace all the steps that intervene between whatever is transmitted in the genes and the eventual blooming of the many and varied aspects of self-monitoring. This course of development is no doubt highly dependent on appropriate environments. That is, although one may be "born" with a genetically given predisposition to become high or low in self-monitoring, one must actually be "made" high or low in self-monitoring through relevant experiences of socialization.

A person may, for example, acquire a genetic predisposition to exercise control over the expressive musculature of the face and body. But, actually being able to use this ability to create naturally appearing social images may require considerable fine-tuning over a long series of learning experiences. In addition, the motivation to employ expressive self-control abilities for impression-management purposes may be itself the product of life experiences.

Not incidentally, the biological-genetic perspective may provide some insight into whether motivation precedes ability or ability precedes motivation in the origins of self-monitoring. Consider, first, the possibility that ability develops before motivation. If the ability to practice finely tuned control over expressive behavior is genetically determined, and if actual use of this ability is later potentiated by experiential factors, then there should be people who are endowed with well-developed self-presentational skills but who are not motivated to practice impression management. Indeed, many extraverts seem to possess some of the same self-presentational skills characteristic of the high self-monitoring orientation. Yet, these people may not apply these skills differently from situation to situation; instead, they appear consistently "extraverted." In sharp contrast, high self-monitors can and do use their self-presentational abilities to appear extraverted in some situations and introverted in others, depending on situational cues (Lippa, 1976*b*).

Now, if it were motivation that came before ability, then when people became motivated to engage in impression management, they would develop the skills needed to do so. If motivation and ability go hand in hand, then there should *not* be any people with motivation who lack ability. Yet, such people clearly do exist, such as those with a high need for social approval (Crowne and Marlowe, 1964). As motivated as these people are to seek and gain the social approval of others, many of them do not act in ways that actually elicit that approval. In fact, as a group, they tend to be somewhat lacking in social skills and make very few friends (Crowne and Marlowe, 1964). Whatever motivation these people possess, it clearly is not accompanied by the ability to fulfill their motivational desires.

Taken together, these cases lead us to this conclusion: The person with the extraverted disposition (who may possess some high self-monitoring abilities but lack high self-monitoring motivations) and the person with the high need for social approval (who may be motivated to engage in self-monitoring but lack the self-presentational abilities to do so) suggest that, with respect to self-monitoring, ability *precedes* motivation.

The Emergence of Self-Monitoring

Needless to say, pointing to biological-genetic origins does not suggest that all of the adult behavioral aspects of self-monitoring will appear, in full bloom, in childhood. Instead, it is more likely that self-monitoring first emerges in limited domains and that these initial differences are amplified and extended over time. At least two candidates for the domains of these initial manifestations suggest themselves.

The first candidate is differences in temperament, observable in early infancy. Very young infants (even a few months old) differ in, among other temperaments, their adaptability to changes in their environments and their responsiveness to social stimuli (e.g., Thomas, Chess, and Birch, 1968). Perhaps these differences are very early indicators of self-monitoring. Greater adaptability to environmental change and greater social responsiveness may be precursors of the high self-monitoring orientation; lesser reactivity to situational events may be a precursor of the low self-monitoring orientation.

In fact, differences in temperament may be inherited (e.g., Buss and Plomin, 1984; Goldsmith and Campos, 1982; Goldsmith and Gottesman, 1981; Harris and Rose, 1977; Matheny, 1980; Plomin and Rowe, 1977). As such, they may be associated with the biological-genetic origins of self-monitoring. Moreover, temperaments have some continuity over time (e.g., Beckwith, 1979; Dunn, 1980; Lewis and Starr, 1979). Thus, as they emerge and develop, temperament differences may come to be associated with self-monitoring styles. As intriguing as this possibility may be, a word of caution is in order: Little is known about the actual validity of the measures used to assess infant temperament (Hubert, Wachs, Peters-Martin, and Gandour, 1982).

There is, however, a second candidate for the domain in which self-monitoring makes, if not its first, then a very early appearance, which bears more than a passing resemblance to manifestations of self-monitoring in adulthood. In fact, so strong is this resemblance that it would be difficult not to regard it as a family resemblance. Systematic differences in how children acquire language that can be detected in children as young as $1\frac{1}{2}$ years old may be related to self-monitoring.

Some children, described by Nelson (1973, 1981) as "referential," acquire language as a system for conveying information about events in the world. Early on, they develop large vocabularies of nouns.

Other children, called "expressive" by Nelson, acquire language as a social vehicle for capturing the attention of others. They are quick to learn how the pattern, structure, and intonation of linguistic expressions are reflections of social context. In addition, these children focus on the social structure of events and the different roles that people can and do play in social situations. They also have a flair for telling dramatic stories and for displaying elaborate forms of imitation. Little wonder that Wolf and Gardner (1979) have called them "dramatists."

These differences in young children are, of course, strikingly similar to self-monitoring differences in adults. Referential children and low self-monitoring adults are rather insensitive to social context, whereas expressive children and high self-monitoring adults are highly attentive to such considerations. At the same time, expressive children and high self-monitoring adults are "dramatists" who put on social performances. They are sensitive to the attention that dramatic performances gain and they are skilled at imitating others. By comparison, referential children and low self-monitoring adults tend to be nondramatic in their orientation to social situations. The undeniable overlap between these two sets of behavioral differences suggests that they may be reflections of the same underlying causal variable, namely self-monitoring, operating at different ages.

A Radical Approach?

To be sure, tracing the roots of self-monitoring to biological-genetic origins may seem to be somewhat out of keeping with a concept as fundamentally social in character as self-monitoring. As contrary to intuition and as radical as it may seem, this approach to discovering the origins of self-monitoring has been a productive one. It has been possible to propose, and to find evidence for, an etiology for self-monitoring. And it has been possible to identify possible initial manifestations of self-monitoring in infancy and very early childhood.

Moreover, self-monitoring is not alone in having possible biological-genetic origins. A growing body of evidence suggests that genetic variation plays a meaningful role in the development of personality and social behavior (e.g., Henderson, 1982; Plomin, DeFries, and McClearn, 1980). Although it is unlikely that any single gene has large effects on psychological functioning, more complex genetic systems may have wide-ranging effects on the development of personality and social behavior. In the case of self-monitoring, the precise nature of this genetic system remains to be specified.

As intriguing and provocative as genetic origins for self-monitoring may be, I must underscore the fact that the saga of the development of self-monitoring is far from complete. A specific etiology and some initial manifestations are but the prologue to a much longer story. After all, the biological-genetic etiological factor is only a *predisposition* to *develop* a behavioral orientation, not the behavioral orientation itself. And, almost by definition, the early manifestations of self-monitoring are a more limited set than those observed in adults. There may be early cognitive differences that lead children to develop their language styles. But, there may not yet be any motivational differences regarding concern for the situational appropriateness of self-presentation. These and other differences involved in self-monitoring only develop over an extended period of time. It is as important to trace the steps in that developmental sequence as it is to identify the etiology of self-monitoring.

This development over time occurs, of necessity, in an environmental context. For the activities that define the high and low self-monitoring interpersonal styles can only occur in social situations. Thus, although a person may be predisposed to become high or low in self-monitoring, the interpersonal style that results will depend heavily on environmental factors that influence personality and social development. There probably are environments that are conducive to the development of the high self-monitoring orientation and others conducive to the socialization of the low self-monitoring orientation. Most likely, biological-genetic predispositions combine or interact with these environmental influences in the development of self-monitoring. The question is: How does this interaction work? The next chapter provides some answers to this question about the socialization of self-monitoring.

CHAPTER 11

The Development of Self-Monitoring

■

IF PEOPLE ARE born to be either high or low in self-monitoring, how do they actually develop the corresponding orientation? One possible scenario involves a process known as *divergent causality*. Divergent causality occurs when initially small differences become amplified or extended over time (Langmuir, 1943; London, 1946; Meehl, 1978). For self-monitoring, divergent causality might begin with small differences observable in young children that then "snowball" into the extensive differences in wide-ranging domains seen in adults.

What are the events of this "snowballing" developmental scenario? In the beginning, as we have just seen in Chapter 10, self-monitoring may involve tendencies to attend to different features of the social world, tendencies later expressed as actual differences in knowledge of the social world. Similarly, children may begin by having different potentials for acquiring dramatic role-playing skills; later they may actually differ in possession of these skills and use of them. Still later on, as children with these skills learn their purposes, they may become motivated to use them in social situations. Over time, then, the network of self-monitoring phenomena may expand through the acquisition of knowledge, skills, and motives (Gangestad and Snyder, 1985).

A Divergent Causality Scenario

More specifically, how might a process of divergent causality operate in the development of self-monitoring? One theory proposes that the latent causal factor involved in the origins of self-monitoring may influence choices of situations so that people gravitate toward environments conducive to their emerging self-monitoring propensities (Gangestad and Snyder, 1985). By virtue of spending time in situations conducive to their initial tendencies, people will develop repertoires increasingly consistent with these initial tendencies. Those predisposed by the latent causal factor to be low in self-monitoring may gravitate toward situations that provide supports for acting in accord with their attitudes, traits, and emotions. And those predisposed by the latent causal factor to be high in self-monitoring may gravitate toward situations that provide opportunities for enacting roles based on clearly defined situational guidelines.

This scenario also suggests that people may behave in ways that elicit different treatment from others, which may further reinforce the emerging self-monitoring orientations. Young children, by virtue of early displays of their self-monitoring tendencies, may prompt different parenting, caretaking, and caregiving styles from adults (cf. Bell, 1968, 1971). Thus, when adults are faced with young children who have referential communication styles (possible early low self-monitoring signs; see Chapter 10), they may react by providing more opportunities for these children to behave in a low self-monitoring manner. And when children have expressive social styles (possible early high self-monitoring signs), adults may respond by providing added opportunities for these children to behave in a high self-monitoring fashion.

In this way, early displays of self-monitoring may, in effect, influence the circumstances in which development occurs. Over time, high and low self-monitoring children will come to differ increasingly in their behavioral repertoires and their interpersonal styles. For elaboration of the role of choosing situations in developmental processes, see Snyder (1981*b*, 1983); also see Bell (1968, 1971) and Plomin, DeFries, and Loehlin (1977).

People, in fact, do structure their situations and choose their friends in ways conducive to their self-monitoring orientations (see Chapters 4, 5, and 6). Could it also be that children choose situations that correspond to their biological-genetic predispositions to be high or low in self-monitoring? Although young children have little control over many aspects of their environments (they don't choose their homes, families, neighborhoods, or schools), they can choose their friends and activity partners. Perhaps children disposed to become high self-monitors tend to choose friends who are skilled activity partners. And perhaps children disposed to become low self-monitors tend to choose friends who are well-liked and similar to them. By spending time with their chosen friends, then, high self-monitoring children may develop increasingly diverse behavioral repertoires, whereas low self-monitoring children may develop increasingly uniform ones. The net effect, of course, is yet more divergence in the situations and relationships of high and low self-monitoring children.

To the extent that parents encourage these choices of friends, the impact of these choices on the developing self-monitoring propensities will be enhanced. Parents may be most likely to support the friendship choices of their children when these choices reflect the same considerations that the parents themselves invoke when selecting their own friends. Thus, the impact of parental encouragement may be greatest in those cases where parents and children have matching self-monitoring orientations.

In like fashion, other choices of situations may add to the emerging pattern of differences between high and low self-monitoring children. Among these choices may be children's use of the space within the home. For example, in homes with many rooms, children can engage in various activities in separate locales, perhaps playing different roles in different places. In fact, high self-monitoring adults report that they grew up in houses with more rooms and fewer people per room than those who have grown up to be low in self-monitoring (Zaidman and Snyder, 1983).

There are, to be sure, many possible scenarios for the development of self-monitoring. This one, in which initial predispositions guide and direct (and are in turn reinforced and amplified by) choices of social situations is certainly plausible enough. But does it occur? To test it (or any other developmental scenario for self-monitoring), researchers will need some way to classify relatively young children as high or low in self-monitoring. At least two instruments are now available to measure self-monitoring in children.

Self-Monitoring in Early Childhood

Eder (1984) has developed a measure of self-monitoring that can be used with children as young as three years. This measure permits an adult who knows a child fairly well (for example, a teacher in a preschool setting) to describe that child with 25 statements derived from the adult Self-Monitoring Scale. More specifically, the adult would indicate whether items such as the following were true or false for the child in question: "Finds it hard to imitate others"; "Usually behaves consistent with his/her true inner feelings"; "In social situations does not attempt to do or say things that others will like"; "Looks at the behavior of others for cues of how to act in a situation where s/he is uncertain"; "Is a little entertainer"; and "Is rarely the center of attention in a group of people" (for a complete listing of the items, see Table 11-1).[1]

This self-monitoring measure for young children has the potential to reveal much about the developmental course of self-monitoring. For example, researchers could conduct a longitudinal investigation, using Nelson's (1973) classification system, in which they identify referential and expressive children at age $1\frac{1}{2}$ to two years and follow their development to see whether, at age three or four, they have become low or high self-monitoring children, as classified by Eder's measure. Such a demonstration could provide persuasive evidence that referential and expressive linguistic styles are, indeed, early forms of self-monitoring. Other researchers could examine the domains in which self-monitoring occurs in young children. Do high self-monitoring children have different self-presentational styles with parents and peers? Do low self-monitoring children show evidence of consistency between the beliefs, feelings, and intentions they express and their subsequent actions?

Still other researchers could investigate the role of choosing friends in the development of self-monitoring. Do high self-monitoring children associate with other children on the basis of their skills as activity

---

[1] An initial study of children between the ages of three and five revealed that this measure has an internal consistency of +.7 (coefficient alpha) and a test-retest reliability of +.7 (one-month time interval). This measure has an internal factor structure comparable to that of the adult Self-Monitoring Scale (see Chapter 12).

partners? Do they, for example, choose teammates for different sports on the basis of each potential teammate's track record in that particular sport? Do low self-monitoring children affiliate with other children on the basis of their general likability? Do they, for instance, choose their best friends as teammates, no matter what the sport? At what age do some children begin to develop the compartmentalized social networks (different friends for different activities) that, as we know (Chapter 5), are so typical of the high self-monitoring orientation? And, at how early an age do other children start developing the homogeneous social networks (a single, all-purpose "friend for all seasons") that are so much a part of the low self-monitoring orientation?

Furthermore, a self-monitoring measure geared to early childhood may help answer some fundamental questions: What are the links between parents' self-monitoring orientations and those of their children? Do children high or low in self-monitoring have parents who themselves are high or low self-monitors? If so, is the self-monitoring status of one parent a better guide than that of the other to the self-monitoring type of their children? In addition, studies of interactions between parents and children may be revealing. When it comes to social influence, young children identified as low self-monitors may elicit and respond to parental appeals of the form, "Eat this because you will like it" (an appeal to personal considerations), whereas high self-monitoring children may evoke and comply with parental appeals of the form, "Eat this because I want you to" (an appeal to social considerations).

Similarly, young children, when given the opportunity to influence other children, may employ tactics associated with their self-monitoring orientations. Low self-monitoring children may try to get their way with requests framed in terms of the other child's personal qualities ("Come play with me in the sandbox because you like me"); high self-monitoring children may seek to work their will with overtures geared to the other child's social interests ("Come join me on the swingset because that will make me like you").

Self-Monitoring in Middle Childhood

Graziano, Leone, Musser, and Lautenschlager (1985) have developed a measure of self-monitoring suitable for use in middle childhood (ages 6–9 through 10–13 years old). It consists of 24 true-false items de-

Table 11-1   Assessing Self-Monitoring in Early Childhood:
             A 25-Item Measure

1. Finds it hard to imitate others. (F)

2. Usually behaves consistent with his/her true inner feelings, attitudes and beliefs. (F)

3. At social gatherings and parties does not attempt to do or say things that others will like. (F)

4. Can only express ideas which s/he believes completely. (F)

5. Can talk or act like s/he knows a lot more about topics than s/he actually does. (T)

6. Puts on a show to impress people. (T)

7. Looks at the behavior of others for cues of how to act in a situation when s/he is uncertain. (T)

8. Would probably make a good actor. (T)

9. Rarely seeks advice of others to choose movies, books, records, or television programs. (F)

10. Sometimes appears to be experiencing deeper emotions than s/he actually is. (T)

11. Probably laughs more when seeing a funny show on television with others than when alone. (T)

12. Is rarely the center of attention in a group of people. (F)

13. In different situations and with different people, acts like very different children (persons). (T)

14. Is not particularly good at making others (peers and adults) like him/her. (F)

15. Often pretends to have a good time even when not really enjoying him/herself. (T)

16. Is not always the person s/he appears to be. (T)

17. Is reluctant to change her/his opinions (or the way s/he does things) in order to please someone else or win their favor. (F)

18. Is a little entertainer. (T)

19. In order to get along and be liked, tends to be what people expect rather than anything else. (T)

Table 11-1   *(continued)*

20. Is not very good at games like charades (e.g., "Who am I?"), improvisations, or acting.   (F)

21. Has trouble changing his/her behavior to suit different people and different situations.   (F)

22. Lets others keep people entertained in social situations or parties.   (F)

23. Seems to feel a bit awkward in the presence of company and does not show up quite as well as s/he should.   (F)

24. Can look anyone in the eye and tell a lie with a straight face (*if for a right end*).   (T)

25. May deceive people by being friendly when actually dislikes them.   (T)

For information on administration and scoring, see Eder (1984). Items are keyed in the direction of high self-monitoring (T = true; F = false).

signed to tap the same general content domains as the adult Self-Monitoring Scale (e.g., concern with social appropriateness, attention to social comparison information, ability to control expressive behavior, and situational specificity of self-presentation). Its items, however, are specifically appropriate for middle childhood; examples include "I sometimes wear some kinds of clothes just because my friends are wearing that kind," "I like to know how my classmates expect me to act," "I do not usually say things just because other people want me to," "I usually do what I want and not just what my friends think I should do," "When I'm with my friends I act different than I do with my parents," and "I'm not very good at telling jokes." For a complete listing of the items, see Table 11-2.[2]

This measure of self-monitoring in middle childhood predicts some of the same behaviors as the adult Self-Monitoring Scale. Just as high scorers on the adult measure seek out relevant sources of social com-

---

[2]The Graziano et al. (1985) measure has an internal consistency of .62.

**Table 11-2   Assessing Self-Monitoring in Middle Childhood:
A 24-Item Measure**

1. There are many things I would only tell to a few of my friends.   (Y)

2. I sometimes wear some kinds of clothes just because my friends are wearing that kind.   (Y)

3. I like to know how my classmates expect me to act.   (Y)

4. I would probably be good at acting in a school play.   (Y)

5. When I grow up, I would rather be a famous writer or painter than be in movies or be on TV.   (N)

6. I act better when my teacher is in the room than when my teacher is out of the room.   (Y)

7. When I don't know what to wear, I call my friends to see what they are going to wear.   (Y)

8. Even if I am not having a good time, I often act like I am.   (Y)

9. Sometimes I clown around so my classmates will like me.   (Y)

10. When I am not sure how to act I watch others to see what to do.   (Y)

11. I laugh more when I watch funny TV shows with other people than when I watch them alone.   (Y)

12. I do not usually say things just because other people want me to.   (N)

13. When I'm with my friends I act different than I do with my parents.   (Y)

14. I'm not very good at telling jokes.   (N)

15. When I'm afraid of someone, I try to be nice to them so they will not bother me.   (Y)

16. I usually do what I want and not just what my friends think I should do.   (N)

17. I try to figure out how each teacher wants me to act and then that's how I try to act.   (Y)

18. There are some things about me that I wouldn't want to tell anyone.   (Y)

19. I feel embarrassed when I don't have the same kind of clothes as my classmates.   (Y)

Table 11-2 *(continued)*

20. When a new person comes to school, I listen to what my classmates say before I decide whether I like the new person.   (Y)

21. Sometimes I help my mom without her asking me, so she will let me do something I want to do later.   (Y)

22. I can make people think I'm happy even if I'm not happy.   (Y)

23. I can be nice to people I don't like.   (Y)

24. I feel unhappy when I don't have the things that my friends have.   (Y)

For information on administration and scoring, see Graziano, Leone, Musser, and Lautenschlager (1985). Items are keyed in the direction of high self-monitoring (Y = yes; N = no).

parison (Snyder, 1974), so too do high-scoring grade school students (Graziano, Leone, Musser, and Lautenschlager, 1985). Presumably, these grade schoolers can put this information to work in their early efforts to act out situationally appropriate roles.

Any measure focusing on middle childhood ought to be particularly useful for charting the growth of self-monitoring. Middle childhood, after all, is a particularly critical period in development. It marks the transition between the Piagetian stages of preoperational and concrete-operational thinking (Piaget, 1970). One feature of the concrete-operational stage is the capacity to "decenter" and engage in non-egocentric thought (Ford, 1979; Keating, 1980). This capacity is, no doubt, involved in role-playing and impression management; before children can begin to control the images they convey to others, they must first know how they appear to others. A concern with social identity also emerges in this developmental stage (e.g., Selman, 1980) as does an awareness that other people's actions may have an impact on the self (e.g., Ruble, Feldman, Higgins, and Karlovac, 1979). Both of these features may motivate some children to use self-presentation as a way to fashion social identities and influence the treatment they receive from others.

Middle childhood is also a time when children's perceptions of others shift from concrete descriptions of their behavior to abstract inferences about their personalities (e.g., Livesley and Bromley, 1973;

Peevers and Secord, 1973). Also during this period, children's perceptions of others become substantially more accurate (e.g., Higgins, Feldman, and Ruble, 1980). Accordingly, children ought to be able to use their perceptions, should they be so motivated, to choose self-presentations to fit those of their interaction partners. Finally, and associated with these shifts, some rather dramatic increases occur in attention to social comparison information during middle childhood (e.g., Ruble, 1983). These increases may set the stage for some children to use other people as guides for their own social behavior.

Aspects of social and cultural development during middle childhood may also signal the importance of this period in the development of self-monitoring. Middle childhood is a time of increasing opportunity for interaction with peers (e.g., Wright, 1967), opportunities made all the more important by increases in the reward value of peers also occurring in middle childhood (e.g., Charlesworth and Hartup, 1967). In addition, it is a time when children begin to interact with an increasingly diversified set of adults who influence socialization. These factors may provide opportunities for different motivational concerns to emerge and influence the development of self-monitoring.

For all of these reasons, middle childhood seems to be a period of major importance in the divergent causality scenario for self-monitoring. In middle childhood, children disposed to become high or low in self-monitoring will find ample opportunity to develop the patterns of thought, motivation, and behavior that make up their social styles. The measure of self-monitoring in middle childhood developed by Graziano, Leone, Musser, and Lautenschlager (1985) seems ideally suited for studying self-monitoring propensities as they emerge during this critical developmental stage.

Self-Monitoring in Adolescence

Adolescence is a time when developments in the social and personality spheres are often rapid, dramatic, and far-reaching. Not the least of these developments is the quest for romantic and sexual partners. Do the committed versus uncommitted orientations to dating relationships and the restricted versus unrestricted orientations to sexual relations seen in low and high self-monitoring adults (see Chapter 6) have their beginnings in the social lives of adolescents? Are the dating activities of low self-monitoring youths centered on a single partner with whom they seek an increasingly close, intimate, and exclusive relationship? Are the initial dating habits of high self-monitoring youths characterized by a larger set of partners with whom they maintain relationships of less closeness and short duration? Similarly, do the initial sexual experiences of low self-monitoring adolescents occur in the context of romantic relationships characterized by personal intimacy and emotional investment? And do the early sexual encounters of high self-monitoring adolescents involve partners to whom they are physically attracted but not psychologically close? If these features characterize the dating, romantic, and sexual lives of adolescents—and if high and low self-monitoring adolescents are actively structuring their relationships to create these features—these facts would point yet another finger at the role of choosing situations in the development of self-monitoring.

Of course, romantic and sexual pursuits are but one aspect of adolescence—although, to be sure, a prominent feature. Other events in adolescence may also be revealing about the developmental course of self-monitoring. Adolescence is often a time of momentous (or at least what often seem momentous) conflicts between the expectations of parents and peers. The need for some resolution of these conflicts and the modes used to achieve resolutions may tell us something about the emerging self-monitoring styles. Resolving these conflicts may provide high self-monitoring adolescents with opportunities to refine the skill of being a different person in the company of different reference groups and to increasingly appreciate such pragmatic "creature of the situation" resolutions of conflicting role demands. Low self-monitoring adolescents may resolve these same conflicts by articulating values and defining behavioral patterns that permit them to think and act consistently with both parents and peers.

Further, adolescent relationships with parents and peers may provide a setting for consolidating the emerging self-monitoring propensities. Parents, in their interactions with adolescent children, may be more able than peers to draw on deep and enduring values. Hence, they may have a relatively heavy impact on the behavior of low self-monitoring adolescents. Peers, by contrast, operate more on the level of immediate social and normative pressures and therefore may have a comparatively greater impact on the actions of high self-monitoring adolescents.

Self-Monitoring across Generations

Ideally, in tracing the development of self-monitoring, researchers should conduct an extensive longitudinal study, following the same people as they move through the stages of their lives. As desirable as such a lifespan longitudinal study would be, it does of course represent a rather monumental undertaking. It would literally take a lifetime to conduct. A more modest research strategy involves concurrent studies of separate groups of people at different age levels to see if events occurring in the separate groups share common features of self-monitoring. However, even in this research strategy, it is critically important to study a wide range of age levels, from the very young to the very old. Only then will it be possible to account for self-monitoring across the entire lifespan.

Whatever the research strategy, a key question to be answered is: In what ways are self-monitoring propensities stable and in what ways do they change across the stages of life? Certainly, scores on the Self-Monitoring Scale are stable over a period of months (see Chapter 2). But are they stable over years and decades? And perhaps of greater importance, do the self-monitoring orientations manifest themselves in the same fashion at different stages of life? It is possible that the latent causal entity thought to dispose people to one orientation or the other may generate an underlying stability in whether people are high or low in self-monitoring. Nevertheless, even though these inherent self-monitoring orientations may remain the same, there may be changes over the years in the precise signs of these orientations as people successively adopt the behavior patterns typical of childhood, adolescence, and adulthood.

In addition, there may be certain critical periods or life events that lead people, whether they are disposed to be high or low in self-monitoring, to behave in ways typical of the other self-monitoring orientation. For example, in transitional periods that mark the passage from one role to another (such as from child to adult) or that require the adding of roles (such as becoming a parent), people may temporarily show more signs of the high self-monitoring orientation. In fact, when events make people uncertain of their emotional reactions, they look to the behavior of others for cues to define their private experiences and their public expressions of emotion (e.g., Schachter and Singer,

1962). On the other hand, there may be periods of life marked by great anonymity and de-individuation (Zimbardo, 1969) that prompt direct expressions of attitudes and impulses typically held in check by norms of social appropriateness and expectations of social sanctions. These periods may be characterized by increases in signs of the low self-monitoring orientation. When such critical periods are behind them, people may revert to their more long-standing orientations, unless, of course, the impact of these periods has been so strong and is so long-lasting that the behavioral habits acquired in them gain an autonomous life of their own. Naturally, only relevant studies can pin down the impact of such critical periods on stability and change over time in social styles and interpersonal orientations.

Conspicuous in Their Absence

At this point, it is appropriate to consider some factors that are conspicuously absent from the developmental scenario I have sketched for self-monitoring. These are the gross demographic variables (social class, economic status, geographical region, religious affiliation, and so on) often thought to be critically important in development because of the differing socialization practices associated with them. The absence of these variables in the developmental scenario is neither an oversight nor a reflection of the sketchy nature of the scenario. As we saw in Chapter 10, surveys and questionnaires have indicated no associations between these variables and self-monitoring.

However, demographic variables and the socialization practices associated with them may be implicated in the development of self-monitoring propensities to a greater extent than these negative survey findings would suggest. Indeed, in innovative investigations of the impact of role transitions and environmental relocations on the self, Hormuth (1984a, b, c; Hormuth and Lalli, 1984) has discovered hints of just such implications. In his research, he has employed the technique of autophotography developed by Ziller (e.g., Ziller and Lewis, 1981; Ziller and Smith, 1977). With this technique, people are given a Polaroid camera, instructed to take photographs of people and objects they consider to be part of or expressive of their selves, and asked to return each photograph accompanied by a one-line commentary. Judges then evaluate the content and self-relevant implications of the photographs.

In his investigations, Hormuth has discovered that people whose photographs represented urban environments were higher in self-monitoring than those whose photographs contained no urban environments (Hormuth and Lalli, 1984). These "urban environmentalists" frequently reported that they had had to "make a new beginning" (i.e., had undergone transitions, perhaps involving a move to an urban area) in the last 12 months. There are, of course, several interpretations of these findings. One is that people who are high in self-monitoring may be particularly likely to regard pictures of urban environments as representative of their selves. They are well aware that the diversity of urban settings symbolizes the diversity in their self-presentations. Another possibility is that those who have recently made the transition to urban living may also have had the opportunity to monitor their expressive self-presentation as they adjusted to their new circumstances, and hence have become higher in self-monitoring.

Hormuth himself interprets his findings in terms of a larger theoretical framework that proposes that transitions and relocations motivate an increased orientation toward and reliance on cues in the social and physical environment. Furthermore, it may be—in keeping with Hormuth's theory—that other role and environmental transitions (as well as experiences that challenge and question the self-concept, another key ingredient in Hormuth's theory) will prove relevant to understanding the motivational side of self-monitoring, whether because self-monitoring motivates such transitions or because such experiences motivate self-monitoring propensities.

Whichever explanation of the associations between autophotography and self-monitoring proves correct, it is important to recognize that each has a decidedly *motivational* flavor to it. As such, these explanations raise the possibility that the role of life experiences will be most pronounced and most noticeable in the motivational aspects of self-monitoring. Moreover, this possibility may point the way toward an integration of biological-genetic and environmental-socialization perspectives on the origins and development of self-monitoring.

If there is an inherited biological-genetic component to self-monitoring and if it is primarily an ability component (as it seems to be, see Chapter 11), any factors implicated in the motivation to translate differences in self-monitoring abilities into high and low self-monitoring behavioral styles might fare poorly as predictors of *overall* differences in self-monitoring. Perhaps the motivation to draw on expressive self-control abilities to create situationally-appropriate images stems from life experiences associated with particular socioeconomic circumstances and socialization practices. If so, developmental researchers may need separate and independent measures of self-monitoring abilities and self-monitoring motivations. With these measures, it may be possible to show that differences in self-monitoring abilities reflect biological-genetic influences and differences in self-monitoring motivations are predicted by demographic and socialization variables.

Self-Monitoring: Born or Made?

When it comes to self-monitoring, are people born or are they made? With this fundamental question, we began our journey over the course of the origins and development of self-monitoring. And, the answer to this fundamental question seems to be one of combined and combining influences. People appear to be born with a biological-genetic predisposition to be high or low in self-monitoring. Then, over an extended course of socialization, small initial differences emerge in relatively restricted domains. They are then amplified and extended over time to eventually become the many and varied manifestations of self-monitoring. Moreover, in this "born then made" scenario, biological-genetic and environmental-socialization influences are thought to work hand in hand. That is, the social circumstances and life experiences that bring out the diverging self-monitoring orientations may be ones toward which people gravitate precisely because of their self-monitoring predisposition. It is in this sense that, when it comes to self-monitoring, it is proper to say that people are *first* born, and *then* made.

PART V

The Nature of Self-Monitoring

OVER THE YEARS of research, there have been growing indications that self-monitoring propensities are generalized orientations that exert substantial influence on the ways people think, feel, and act in social situations and interpersonal relationships. As I have reflected on this considerable body of evidence about self-monitoring, and as I have discussed its meaning with my colleagues and my students, I have found that several questions keep cropping up. These questions—and, of course, their answers—have turned out to be critically important to understanding the very nature of self-monitoring.

Among these questions are: Is there some causal entity that underlies and accounts for the extensive network of self-monitoring phenomena? If so, what is the nature of this latent entity? Does it, perhaps, involve a single major causal variable? Moreover, if one can be identified, what are its implications for how self-monitoring should be conceptualized and measured? These are the questions that have guided considerations of the underlying nature of self-monitoring.

Chapter 12 provides an account of the search for that causal entity. Let the reader be forewarned: Portions of this chapter, namely psychometric analyses of the internal structure of the Self-Monitoring Scale, are somewhat technical in nature. Its conclusion, however, is intriguing: At an underlying level, people come in only two kinds—the high and the low in self-monitoring. The implications of this conclusion are considerable, and not just for understanding the nature of (and even the origins of) self-monitoring. What this conclusion says about the nature of self-monitoring may have something to say about the "units" of personality, how differences between people should be thought of and how they should be measured.

Further implications of this conclusion are revealed when inquiries about the nature of self-monitoring are viewed in the context of more general approaches to employing measures of differences between people as vehicles for developing and elaborating psychological theory. Thus, Chapter 13 contains an examination of the growth, development, and evolution of self-monitoring as a psychological construct. One product of this evolution is a new 18-item measure of self-monitoring, unveiled in Chapter 13.

CHAPTER 12

The Underlying Structure
of Self-Monitoring

ACCORDING TO THE emerging portrait of self-monitoring, people adopt one of two interpersonal orientations. High self-monitors usually adopt (what they regard as) a "pragmatic" orientation; they are able to strategically guide their interactions toward situationally appropriate outcomes. It is as if their actions are answers to the question "Who does this situation want me to be and how can I be that person?" Low self-monitors typically adopt (what they see as) a "principled" orientation, reflected in correspondence between their feelings and attitudes and their behavior. Their actions seem to be answers to the question "Who am I and how can I be me in this situation?"

Presumably, there must exist "something" that underlies, accounts for, and causes the rich network of social phenomena that involves self-monitoring. Of course, as with any underlying causal entity, it is not possible to observe that "something" directly and therefore define it *explicitly*. Nevertheless, it is possible to think about this "something" underlying self-monitoring and to understand it *implicitly* in terms of its role in a theoretical network that explains the phenomena of self-monitoring (cf. Cronbach and Meehl, 1955). That "something," if it exists, would constitute a *latent causal structure* for self-monitoring.

Theoretical analyses of the origins and development of self-monitoring (see Chapters 10 and 11) have prominently featured a causal entity thought to, first, dispose people to be high or low in self-monitoring and then guide them toward socialization experiences that amplify and extend their emerging self-monitoring propensities. Quite possibly, this entity is the "something," the latent causal structure that underlies and accounts for the extensive network of self-monitoring phenomena.

More precisely, though, what is the underlying nature of self-monitoring? To answer this question requires, first, that it be placed in the larger context of the nature of differences in personality. Typically, in personality theories, the features that distinguish one person from another have been treated as comparative differences, on the assumption that any two people can be compared in terms of the same variables. These personality variables, in principle, may be of at least two varieties—*dimensions* and *class variables* (Gangestad and Snyder, 1985).

Dimensions are characteristics thought to be possessed to some degree by all people. As a result, the distributions of such characteristics are continuous. For example, dominance is a dimension of personality assumed to be distributed continuously and measured by a scale on the Personality Research Form (Jackson, 1974). On the other hand, certain units of personality may not be dimensions but class variables, which are expressed as differences distributed into discrete categories. Thus, these differences can be introduced by the colloquial expression "There are two (or, for that matter, any finite number of) types of people in the world."

A Class Model of Self-Monitoring

Is self-monitoring a continuous dimension, possessed in some degree by all people or is it a class variable, with people belonging to one of two discrete classes, the high self-monitoring class or the low self-monitoring class? To be sure, researchers (myself included) have often written about self-monitoring as if the world were populated by just two kinds of people, high and low scorers on the Self-Monitoring Scale. This book is no exception: Implicitly, at least, I have written as if there are just two types of people in the world. Many readers have probably regarded this as a mere expository shortcut, since they know that many people's scores fall in the mid-range of the Self-Monitoring Scale. Asking whether self-monitoring is a dimension or a class variable makes explicit the possibility that people actually do come in two kinds—the high and the low in self-monitoring.

The answer to the question "Is self-monitoring a dimension or a class variable?" may depend on the kind of classification to which the question refers. At a *phenotypic* level, of course, self-monitoring tendencies are distributed continuously. That is, the extent to which people actually exercise self-control over their expressive behavior exists in all degrees and thus is continuously distributed, as are scores on the Self-Monitoring Scale itself. Even so, however, at a *genotypic* level there may exist one *latent* causal entity that is discretely distributed into two types (high and low self-monitoring) and is thus a class variable. The case of self-monitoring may not be all that different from that of masculinity, femininity, and biological sex. At a phenotypic level, masculinity and femininity are continuously distributed dispositions. That is, people possess, in varying degrees, masculine and feminine characteristics that discriminate between the sexes. Yet, there exists, at a latent level, a discretely distributed variable—male or female biological sex—that plays a role in the causal network giving rise to expressions of masculinity and femininity.

Is there, then, a latent causal entity underlying self-monitoring phenomena? If so, is it a class variable? As we have seen (Chapter 4), distinctly different self-structures may guide and direct the activities of people high and low in self-monitoring, suggesting—implicitly, at least—that the underlying structures that organize, guide, and direct expressive self-presentation differ not just in degree, but in *kind*. That is, they hint that the causal variable underlying self-monitoring propensities is not distributed continuously but rather is distributed discretely into two latent classes—the high self-monitoring class and the low self-monitoring class.

How are variables that entail discrete classes to be distinguished from those that involve continuous dimensions? Generally speaking, if a class variable exerts a strong influence on some domain of behavioral characteristics, then people will be discontinuously distributed in the multidimensional space defined by these behavioral characteristics. To the extent that unusual clustering of people can be detected in this multidimensional space, there exists empirical evidence consistent with a class model.

My colleague Steve Gangestad and I have tested the class model of self-monitoring propensities. Our efforts involved a two-stage process. First, we performed a *structural analysis* in which we examined people's responses to items of the Self-Monitoring Scale for discontinuities consistent with a class model. Then, we conducted an *external analysis,* in which we examined the relations between a classification scheme based on these discontinuities and actual criterion behaviors relevant to self-monitoring. For a detailed treatment of our test of the class model, see Gangestad and Snyder (1985).

The Structural Component of the Class Model   Over the years, Paul Meehl and his colleagues have developed *taxometric methods* to detect latent class structures in sets of empirical data (e.g., Meehl, 1978; Meehl and Golden, 1982). These methods can be applied when researchers believe that a dichotomous class variable exists and they can supply a set of indicators thought to discriminate between the two classes. For self-monitoring, previous research and theory had already hinted that self-monitoring might be a class variable, and the items of the Self-Monitoring Scale clearly constitute a set of indicators believed to discriminate between the two classes.

In essence, what the taxometric methods assess are deviations from multivariate normality of the conjectured indicators, deviations consistent with a model stipulating two latent classes underlying the indicators. Indeed, when these so-called "maximum covariance" methods are applied to an appropriate set of the self-monitoring indicators, they suggest that a class model is the appropriate model for self-monitoring propensities (Gangestad and Snyder, 1985).

Maximum Covariance Analysis. We began by identifying a subset of the items of the Self-Monitoring Scale that would meet the assumptions and requirements of the taxometric procedures—items that ought to discrminate between the conjectured classes but not correlate within the conjectured classes. We then selected pairs of these items and constructed scales from the remaining items. Out of a large sample of people (almost 2000) who had taken the Self-Monitoring Scale, we next formed subsamples with each of the possible scores on these constructed scales. If a class variable underlies the responses to the items as conjectured, then the sample covariances between the pairs of items plotted as a function of the values on the constructed scales associated with the samples should be *peaked,* maximal toward the

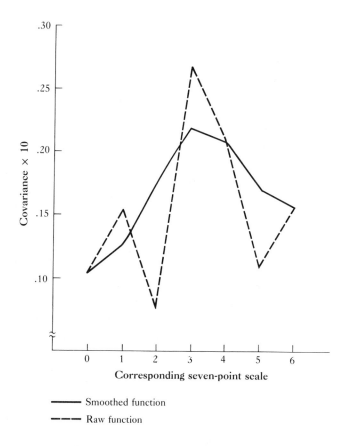

Figure 12-1   The underlying nature of self-monitoring. The figure depicts a peaked covariance curve representing covariance between self-monitoring indicators averaged across all pairs of the indicators. (Gangestad & Snyder, 1985.)

middle values and nearer to zero toward the extremes (see Gangestad and Snyder, 1985, for a complete explication of this prediction). Figure 12-1 depicts the covariance curve between the pairs of items, averaged across all sets of observations for all pairs of indicators. Its peaked function is of precisely the form expected if a class model is appropriate for self-monitoring propensities.

Estimates of Base Rates. Additional analyses have provided further evidence for the class model. If a dichotomous class variable underlies a set of its purported indicators, then two values—the proportions of people belonging to each of the classes—define the distribution of the class variable. If real classes do exist, then these "base rates" are fixed within any sample of people. Hence, different mathematical formulae derived from the class model ought to yield consistent estimates of the base rates. In the case of self-monitoring, six quasi-independent methods of base-rate estimation have yielded remarkably consistent estimates of the proportions of people belonging to the high self-monitoring class (.41) and the low self-monitoring class (.59). In addition, it is possible to calculate for each person the probability, under the class model, of belonging to the high or to the low self-monitoring class. Indeed, when people are assigned to self-monitoring classes on the basis of these calculations, we estimate that 89 percent of these classifications are correct (for details, see Gangestad and Snyder, 1985).

Factor Analysis and the Class Model   These taxometric analyses, then, suggest that the latent causal entity underlying self-monitoring, the "something" that explains and accounts for self-monitoring phenomena, is a class variable. Furthermore, it is possible to locate this self-monitoring class variable in the factor structure of the Self-Monitoring Scale. Several published factor analyses have indicated that multiple factors underlie the Self-Monitoring Scale (e.g., Briggs, Cheek, and Buss, 1980; Furnham and Capon, 1983; Gabrenya and Arkin, 1980; Sparacino, Ronchi, Bigley, Flesch, and Kuhn, 1983; Tobey and Tunnell, 1981).

None of these factor analyses, however, has yielded a factor that the authors have interpreted as a "self-monitoring" factor. Consider, for instance, that of Briggs, Cheek, and Buss (1980), perhaps the most frequently cited of the factor analyses. They have interpreted their three factors as "extraversion," "other-directedness," and "acting." If a self-monitoring class variable exists and underlies the items of the Self-Monitoring Scale, why does it not appear in these factor analyses? Perhaps, it does not appear because, quite simply, it is *not* a major source of variation underlying the Self-Monitoring Scale.

Although this conclusion may seem to follow from the factor analyses, it is not a justified one. Although the identification of a factor space is (for a given method) unique, the precise identification of the axes defining it is far from unique. Typically, to identify the axes, factor analysts have pointed to simple structure, a location of the axes that makes for easy description of the factors (see Thurstone, 1947). In fact, all of the factor analyses cited here have involved interpretations of factor structures *rotated* in accord with simple structure criteria. Unfortunately, there is no indisputable justification for believing that a rotated factor structure identifies "real" sources of underlying variation (e.g., Eysenck, 1950; Guilford and Zimmerman, 1963; Overall, 1964).

Accordingly, the self-monitoring class variable need not appear as one of the axes in a factor solution involving rotation to simple structure. Where, then, ought it to appear? If certain assumptions hold (which they do for self-monitoring; Gangestad and Snyder, 1985), the class variable should emerge as the first *unrotated* factor extracted in a principal components analysis of variance (the first unrotated factor being the inferred variable that maximally accounts for the variation in the items; Rummel, 1970). Indeed, our principal axes factor analysis confirms that the first unrotated factor corresponds very closely to the self-monitoring class variable (Gangestad and Snyder, 1985). Specifically, the factor loading for a given self-monitoring item is a near perfect estimate of that item's ability to predict membership in the latent self-monitoring classes. Thus, the class variable appears to be expressed as a factor that lies very close to the first unrotated factor in the Self-Monitoring Scale, that is, very close to the variable that accounts for the maximal amount of variance in the self-monitoring items.

What meaning, then, should be attached to this first *unrotated* factor? The first unrotated factor gives every indication of being a *general* self-monitoring factor. Fully 24 of the 25 items of the Self-Monitoring Scale have positive loadings on it; 18 of these 24 have loadings of +.15 or greater (Gangestad and Snyder, 1985). Also the second and third unrotated factors are weak relative to the first and are bipolar. Therefore, the answer to the question "How is the total score on the Self-Monitoring Scale to be interpreted?" is clear. The total score on the Self-Monitoring Scale reflects a person's standing on the first unrotated factor. Those who are high on the first unrotated factor will tend to receive high Self-Monitoring Scale scores; those who are low on it will receive low Self-Monitoring Scale scores. Moreover, the close correspondence between the first unrotated factor and the self-monitoring class variable suggests that those with high Self-Monitoring Scale scores are likely to belong to the discrete high self-monitoring class; those with low Self-Monitoring Scale scores are probable members of the discrete low self-monitoring class.

The general self-monitoring factor should answer other questions of interpretability of the Self-Monitoring Scale. There have been claims that the three rotated factors make it impossible to interpret total scores on the Self-Monitoring Scale (e.g., Briggs, Cheek, and Buss, 1980; Lennox and Wolfe, 1984). In this view, total scores represent a linear composite of three separate components. Thus, the same total score may represent a very different pattern of factor scores for one person than for another person. On what basis, it has been asked, should these two people be represented by the same score? The basis, to answer this question, is the general self-monitoring factor. It permits interpretation of Self-Monitoring Scale scores in terms of each person's standing on the first unrotated factor, a general factor best interpreted as a reflection of the latent self-monitoring class variable.

What meaning, furthermore, should be given to the *rotated* factors? Our own oblique rotation yielded three factors (Gangestad and Snyder, 1985). These three (which are similar to those reported by Briggs, Cheek, and Buss, 1980) are all positively correlated with the first unrotated factor. These rotated factors appear to define content domains that discriminate between the high and low self-monitoring classes.[1] In order of importance to the self-monitoring class variable (as reflected in their correlations with the first unrotated factor), these domains are "expressive self-control," "social stage presence," and "other-directed self-presentation."[2]

---

[1]Briggs, Cheek, and Buss (1980) have labeled these factors Acting Ability, Extraversion, and Other-Directedness. Their labels may connote too broad an interpretation. For instance, the items that define the Social Stage Presence content area correspond not to extraversion in general, but to concern with feeling comfortable performing in typical group situations.

[2]Concerns have been expressed that individual rotated factors have correlated differently with measures of other psychological variables (Briggs, Cheek, and Buss, 1980; Lennox and Wolfe, 1984). For example, trait anxiety correlates *negatively* with Social Stage Presence but *positively* with Other-Directed Self-Presentation (Cheek and Briggs, 1981). How can two content domains correlate with a third variable in *opposite* directions and still tap the *same* underlying construct? Quite easily: It can be demonstrated mathematically that the rotated factors can have modest but opposing correlations with other variables at the same time as they are all meaningful reflections of the same underlying self-monitoring variable (for details, see Snyder and Gangestad, 1986).

The rotated factors may correspond to dimensional variables that discriminate between the self-monitoring classes and yet are, in part, independent of the latent class variable (for relevant analyses, see Gangestad and Snyder, 1985). With respect to these dimensional variables, then, the self-monitoring class variable may be a higher order disposition that *potentiates* lower order dispositions corresponding to these three dimensions. Thus, the self-monitoring class variable may potentiate the development of the ability to control one's expressive behavior, the ability to maintain a social stage presence, and a propensity for conscious self-presentation.[3]

The External Component of the Class Model   Clearly, a dichotomous class model is highly consistent with the internal structure of the Self-Monitoring Scale. To demonstrate that the class variable is appropriately interpreted as a *self-monitoring* class variable, we have examined relations between the class variable and relevant behaviors. These examinations constitute the external component of the class model. In fact, the self-monitoring class variable successfully accounts for relations between the Self-Monitoring Scale and behavioral criteria predicted by self-monitoring theory. To be more precise about it, across a wide variety of studies involving self-monitoring phenomena, the classification scheme emerging from the taxometric analyses outperformed the full Self-Monitoring Scale treated as a continuous dimension. It did so by approximately 50 percent (for further details on these analyses, see Gangestad and Snyder, 1985; Snyder and Gangestad, 1986). These relative performances, it should be noted, are very near what would be expected if the class variable were the *sole* source of influence linking the Self-Monitoring Scale and the external behavioral criteria.

In these assessments of criterion-oriented validity, each rotated factor (e.g., those reported by Briggs, Cheek, and Buss, 1980) has been,

---

Furthermore, such opposing correlations do not mean that it is wrong to sum across items to obtain a *single score* to measure self-monitoring. In fact, it is possible to measure the latent self-monitoring entity with nearly 90 percent accuracy using items selected from all three rotated factors (Gangestad and Snyder, 1985).

[3]These three phenomena may be affected by influences other than self-monitoring in their development. Thus, there may exist meaningful differences in these phenomena *independent* of self-monitoring. These differences need not threaten the validity of the general self-monitoring factor. For elaboration, see Snyder and Gangestad (1986).

in general, *weakly* related to the criterion variables compared with either the taxometrically derived classification scheme or the full Self-Monitoring Scale. Moreover, in these analyses, no one factor consistently outperformed any other; rather, the factors tended to perform similarly to one another, and less powerfully than the full Self-Monitoring Scale. Indeed, as a whole, the rotated factors tend to be correlated with criterion variables to the extent that the factors themselves are correlated with the self-monitoring class variable (see Gangestad and Snyder, 1985; Snyder and Gangestad, 1986, for fuller discussions of these results).[4] Finally, the fact that any one factor's performance is similar to the others' calls into question any general claims that effects in certain studies of self-monitoring may be attributable to one factor, effects in other studies to a second factor, and effects in still other studies to a third factor (e.g., Briggs, Cheek, and Buss, 1980).[5]

It appears, then, that a measure of the class variable detected by the taxometric procedures can effectively stand in for the entire Self-Monitoring Scale. It can account successfully for relations between the Self-Monitoring Scale and behaviors relevant to self-monitoring. Moreover, at least for the phenomena examined, it can do so more effectively than any component factorial portion of the Self-Monitoring Scale. Clearly, too, the taxometrically-identified class variable is appropriately interpreted as a *self-monitoring* class variable.

Implications of the Class Model

What, then, does it mean to say that the latent causal factor underlying self-monitoring phenomena is a discretely distributed class variable

---

[4]The three rotated factors all correlate positively with the general factor, but not equally: Expressive Self-Control, $r = +.6$; Social Stage Presence, $r = +.5$; Other-Directed Self-Presentation, $r = +.3$ (Gangestad and Snyder, 1985). The relative abilities of the factors to predict criterion variables in the studies reanalyzed by Snyder and Gangestad (1986) correspond to their relative correlations with the general factor.

[5]Some researchers may want, in addition to analyzing their studies using the Self-Monitoring Scale (which taps the general self-monitoring factor), to examine the relations of the rotated factors to their criterion variables. For guidelines on appropriate inferential statistics and methodological standards for evaluating factor effects, see Snyder and Gangestad (1986).

rather than a continuously distributed dimensional variable? At the very least, it reveals that it is no mere expository shortcut to claim that, in the case of self-monitoring, the world is composed of just two kinds of people. When it comes to self-monitoring, at an underlying level there really are just two types of people. However, the significance of this latent class variable goes beyond making explicit what had once been only implicit. It takes on particular meaning in the context of issues concerning the nature of self-monitoring (and, for that matter, of personality).

In considering these issues, the reader should be aware that the very fact of even possessing an answer to the "dimension or class variable?" question is itself something of an oddity. Rarely does the question of whether differences between people are properly thought of as dimensions or class variables even get asked, let alone answered. The reason is that this fundamental issue is almost universally prejudged. With few exceptions, it is widely presumed that the basic units of personality are continuous dimensions. This pervasive assumption is bolstered by an enduring prejudice against the viability of class models in personality, rooted in part in claims that class variables constitute curiosities, oversimplifications of reality, or arbitrary fictions (e.g., Jackson, 1971; Mendelsohn, Weiss, and Feimer, 1982; Mischel, 1976).

Are class variables oversimplifications? Are they arbitrary fictions? The answer to this question may depend on what form of classification system is under scrutiny. *Phenotypic* classifications (which are undertaken primarily for descriptive convenience, and in which classes are defined by covariance of phenotypic characteristics with no underlying meaning being ascribed to the classes) definitely are vulnerable to criticism. Indeed, it is unlikely that there are discrete classes at the phenotypic level of behavior (cf. Everitt, 1974; Farris, 1979).

By contrast, *genotypic* approaches to classification (in which classes exist when all members of a class share some latent underlying entity that affects their current behavior) are not as vulnerable to being labeled as, at best, oversimplifications and, at worst, arbitrary fictions. These class variables purport to identify real causal entities—latent constructs that really exercise genuine influences upon phenotypic behavioral characteristics.

Such a genotypic approach to class variables ought to be particularly appealing to researchers in personality and social psychology. It identifies the class variable as a causal-dispositional construct that refers to an underlying structure within the person thought to account for some domain of behavioral events. As such, this approach to class variables is highly compatible with one of the fundamental goals of personality and social psychology, that of identifying dispositional properties that underlie, organize, and structure individual and social behavior (cf. Snyder and Ickes, 1985).

As appealing as genotypically explicated class variables ought to be to students of personality and social behavior, no such class variable exerting widespread influence on human social behavior (with the exception of biological sex) has, until now, been shown to exist. Now, however, the existence of a genotypically-explicated, discrete class variable underlying self-monitoring phenomena has been demonstrated (by the taxometric analyses) and its influence on human social behavior corroborated (by the external validation of the class model).

If the class variable that underlies self-monitoring phenomena is a *genotypically* explicated one, is it to be identified with the *genetically* influenced causal entity implicated in the origins and development of self-monitoring (see Chapters 10 and 11)? Apparently so. For, where identical twins show their virtually perfect rates of concordance is in their status on the latent class variable; they are just about always members of the same latent self-monitoring class (Gangestad, 1984). Thus, the "something" that underlies self-monitoring phenomena, its latent causal structure, may be not only a discrete class variable, but also one with biological-genetic origins that plays a guiding and directing role in the socialization of self-monitoring propensities.

The discovery of a latent causal structure may be critically important in charting the developmental course of self-monitoring over the lifespan. With the taxometrically derived classification techniques, it may be possible to determine whether people remain members of the same latent self-monitoring class (either high or low) while their expressions of self-monitoring propensities are changing (see Chapter 11). Perhaps, at a genotypic level, once high or low in self-monitoring, always high or low. But, as the roles that define one's life evolve and shift over time, the phenotypic manifestations of these stable self-monitoring propensities may change. Thus, the footloose young man, unburdened by professional responsibilities, may reveal his high self-monitoring disposition primarily at parties and social gatherings. Many years later, pursuing a career in medicine that leaves him little time for partying, he may display his unchanged high self-monitoring disposition primarily in the context of his professional activities.

There is, in fact, some evidence that the distribution of self-monitoring propensities is stable across generations. In adults a generation older than college students (namely, their parents), there are signs of a dichotomous class variable underlying their responses to the Self-Monitoring Scale (Gangestad and Snyder, 1985). In spite of all the differences in the circumstances of their lives (think for a moment of all the occupational, personal, and familial roles that can and do separate parents and children), at the underlying level of the latent class variable the relative proportions of low and high self-monitors among the middle-aged parents are remarkably similar to the approximately 60 to 40 percent split among their college-aged children. This finding suggests that the latent self-monitoring classes remain stable across generations, as one would expect if membership in the latent classes were genetically determined. If so, and if the same distribution of membership in the two classes holds across a wide range of age levels, from the very young to the very old, this conclusion would be irresistible: The same latent causal entity may underlie self-monitoring across the entire lifespan.

As intriguing as these possibilities may be, they do not exhaust the implications of the discovery of a latent causal structure. To the contrary, what these discoveries have revealed about the underlying nature of self-monitoring take on particular meaning in the context of issues concerning how self-monitoring should be defined and how it should be measured. We next turn our attention to an examination of evolution in the conceptualization and measurement of self-monitoring.

CHAPTER 13

The Evolution of
Self-Monitoring

■

WHEN I FIRST introduced the concept of self-monitoring, I did so in the context of differences in the extent to which people monitor, through self-observation and self-control, their expressive behavior and self-presentation. I thought that those people high in self-monitoring regulated their expressive self-presentation for the sake of desired public appearances and thus would be highly sensitive to social cues to situationally appropriate performances. Those low in self-monitoring, I thought, either lacked the ability or the motivation to do so. They, instead, would display expressive behaviors that truly reflected their own attitudes, traits, feelings, and other enduring and momentary inner states.

A number of hypotheses—concerning, among other things, the determinants of specificity and consistency in social behavior, the origins of links between attitudes and action, the dynamics of social interaction, and the nature and consequences of conceptions of self—have followed from these basic initial propositions. Research involving a measure of self-monitoring, the Self-Monitoring Scale, has provided—as we have seen—empirical support for these and other hypotheses about the cognitive, behavioral, and interpersonal consequences of self-monitoring. Self-monitoring propensities, these investigations have suggested, are substantially and meaningfully involved in how people think, feel, and act in social circumstances.

To be sure, some investigations have failed to confirm hypotheses about self-monitoring (e.g., Arkin, Gabrenya, Appelman, and Cochran, 1979; Cheek, 1982; Santee and Maslach, 1982; Schneiderman, 1980; Wolfe, Lennox, and Hudiburg, 1983; Zuckerman and Reis, 1978). Nevertheless, given the number and size of effects that have successfully and effectively been identified with the Self-Monitoring Scale, the reports of "failures" have been few and far between (see Snyder, 1986, for a bibliography of sources on self-monitoring). Of course, some unsuccessful studies may be the result of sampling variability, ill-taken hypotheses, or faulty auxiliary assumptions. Nevertheless one should fully expect some specific, well-formulated hypotheses about self-monitoring to be proved false in carefully conducted studies. After all, it is extremely unlikely that any relatively complex dynamic theory (the case of self-monitoring being no exception) is absolutely and completely true. For elaborations on this argument, examples of each type of purported failure to support hypotheses about self-monitoring, and suggested guidelines for evaluating the theoretical implications of confirmed or discredited hypotheses, see Snyder and Gangestad (1986).

In sum, though, the Self-Monitoring Scale and the self-monitoring construct itself have been demonstrated to possess considerable construct validity (e.g., Cronbach and Meehl, 1955). That is, the Self-Monitoring Scale does appear to tap a latent causal variable that partially accounts for a specifiable, yet extensive and extendable, domain of observable behavior. Furthermore, it is in part explicated by the theoretical statements with which I first introduced the self-monitoring construct (Snyder, 1972, 1974).

Elaboration of the Construct:
How Should Self-Monitoring Be Conceptualized?

Nevertheless, we should not be satisfied by the fact that the phenomena associated with the Self-Monitoring Scale can be explicated in part by the initial propositions concerning self-monitoring. In fact, the construct of self-monitoring should not, and cannot, be identified solely with these initial statements. A construct is an interpretation (Loevinger, 1957). Thus, the self-monitoring construct is an interpretation of the latent entity that underlies self-monitoring phenomena. An interpretation should be responsive to, and open to elaboration by, new empirical findings and new theoretical insights (Meehl, 1978). In fact, examining systematic treatments of self-monitoring over the years reveals not a *single* interpretation, but a *series* of interpretations, elaborations, refinements, re-emphases, and new conceptual directions.

Thus, the construct of self-monitoring has evolved from my initial concerns with the control of expressive behavior into a much broader theory of interpersonal orientations. High self-monitors tend to adopt what they see as a "pragmatic" interpersonal orientation, strategically creating social interaction patterns that promote situationally appropriate interaction outcomes. Conversely, low self-monitors tend to adopt what they regard as a "principled" interpersonal orientation, which is reflected in correspondence between their feelings and attitudes and their behavior.

Indeed, as the theory has evolved, it has become increasingly clear that there really are two separate, distinct, and independent self-monitoring orientations. It is apparent that the low self-monitoring orientation is more than the absence of the high self-monitoring orientation. Low self-monitors do not simply lack acting ability and the social flexibility that it may bring. To the contrary, as studies of how people choose and structure their situations (see Chapter 4) have revealed, the low self-monitoring orientation is very much the product of motivated and strategic activities. Indeed, it may take a considerable amount of careful staging to display one's true beliefs and feelings in order to create a social world conducive to one's own personality and sense of self.

Empirical and theoretical investigations continue, oftentimes leading the self-monitoring construct into new—and, at times, unexpected—domains of applicability. Some of the new domains in which self-monitoring has proved relevant include, for example, explorations of the nature of friendships (see Chapter 5), romantic relationships (see Chapter 6), and sexual involvements (see Chapter 6), as well as applications of self-monitoring to the psychology of advertising (see Chapter 8), personnel selection (see Chapter 7), and psychopathology (see Chapter 9). At times, these new explorations have led to conceptual elaborations, extensions, and clarifications of self-monitoring theory. For these reasons, when one examines the nature of self-monitoring, one finds not a static entity but instead a dynamic, evolving

construct that is sensitive to new empirical findings and new conjectured meanings.

Indeed, to some extent, this evolution makes clear why no value
judgments should be attached to the interpersonal styles of either self-
monitoring type. The more that is learned about the many facets of
self-monitoring, the more it becomes apparent that no one orientation
is inherently "better" than the other. With a careful choice of words,
someone who cared to do so could give either orientation a good name
or a bad name. I could, for example, describe the high self-monitor in
rather complimentary terms, pointing to his or her flexibility and
adaptability in coping with the diversity of roles required of a person
in an increasingly complex society. Or, I could paint a rather unflat-
tering portrait of this same person, depicting him or her as a "silly
putty" creature forever being squeezed and shaped into new and different molds, always posturing and gesturing, forever pretending and
occasionally deceiving.

By the same token, I could characterize the low self-monitor in
glowing terms—an honest, forthright, and direct type, an easy-to-read
"open book" in dealings with others, someone with the virtues of being
true to his or her values and principles, who can be counted on to be
the same person all the time. Yet, I could also turn these virtues into
vices. What I had once described as consistency and reliability, I could
now label rigidity and stubbornness. If so inclined, I could cite as
examples those bosses who are as autocratic and dictatorial with their
families as with their employees or those teachers who lecture their
friends as if they were their students.

Therefore, we should avoid making value judgments and instead
recognize that the two self-monitoring orientations each represent a
different approach to life. We should regard these different approaches
as unique lifestyles with their own assets and liabilities. And, until
there are clear indications that life's pleasures and pains are dispropor-
tionate in one or the other type, I, for one, see no reason to grant more
favored status to either the high or the low self-monitoring lifestyle.

There is, however, every reason to expect that theory and research
on self-monitoring will continue to reach out in new directions, ven-
turing into as-yet-unexplored territory and testing new conjectures
about the ramifications of self-monitoring. Because such new conjectures will continue to provide impetus for fresh research directions,
self-monitoring theory will continue to grow and evolve. Some of these

developments in theory and research may prove to be ones not even anticipated in early statements about self-monitoring or even in subsequent treatments.

I must admit that I would have been surprised if, very early in the history of my work on self-monitoring, someone had gazed into a crystal ball and told me that someday self-monitoring theory and research would have something to say about, for instance, the psychology of advertising and consumer behavior or about the psychology of occupational choice and career planning. Yet, within a few years of its inception, self-monitoring theory and research were speaking to these and other critical issues—both in terms of personality and social psychology. These applications and extensions of self-monitoring certainly have been welcome ones. Even the unanticipated developments have turned out to be logical extensions of self-monitoring theory and have provided their own insights into a growing and developing understanding of self-monitoring.

That some of these avenues of inquiry may not have been projected explicitly in the initial characterization of self-monitoring should *not* be taken as a source of concern. To the contrary, one ought to take a positive view of this growth and development. Indeed, if after many years of theory and research, there had been no elaborations, extensions, or even changes and surprises, I might have been tempted to conclude, however reluctantly, that all the years of research were not very fruitful after all.

This evolution of theory and research on self-monitoring is but one example of a more general approach to employing a measure of differences between people as a vehicle for developing and elaborating psychological theory. To use a measure for these purposes, researchers and theorists must first admit that, although they have some ideas about what the measure taps, they don't *really* know for sure. Indeed, they may never know precisely what it measures. They hope, however, that over time their interpretations get closer and closer to the truth about whatever underlies the measure (for further discussion of this point, see Loevinger, 1957). These have been my aims and goals during my research and theory on self-monitoring.

No researcher should construct a measure of personality and social behavior, insisting that the initial interpretation is fully adequate. Researchers must expect some gaps in their understanding of how their measures relate to important domains of social behavior. Moreover, they should use these gaps as opportunities to discover the true nature of their constructs. Thus, researchers should be encouraged to elaborate, extend, and refine their interpretations of their constructs and their measures. In this sense, researchers are much like detectives tracking down clues that bring them ever closer to solving their cases. Nevertheless, at the same time as their interpretations move closer and closer to the "truth," they should be prepared for some "conceptual drift" away from their original notions to occur in the course of their research activities (Meehl, 1978).

In the case of self-monitoring, analyses of latent causal structure (see Chapter 12) have been informative in the search for the "true" underlying nature of self-monitoring. These analyses first postulated the existence of some latent causal structure underlying self-monitoring phenomena. And, by following the trail of clues to the true nature of self-monitoring, they in fact have pointed to an underlying causal entity, one that gives every indication of genuinely being a self-monitoring causal variable.

In the context of these analyses of latent causal structure, how are the *items* of the Self-Monitoring Scale to be regarded? Do they represent *samples* of behavior selected from some semantically coherent behavioral domain defined by the investigator? Or, are they *signs* of an underlying latent reality? If there is a "real" causal entity underlying self-monitoring phenomena, then the items of the Self-Monitoring Scale are more than summary descriptions of past behavior. Instead, they should be viewed as *indicators* of this latent causal reality.

How the items of the Self-Monitoring Scale are to be interpreted has implications, as we shall see shortly, for the measurement of self-monitoring. Before examining them, it is first necessary to underscore the fact that the presumption about items as signs rather than samples is, by the current standards of many personality theorists, a risky assertion. Indeed, it is often assumed that one postulates "real" latent structures underlying personality tests only with great trepidation. According to this view, responses to personality test items should be interpreted as summary statements of behavior, responses that are themselves maintained rather tenuously by readily changeable social contingencies. According to this way of thinking, assessment devices should *not* be viewed as measuring causal structures that are properties of the person making the responses. Although many social learning theorists hold this view (e.g., Bandura, 1971; Mischel, 1968, 1973;

Nicholls, Licht, and Pearl, 1982), it is certainly not limited to them. Even some defenders of trait theory reject the claim that personality scales measure real latent structures (e.g., Hogan, 1976; Wiggins, 1974; see also Hogan, DeSoto, and Solano, 1977).

Influenced by this view, some researchers have endorsed the descriptive role of assessment devices and have attempted to develop procedures to accurately summarize behavior (e.g., Buss and Craik, 1983a, b). In their approach, personality measures of the self-statement variety may still serve a function, but that function is essentially descriptive, consisting "in part in their often impressive efficiency in serving as brief surrogates for the long-term observation and acquaintance process entailed by the monitoring of act-trends" (Buss and Craik, 1983b, p. 407). It is undeniably possible that personality measures may represent only summary statements of behavior. Nevertheless, just because some argue against the possibility of identifying real causal structures underlying personality measures does not mean that no such attempts should be made. There *may* be real latent causal structures that are amenable to empirical study underlying *some* personality measures. Thus, it may be possible to identify major causal variables underlying personality. Investigations of the latent causal structure underlying self-monitoring represent one instance in which a latent causal structure has been identified and explicated. Perhaps this one instance will serve as a model for identifying other latent structures of personality.

Such identifications may serve a larger and more fundamental goal—that of shoring up the foundations of the theory of traits in personality. Many years ago, Gordon Allport (1937) argued that the concept of trait was central to understanding the nature of personality. For Allport, traits were more than descriptive conveniences. He granted traits the status of existing causal entities, which might even be identified with neurological structures. If traits are to be a core construct (if not *the* core construct) of personality theory, one would hope that they are real entities, whether or not they have the precise structure envisioned by Allport. In this regard, identifying real latent causal structures is one means of trying to verify that traits are real.

The Means of Assessment: How Should Self-Monitoring Be Measured?

These considerations about latent causal structures have implications for personality and assessment, implications illustrated by the measurement of self-monitoring. Throughout the growth and development of self-monitoring theory, researchers have employed the same means of assessing self-monitoring—the 25-item Self-Monitoring Scale developed in 1972. Over the years, this instrument has been a faithful servant, contributing the empirical bases for theoretical insights into the nature of self-monitoring.

Nevertheless, the extensive evidence for the construct validity of self-monitoring notwithstanding, concerns have been expressed over the years that the psychometric properties of the Self-Monitoring Scale may threaten its ability to reliably and validly measure self-monitoring (e.g., Briggs, Cheek, and Buss, 1980; Lennox and Wolfe, 1984). Thus, questions have been raised about the interpretability of scores on the Self-Monitoring Scale and about the degree of correspondence between the construct and its operationalization in the Self-Monitoring Scale.

These concerns, are, of course, serious. They invoke, in the specific case of self-monitoring, the two fundamental questions that Loevinger (1957) has posed in the general case of establishing the construct validity of objective tests as instruments of psychological theory. The first question is that of intrinsic validity: *Does the Self-Monitoring Scale measure "something"?* The second question is that of the validity of the interpretation: *Does the Self-Monitoring Scale measure the construct of self-monitoring?* The answer to each of these questions would seem to be yes. The Self-Monitoring Scale does possess intrinsic validity. As examinations of latent causal structure (see Chapter 12) have suggested, it measures an entity or structure that really exists, one that has important implications for many domains of individual and social behavior. Moreover, the Self-Monitoring Scale appears to measure something very much akin to what is specified by the self-monitoring construct. As examinations of the network of associations between the Self-Monitoring Scale and external criterion behaviors (see Chapter 12) have demonstrated, the validity of the interpretation seems to be very much in keeping with that entailed by the construct of self-monitoring. (For a fuller treatment of these issues concerning the Self-Monitoring Scale, see Snyder and Gangestad, 1986.)

Nevertheless, the validity of the existing Self-Monitoring Scale does not preclude the possibility of constructing a "better" measure of self-monitoring. In fact, it has been possible to increase the reliability of the Self-Monitoring Scale and, at the same time, to retain its established intrinsic validity. The same latent structure analyses that indicate the existence of a discretely distributed causal variable underlying the Self-Monitoring Scale also point the way toward a new measure of self-monitoring.

Although virtually all of the 25 items of the original Self-Monitoring Scale are correlated with the latent self-monitoring causal variable, there is considerable variation in the magnitude of these relations. Of the three content domains discriminating between the self-monitoring classes (see Chapter 12), items that belong to the "expressive self-control" and the "social stage presence" domains correlate most strongly with the latent class variable. Examples of the most discriminating items are "I would probably make a good actor," "I have never been good at games like charades or improvisational acting," "In a group, I am rarely the center of attention," "At a party, I let others keep the jokes and stories going," and "I guess I put on a show to impress and entertain others." Items that discriminate moderately well between the classes concern acting like different people in different situations and attempting to be pleasant to others.

Thus, the portrait of the prototypical high self-monitor that emerges from these items is of someone who treats interactions with others as dramatic performances designed to gain attention, make impressions, and at times entertain. The portrait of the prototypical low self-monitor is of someone who is unable or unwilling to engage in histrionics in social situations and who typically does not use dramatic performances to impress others or gain their attention. This person's behavior is, instead, likely to communicate what he or she feels at the moment.

These descriptions are, of course, largely consistent with theoretical definitions of self-monitoring, although they do suggest which features of the original theoretical portraits deserve to be highlighted and to receive the most emphasis in current characterizations of self-monitoring. They are also consistent with recent analyses indicating that the scales of the Personality Research Form (Jackson, 1971) that best discriminate between people high and low in self-monitoring are exhibitionism, play, and dominance (Riggio and Friedman, 1982; Tunnell, 1980).

The analyses of latent structure also have revealed that there are several self-monitoring items that discriminate rather poorly, if at all, between the latent high and low self-monitoring classes. Several of

Table 13-1   The 18-Item Measure of Self-Monitoring

1. I find it hard to imitate the behavior of other people.   (F)

2. At parties and social gatherings, I do not attempt to do or say things that others will like.   (F)

3. I can only argue for ideas which I already believe.   (F)

4. I can make impromptu speeches even on topics about which I have almost no information.   (T)

5. I guess I put on a show to impress or entertain others.   (T)

6. I would probably make a good actor.   (T)

7. In a group of people I am rarely the center of attention.   (F)

8. In different situations and with different people, I often act like very different persons.   (T)

9. I am not particularly good at making other people like me.   (F)

10. I'm not always the person I appear to be.   (T)

11. I would not change my opinions (or the way I do things) in order to please someone or win their favor.   (F)

12. I have considered being an entertainer.   (T)

13. I have never been good at games like charades or improvisational acting.   (F)

14. I have trouble changing my behavior to suit different people and different situations.   (F)

15. At a party I let others keep the jokes and stories going.   (F)

16. I feel a bit awkward in company and do not show up quite as well as I should.   (F)

17. I can look anyone in the eye and tell a lie with a straight face (if for a right end).   (T)

18. I may deceive people by being friendly when I really dislike them.   (T)

Keying is given by either T (true) or F (false) in parentheses following the items, with items keyed in the high self-monitoring direction.

these items concern very insincere behaviors (e.g., "I sometimes appear to others to be experiencing deeper emotions than I actually am," or "In order to get along and be liked, I tend to be what other people expect me to be rather than anything else"). It may, therefore, be incorrect, or at least something of an exaggeration, to characterize—as some might be tempted to do—high self-monitors as presenting themselves in an overly ingratiating manner or as reflecting only that identity conferred on them by others.

Whatever the reason that these items do not discriminate well between the classes, the fact that they do not has implications for the measurement of self-monitoring. Because several of the original 25 items of the Self-Monitoring Scale are not good discriminators, and because the latent causal variable accounts for most of the covariation between the Self-Monitoring Scale and relevant external criterion behaviors, an alternative measure of self-monitoring has been developed. This new, 18-item measure consists of items with a correlation of at least +.15 with the latent self-monitoring causal variable (as estimated by their loadings on the first unrotated factor emerging from a principal axes factor analysis). These items are presented in Table 13-1.

The new 18-item measure has an internal consistency (coefficient alpha) of +.70, slightly higher than that (+.66) of the original 25-item measure. Moreover, the new measure is factorially purer than the original. The first unrotated factor accounts for 62 percent of the common variance, compared to 51 percent accounted for by the first unrotated factor of the 25-item measure. More important, total scale scores for the new 18-item measure are not correlated with an estimate of the second, relatively minor, source of variation. By contrast, total scale scores on the original measure are slightly correlated with an estimate of the second source of variation.[1]

Because the underlying latent variable measured by the new instrument is a class variable, increasing scores indicate a higher probability

---

[1]Lennox and Wolfe (1984) have offered what they regard as a "more adequate measure" (p. 1350). The correlation between that measure and the Self-Monitoring Scale is +.52 (Snyder and Gangestad, 1986). Correcting for attenuation yields an estimated correlation of +.72. The two measures, then, share over 50 percent of their reliable variance—a substantial figure, given all of the differences Lennox and Wolfe have claimed between their measure and the original Self-Monitoring Scale. In comparing the two measures, the question is: Of the 50 percent reliable variance

of belonging to the high self-monitoring class. Thus, appropriate splits should be used to classify people. For college students, the probability of belonging to the high self-monitoring class is estimated to be greater than .5 for those with scores of 11 or greater (Gangestad and Snyder, 1985). Accordingly, a split between scores of 10 and 11 would be a reasonable guideline for research using North American college students. Of course, using more extreme selection criteria, such as upper and lower quartiles on the 18-item measure (13 and over and 7 and under, respectively, for college students) would increase the purity of the class samples.

Researchers who conduct studies that allow replications of past self-monitoring findings may wish to use both the 18-item and 25-item measures in analyses of their data. It is doubtful, however, that these researchers will discover different patterns of findings because there is a substantial correlation (+.93) between the 18-item and the 25-item measures. Nevertheless, the fact that the estimated correlation with the latent self-monitoring causal variable is higher for the 18-item measure (approximately +.70) than for the 25-item measure (approx-

---

not shared by the measures, which contains more intrinsic validity: that in the Self-Monitoring Scale *not shared* with the Lennox and Wolfe measure, or that in the Lennox and Wolfe measure *not shared* with the Self-Monitoring Scale?

There are several reasons to believe that a portion of the variance in the Lennox and Wolfe measure not shared with the Self-Monitoring Scale is *not* intrinsically valid variance, and thus will *not* covary with important criterion features of social behavior. *First*, they constructed their measure very narrowly. Many of their items are virtual restatements, a procedure that increases reliability due to correlated error components rather than to increments in validity (cf. Meehl and Golden, 1982). *Second*, some of the reliable variance in their measure is probably response bias. Eleven items are keyed in the same direction; only two in the other direction. Also, use of a six-point response format in an unbalanced test may add any variation in scale usage to total score variance (Cronbach, 1955; Nunnally, 1967). *Third*, although conventional wisdom advises that items be clear, concise, unambiguous, and easily understandable (Jackson, 1971), most of their items are long and contain terms the average respondent would not use.

These three considerations pose threats to the intrinsic validity of the Lennox and Wolfe measure. In fact, whereas the Self-Monitoring Scale correlates +.65 with the latent self-monitoring causal variable, the Lennox and Wolfe measure correlates only +.4 (Snyder and Gangestad, 1986). Nevertheless, it may possess relations with behavioral variables independently of the latent self-monitoring variable, and hence may correlate with some variables more highly than the Self-Monitoring Scale.

imately +.65) suggests that the 18-item measure is the more effective indicator of the latent self-monitoring causal variable.

Of course, it may some day be possible to construct an even better measure of self-monitoring, an instrument that possesses even greater intrinsic validity than the best one that is currently available. This may require identifying new item contents that tap the causal entity underlying self-monitoring phenomena. Most likely, such new item contents will come out of successful extensions and elaborations of self-monitoring through research involving its current measure (Cronbach and Meehl, 1955). From this perspective, the development of a better measure of self-monitoring would not be motivated by any failure on the part of the current measure. On the contrary, the better measure will have come into being precisely because of the very success of the current measure in pointing the way toward increased understanding of the true nature of self-monitoring.

PART VI

A Theoretical Framework for Self-Monitoring

WHAT ARE THE implications of self-monitoring for understanding human nature? Researchers working like scientific sleuths have followed the trail of self-monitoring up and down many avenues of inquiry. They have collected, examined, and pieced together many bits and pieces of evidence. They have documented the consequences of self-monitoring. They have explored its applications and traced its origins and development. And, they have uncovered the underlying nature of self-monitoring. This scientific detective work having been done, the time has come to place self-monitoring into the broader context of a larger theoretical framework for personality and social psychology.

These integrative conceptual efforts will begin, first, with an examination of the implications of self-monitoring for understanding the nature of the self (Chapter 14). These integrative efforts will then focus, more generally, on the links between personality and social behavior (Chapter 15). From these integrative conceptual efforts, I hope, will come new approaches for understanding people and their social worlds (Chapter 16).

The Nature of the Self

∎

IN THE BEGINNING, my explorations of self-monitoring emerged from concerns about the nature of the self, in particular with the links between the private realities and public appearances of the self. Of critical importance to relations between private realities and public appearances is the extent to which people differ in their ability and motivation to control their expressive and self-presentational behaviors. These differences may reflect the degree to which people identify with the metaphor of life as a stage on which to play one or more roles. Not only does the dramatic metaphor (the "great stage of life," as Plato put it) provide a starting point for the concept of self-monitoring, it also offers a point of origin for considering the nature of the self.

The Self as an Actor

What, then, is acting? Tyrone Guthrie has written:

> By definition Acting is no more than Doing, Taking Action. But in a specialized sense, the term Acting is used for the Art or Craft of Acting. This implies pretending to be someone or something other than yourself; or even, while retaining your own identity, expressing thoughts or feelings which do not in fact correspond with your own thoughts and feelings at a particular moment. Indeed in this sense of the word we all

spend a great deal of our lives in acting, a greater part, I suspect, than most of us realize. (1971, p. 7)

But, is this really acting? Once again, Guthrie's answer:

I think so, because, though you are not pretending to an identity or an appearance other than your own, and though you are inventing your own dialogue and choreography, you are, nevertheless, expressing many different facets of yourself, and this, I believe, means that from time to time you are forced, if the facets are to be convincingly displayed, to think of yourself as many different kinds of people, similar only because they all look like you, wear your clothes, [and] speak in your voice . . . . (1971, p. 7)

When the arts and crafts of acting are applied, as Guthrie put it, "to lubricate the creaking mechanism of social intercourse" (1971, p. 7), the many roles played have very much in common with the many public selves of the high self-monitoring lifestyle. High self-monitors are, in a sense, actors with a large repertoire of roles, willing and able to work from a wide range of scripts; they cast themselves in many different parts in life. By contrast, the low self-monitor may be likened to the performer who has the same part in every production, particularly the performer whose own personality seems to provide the script for his or her every role.

In this regard, it is worth noting that Tyrone Guthrie believed that good stage acting required a talent for which the most natural medium is social life itself and that no amount of training on the stage could make up for the sheer lack of this talent. It is perhaps for this reason that professional stage actors do have relatively high scores on the Self-Monitoring Scale (Snyder, 1974). Moreover, as structural analyses have revealed, the single item that most validly taps the general factor pervading the Self-Monitoring Scale is the item "I would probably make a good actor" (Gangestad and Snyder, 1985).

Self-monitoring is very much a concept about acting in Guthrie's very specialized sense of the term (recognizing, of course, that the drama of life may involve more than the acting of the stage and screen; Buss and Briggs, 1984). But, self-monitoring is also a concept about acting in Guthrie's more general definition of the term. Just as, in its widest sense, acting is doing and taking action, so too is self-monitoring about doing and taking action. Thus, although the concept of self-monitoring draws on the dramaturgical metaphor, it does so in the broadest possible sense.

The Self in Self-Monitoring

Any theory of the self must come to grips with a number of central issues. Gergen (1971), for example, has proposed five:

1. the self as fact versus fiction,
2. the self as knower versus the known,
3. the self as structure versus process,
4. the self as single or multiple, and
5. the self as consistent or inconsistent.

Theoretical treatments of self-monitoring have addressed each of these critical issues in the knowledge base provided by empirical research.

In keeping with most theories, the "self" in self-monitoring theory is a hypothetical construct (a theoretical "fiction"), but one whose manifestations (its "facts") are well-specified and readily observable. Self-monitoring deals both with the knower (people high and low in self-monitoring) and the known (their characteristic conceptions of self). It deals with how knowledge of self is organized (whether in pragmatic or in principled organizing structures) and with how it is used (the processes by which conceptions of self guide and direct activities). Self-monitoring recognizes the existence—at least at the phenotypic level of behavioral presentations of self—of single selves and multiple selves and of consistency and inconsistency, linking these descriptors to, respectively, the low and high self-monitoring types.

Just as self-monitoring has features in common with other theories of the self, so too does it have features that—because of special emphases on particular issues—may set it apart. At the center of its very identity, self-monitoring is a theory of *the self in action*. Its basic premise is that theories that people adopt in defining what they regard as "me," and the impact of these conceptions of self on their lives are of particular importance in understanding the self. Knowing how conceptions of the self are reflected in patterns of social behavior, in the dynamics of interpersonal relationships, and in the structure of people's social worlds will yield, according to self-monitoring theory, an understanding of the nature of the self in action.

The self-monitoring construct has helped researchers identify two theories of the self that people can and do adopt—the pragmatic sense of self and the principled sense of self. And the Self-Monitoring Scale has identified the two categories of people who exemplify these theories of self. Low self-monitors characteristically endorse the principled theory of self; high self-monitors, the pragmatic theory of self (see Chapter 4).

The principled and pragmatic theories, it should be noted, are thought to be *personal* theories that people use to understand their own natures and to guide their own actions. Nevertheless, these personal theories have their counterparts in *scientific* theories of the self. The relatively principled theory is a fundamentally *psychological* theory, written in the psychological terms of enduring traits, stable dispositions, and other features of identity thought to reside within people. For this reason, a psychological definition of the self—such as that offered by Schlenker: "The inner self is . . . a theory of oneself . . . containing the organized, relatively stable contents of our personal experiences . . . basic, enduring, genuine . . ." (1985, xiii)—embraces low self-monitoring views of the self. By contrast, the relatively pragmatic theory is a distinctly *sociological* theory, cast in terms of roles, interpersonal situations, and other properties of the social structures in which people operate; it corresponds to high self-monitoring ideas about the self. Such a definition is proposed by Becker: "The self consists . . . of all the roles we are prepared to take in formulating our own line of action, both the roles of individuals and of generalized others . . . a process in which the roles of others are taken and made use of in organizing our own activities" (1968, p. 197).

The Self as a Guiding Theory

The concept of self is one of the oldest and most enduring in psychological and philosophical considerations of human nature. For centuries, students of the self have been concerned with how people come to know themselves. Within this tradition, many have focused on the social origins of self-conceptions, or the extent to which beliefs about the self are products of social interaction. Indeed, both classical (Cooley, 1902; James, 1890; Mead, 1934) and contemporary (Bem, 1972;

Gergen, 1977) treatments of self and identity have emphasized the social and societal determinants of self-conceptions. (For reviews and sourcebooks, see Gordon and Gergen, 1968; Schlenker, 1985; Suls, 1982; Suls and Greenwald, 1983; Wylie, 1974, 1979.)

In the context of the considerable attention directed at the origins and *antecedents* of self-conceptions, the focal points of self-monitoring theory and research, which are concerned with considerations of the *consequences* of conceptions of self, represent a marked departure from tradition. Self-monitoring theory and research are devoted to answering the questions: Of what consequences are conceptions of self for what people subsequently think, feel, and do? How do beliefs about the self influence the thought processes by which people organize and interpret material relevant to the self? How do beliefs about the self direct patterns of social behavior? How do beliefs about the self channel the unfolding dynamics of interpersonal relationships? And at a more general level: How are the conceptions of self reflected in people's lives?

In its answers to these questions, self-monitoring encompasses a domain of self-conception sufficiently broad and global in scope to capture the essence of people's sense of "me." It appears to capture people's own theories about their personal characteristics, their social situations, and their actions in these situations. These personal theories have an impact in many spheres of life—how people think and how they act (see Chapter 3), how they structure their social worlds (see Chapter 4), and how they conduct their relationships with friends and lovers (see Chapters 5 and 6). This influence extends, too, to domains of jobs, careers, and professions (see Chapter 7), advertising and consumer behavior (see Chapter 8), and personal problems, counseling, and therapy (see Chapter 9).

If the self is a guiding theory, how does it guide? Earlier in this book (see Chapter 3), I characterized self-monitoring orientations in terms of two fundamental questions: "Who does this situation want me to be and how can I be that person?" for high self-monitors and "Who am I and how can I be me in this situation?" for low self-monitors. One way in which the self may function as a guiding theory is in the selection of one of these questions as a formula for choosing actions in social situations. The guiding hand of the self may also be at work in choosing situations and relationships that are conducive to one's self-monitoring propensities (see Chapters 4, 5, and 6). In these ways, principled and pragmatic definitions of the self may promote patterns of behavior that embody these personal theories.

Global Selves and Molecular Selves

The lives of high self-monitors appear to be meaningful reflections of a pragmatic sense of self; those of low self-monitors reflect a principled sense of self. That is, for all people, whatever their self-monitoring propensities, there appears to be a clearly defined congruence between their conceptions of self and their social lives. To witness this congruence, however, it is necessary to consider these two conceptions of self at the *global* level of personal theories. If researchers were to consider conceptions of self at the more *molecular* level of specific traits and attitudes, they would reach a somewhat different conclusion.

At the level of specific traits and attitudes, it is only people low in self-monitoring who, in accord with principled theories of self, show consistency between particular personal attributes and social behavior. At the molecular level, high self-monitoring behavior reflects the prescriptions of immediate situations, rather than personal characteristics. But the high self-monitor's situation-to-situation specificity in social behavior is congruent with a *global* pragmatic conception of self.

Seen in this light, it is easy to understand why empirical searches for consistency between traits and behavior (Mischel, 1968) and between attitudes and behavior (Wicker, 1969) have produced, at best, only equivocal evidence of pervasive consistency. Researchers who use measures of specific traits and attitudes in this endeavor are working with a strategy well-suited for detecting the directive influence of self-conceptions on the behavior of low self-monitors. In keeping with a principled global conception of self, low self-monitors *do* display congruence at the molecular level of specific traits and attitudes. This same strategy, though, is inappropriate for detecting the directive influence of self-conceptions on high self-monitors. These people, in keeping with a pragmatic global conception of self, only display congruence at the level of global conceptions of self.

By examining global conceptions of the pragmatic and the principled self, researchers can employ a strategy well-suited for understanding all people, whatever their self-monitoring type. This strategy reveals that both kinds of people demonstrate meaningful congruence between their global conceptions of self and specific life events. As different and distinct as their characteristic social styles may be, both types may succeed in being faithful to their personal conceptions of self.

The Self as a Motivational Force

The active involvement of the self in structuring social worlds takes on added significance when viewed from the perspective of the "ecology" of the self. Hormuth has suggested that the "elements of the ecology of the self are *others*, as the sources of social experiences and reflections of the self, *things* that make self-relevant activities possible, acquire symbolic value and represent the self toward others, and *environments* that are the setting for social experiences and allow and represent self-relevant activities and interactions" (1984a, p. 2). With their impact on cognitive, behavioral, and interpersonal activities (including, especially, choices of social settings and interaction partners), the principled and pragmatic selves seem to be actively involved in shaping the entire ecology of the self.

This active involvement makes clear the extent to which self-monitoring is a fundamentally *motivational* theory of the self. Indeed, people of both self-monitoring types choose their social situations and structure their interpersonal relationships (see Chapters 4, 5, and 6). These strategic and motivated activities may operate in the service of each type's characteristic conception of self. Whether this guiding theory depicts a principled self or a pragmatic self, the motivational processes and outcomes are the same—a pattern of cognitive, behavioral, and interpersonal activities constructed in the image of each type's personal theory of the self.

In addition, the motivating influence of these personal theories may be seen in certain facets or tasks of the self, as Greenwald (e.g., 1982; Greenwald and Breckler, 1985; Greenwald and Pratkanis, 1984) has suggested. For example, the "ego task" of social accreditation and the evaluation of the self based on reactions from external audiences may be facets of the high self-monitoring self, whereas the "ego task" of individual achievement and self-evaluation based on internal standards may be facets of the low self-monitoring self (cf. Greenwald and Pratkanis, 1984).

This view of the self as a guiding theory—one that exerts a directive influence on life events—should be viewed in the context of other approaches to the self that have invoked the metaphor of the theory. Many scholars have regarded people as naive scientists attempting to develop and test theories about the world around them (e.g., Heider, 1958; Kelly, 1955; Lecky, 1969 [1945]). Most explicitly, Epstein has described the self-concept as a "theory the individual has unwittingly constructed about himself as an experiencing, functioning individual," a theory that is "part of a broader theory which he holds with respect to his entire range of significant experience" (1973, p. 407).

How do people form and test theories about the self? Researchers have documented the ways in which knowledge structures (known variously as schemata, scripts, or prototypes) are actively involved in acquiring knowledge about the self, in interpreting it, in storing it in memory, and in retrieving it (e.g., Abelson, 1976; Cantor and Mischel, 1979; Judd and Kulik, 1980; Markus, 1977; Rogers, 1981; Swann and Read, 1981; Taylor and Crocker, 1981). Other researchers have uncovered several biases of the self as a knowledge generator and a theory tester: egocentricity, the tendency for judgments to center on the self; beneffectance, the tendency to regard the self as good and competent; and conservatism, the tendency to resist change in existing beliefs about the self (for a review, see Greenwald, 1980).

Still other researchers have demonstrated the motivational nature of attention to and awareness of the self (e.g., Buss, 1980; Carver and Scheier, 1981; Wicklund, 1975), as well as of challenges to one's conceptions of self (e.g., Swann, 1983, 1985). Let us examine more carefully the overlapping between the concepts of self-monitoring and self-awareness. According to one treatment of self-awareness (Duval and Wicklund, 1972; Wicklund, 1975), external stimulus events may direct a person's focus of attention either to the self as a distinct object (the state of objective self-awareness) or away from the self to the surrounding situation (the state of subjective self-awareness). According to a related analysis (Buss, 1980), when attention is directed to the self, it may be focused either on relatively private aspects typically not available to outside observers (the state of private self-awareness) or on relatively public aspects observable by other people (the state of public self-awareness).

Could it be that the two self-monitoring orientations reflect chronic differences in typical states of awareness (cf. Schneiderman, Webb, Davis, and Thomas, 1981)? Perhaps high self-monitors, with their attentiveness to situational cues to behavioral appropriateness, reside in a chronic state of subjective self-awareness, and low self-monitors, with their attentiveness to inner guides to action, exist in a chronic state of objective self-awareness. Perhaps, too, high self-monitoring concerns with images projected in social interaction may reflect a chronic propensity to states of public self-awareness, and low self-monitoring concerns with being true to personal attitudes and values may reflect a chronic tendency toward states of private self-awareness.

These arguments for conceptual overlap between self-monitoring and states of awareness would seem to be well grounded. Indeed, the results of experimental investigations (e.g., Schneiderman, Webb, Davis, and Thomas, 1981) have suggested support for specific hypotheses derived from these arguments. Nevertheless, this potential overlap does not seem to occur at the level of measures of self-monitoring and self-awareness. The private self-consciousness and public self-consciousness factors of the Self-Consciousness Scale (Fenigstein, Scheier, and Buss, 1975) would seem to be measures of differences in private self-awareness and public self-awareness. Yet, all indications are that the correlations between these measures and the Self-Monitoring Scale are very minimal indeed (e.g., Tomarelli and Shaffer, in press; Turner, Scheier, Carver, and Ickes, 1978).[1] Nevertheless, although empirical ties have yet to be identified, the concepts of self-monitoring and self-awareness do seem to have shared themes.

Clearly, views of the self that invoke the metaphor of the theory and those that focus on states of awareness have much in common with my own perspective on the self in action. Each view recognizes and emphasizes the active and motivational nature of the self. Each view acknowledges the guiding and directive involvement of the self in acquiring and interpreting information about it. Yet, focusing on the self in action has taught me that there is more to the self than self-knowledge, no matter how intimately involved in information processing the self may be. Focusing on the consequences of the self for understanding social worlds has helped me see the intricate ways that

---

[1] In an analysis of the relations among self-monitoring and the factors of the Self-Consciousness Scale, Tomarelli and Shaffer (in press) have reported that those scoring highest on self-monitoring were low in social anxiety and high in public self-consciousness, and those with the lowest self-monitoring scores were high in social anxiety, low in public self-consciousness, and high in private self-consciousness.

conceptions of self are woven into the entire motivational fabric of social existence, including patterns of social behavior and networks of personal relationships.

The Genesis of the Self

No inquiry into the nature of the self could be complete without at least some hints about the genesis of the self. What are its origins? When does it emerge? How does it develop? In the context of self-monitoring as a theory of the self these general questions become: What can the development of self-monitoring tell us about the self? To answer this particular question, begin by returning to the scenario for the origins and development of self-monitoring (sketched in Chapters 10 and 11).

Evidence is mounting that the causal variable underlying self-monitoring has definite, demonstrable, biological-genetic origins (Dworkin, 1977, in press; Gangestad, 1984). Moreover, it is possible to chart a developmental course in which this causal entity emerges in early childhood and initiates processes of divergent causality for the socialization of the many and varied manifestations of self-monitoring seen in adults (Gangestad and Snyder, 1985). What, then, are the links between a developmental scenario for self-monitoring involving a biological-genetic etiology followed by divergent causality and a conceptualization of the self as a guiding theory with motivational consequences for behavior in social contexts?

Although research-based answers to this question are not yet available, some theoretical ones are. Both the developmental scenario for self-monitoring and the analysis of the self as a guiding theory have emphasized the processes by which people gravitate toward particular situations that provide specific behavioral opportunities. In the developmental scenario, the latent self-monitoring causal entity disposes people toward situations that foster the development of their emerging self-monitoring propensities. In the context of analysis of the self, personal theories of the self guide people into situations that dispose them to act in accord with their own conceptions of self. That is, the latent self-monitoring entity and conceptions of self play functionally equivalent roles, that of guiding and directing people into situations conducive to their characteristic interpersonal orientations.

To say that they serve functionally equivalent purposes is not necessarily to propose that the latent self-monitoring causal entity and conceptions of self are one and the same thing. That would also require proposing the existence, at the time of the very earliest manifestations of self-monitoring, of well-articulated beliefs of the form "I am a pragmatic creature of my situations" or "I am a principled, consistent being." However, it is not at all difficult to imagine initial manifestations of self-monitoring (such as temperament differences in newborn infants or language acquisition in very young children; see Chapter 10) that precede the development of sufficient cognitive capacity to articulate abstract theories about one's self (see Harter, 1983).

It would seem more reasonable to propose that pragmatic and principled conceptions of self are themselves manifestations of the latent self-monitoring causal variable (see Chapter 12). Presumably, these conceptions emerge at a point in the developmental scenario when the capacity to form abstract concepts is present and a sufficient corpus of behavioral and experiential manifestations of the latent self-monitoring entity exists to be organized into a pragmatic or principled sense of self. Once developed, these conceptions of self, if they do function as guiding theories and motivational forces, may constitute a primary vehicle for the influence of the latent entity on self-monitoring phenomena. In this sense, the pragmatic and principled selves may have the status of genuine causal factors in accounting for social behavior.

The Quintessential Question: Is There a "Real" Self?

This psychological inquiry into the nature of the self may answer the philosophical question that I posed at the very beginning of this book: Is there, beneath the appearances and images that people project to each other, a "real" me, an essential "self"? The answer to this question is, on the one hand, yes. There is a real self, but the nature of that self is radically different for different people—a principled sense of self for some and a pragmatic one for others.

But perhaps the reader is tempted to say that the low self-monitoring self is somehow more "real" than the high self-monitoring self. Does not, after all, the kaleidoscope of changing appearances displayed by the high self-monitor lack the unifying coherence of the single, enduring sense of "me for all times and places" found in the low self-monitor? One answer to this question comes from the writings of William James (1890). James' notion of a multiplicity of social selves clearly seems to fit people high in self-monitoring. But his views on the unity of the self just might encompass high as well as low self-monitoring selves:

> If from the one point of view they are one self, from others they are truly not one but many selves. And similarly of the attribute of continuity; it gives its own kind of unity to the self—that of mere connectedness, or unbrokenness, a perfectly definite phenomenal thing—but it gives not a jot or tittle more. And this unbrokenness in the stream of selves, like the unbrokenness in an exhibition of "dissolving views," in no wise implies any farther unity or contradicts any amount of plurality in other respects. (p. 335).

This "separate but equal" view of the principled and pragmatic selves is, to some extent, an empirical question. One could, in principle, assess the "continuity," "connectedness," and "unbrokenness" of either type of self—whether in terms of internal structural properties or in terms of relevant behavioral manifestations.

But the real answer to the philosophical question, "Is there a real me?" may be that this is not *the* question at all. For the message of theory and research on self-monitoring is that what may be most important is not the elusive goal of knowing whether there is a quintessential self but the more tractable goal of understanding the theories that different people adopt in defining what they collectively regard as "me." What may be most important is understanding the impact of these differing conceptions of self on patterns of social behavior and on the dynamics of social relationships. From such an understanding of people and their social worlds, even more profound insights into the nature of the self may yet come.

Understanding the self in action may also reveal the true importance of conceptions of self. No longer will it be necessary to ask plaintively of self-conceptions, as some have asked about other beliefs that people hold: "Of what importance are they to how people actually think, feel, and act?" (Kelley, 1973). No longer will it be necessary to worry about whether conceptions of self are little more than epiphenomenal notions that exist in a vacuum. To the contrary, conceptions of self may be important precisely because of their pervasive influences on people's social lives.

The Several Senses of the Self

As an inquiry into the nature of the self, theory and research on self-monitoring highlight the several senses of the term "self." There is, on the one hand, the private self as it is conceived by the person—the theory in terms of which a person construes his or her nature as an individual and as a social being. And there is, on the other hand, the public self as it is presented to other people—the set of activities into which a person's conceptions of self are translated, expressed, and communicated in social interaction.

From my perspective, self-monitoring is a theory of the self in both of these senses. As a theory of the private self, it is concerned with the private realities of the pragmatic and principled conceptions of self people adopt to understand their own natures. And as a theory of the public self, it is concerned with the public appearances of the presentations of self people display in their dealings with others, presentations that embody pragmatic or principled conceptions of self.

In considering these two senses of the self, it is important to resist the temptation to link one of them (the private self) to the low self-monitoring orientation and the other (the public self) to the high self-monitoring orientation. Private conceptions of self, from my perspective, are employed by all people to understand their natures. Of course, it is a principled framework that is employed by low self-monitors and a pragmatic one that is used by high self-monitors. Similarly, from my perspective, public selves are presented to others by all people. However, for those high in self-monitoring, pragmatic considerations of impression management are paramount in choosing public selves; for those low in self-monitoring, principled considerations of fidelity to one's attitudes and dispositions are of primary importance in public displays of the self.

But, and perhaps more fundamentally, self-monitoring is a theory of self in a *third* sense as well. As a theory of self, self-monitoring is concerned most basically with how private conceptions of self are translated into public presentations of self. That is, the processes of self-monitoring are those by which informational and motivational considerations embodied in personal conceptions of self are integrated with those provided by social contexts to guide and direct behavior. From my perspective, the processes of self-monitoring are those that link the private self and the public self. They weave the complex of intricate patterns that make up the private realities and the public appearances of the self.

Personality and Social Behavior

■

ALTHOUGH FUNDAMENTALLY AN inquiry into the nature of the self, self-monitoring is more generally an inquiry into the nature of personality and social behavior. As a psychological construct, personality refers to regularities and consistencies in behavior. These regularities and consistencies may exist across contexts (Is the person who is dominant on the job also dominant at home?), over time (Is the person who is assertive today also assertive tomorrow, next month, and next year?), and between domains (Is the person who appears to be conscientious on a personality test actually conscientious when given the opportunity to behave that way?). If such stabilities exist, they ought to distinguish one person from another, to render people's actions predictable, and to determine their adjustment to the circumstances of their lives (see Allport's classic definition of the nature of personality, 1937).

That the self and personality have much in common, and that what they have in common has something to do with self-monitoring, is suggested by the origins of the term "personality." At one time in the history of the theater, the actors performed behind masks. Theatergoers knew that a performer who wore a particular mask, or *persona,* would be playing a character with a consistent pattern of behavior and attitudes. Originally, the term *persona* designated only the mask. But as time went by, it came to refer also to the character played by the wearer of the mask and eventually to the actor who played that character. *Persona* is also the Latin root of the psychological term "personality." Just as *persona* referred to regularities and consistencies in characters created on the stage, *personality* refers to regularities and consistencies in people's behavior.

That an actor might acquire a "personality" by putting on a mask and change that personality by changing masks makes me wonder whether personality might not have something in common with the masks of the theater and the actors who wore them. Might not personality, as we experience it in our dealings with others, be a "mask" created by a regular and consistent presentation of self? Might not some people be capable of wearing only one mask, therefore presenting the same "self" to all with whom they interact? Might not other people be capable of wearing many masks, therefore displaying many different "selves"? Clearly, self-monitoring theory and research suggest affirmative answers to these questions. And, the very fact that the questions can be posed suggests that considerations of self-monitoring are also considerations of personality and social behavior.

How are the regularities and consistencies of personality reflected in the behavior of people in social contexts? Kurt Lewin's seminal proposition, "Every psychological event depends upon the state of the person and at the same time on the environment, although their relative importance is different in different cases" (1936, p. 12), suggests three major strategies for investigating personality and social behavior—the *dispositional,* the *interactional,* and the *situational* strategies. These strategies differ in the extent to which they identify personal-dispositional and environmental-situational sources of regularities and consistencies in social behavior. Each of them can be characterized in terms of its theoretical perspective and empirical orientation (Snyder and Ickes, 1985).

In the study of personality and social behavior, there has been something of a sequential progression from the dispositional to the interactional to the situational strategy. This has been not only a historical progression but an evolutionary one. As a consequence of this evolution, the three strategies possess much in the way of family resemblance, with themes voiced by strategies earlier in the sequence echoed by later ones. The net effect has been an increasingly precise and sophisticated understanding of personality and social behavior. (For elaboration of these points, see Snyder and Ickes, 1985).

This evolution also has characterized theory and research on self-monitoring. At appropriate stages, investigators have examined self-monitoring from the dispositional, interactional, and situational vantage points. For this reason, self-monitoring research serves as a case history of the evolving strategies for understanding personality and social behavior.

Self-Monitoring and the Dispositional Strategy

The *dispositional* strategy is guided by a theoretical perspective that assumes that regularities and consistencies in social behavior can be understood in terms of stable and enduring dispositions thought to reside within people and by an empirical orientation that tries to identify categories of people who typically manifest the phenomena of concern to researchers. The dispositional strategy dictates that many of the phenomena of personality and social behavior can be understood by focusing on people who typically display those phenomena. After first identifying categories of people who typically manifest the phenomenon under consideration, the researcher can then use those people to investigate the psychology of that phenomenon (Snyder and Ickes, 1985).

Identifying Categories of People   How might this investigative strategy be applied in the particular case of self-monitoring? To apply the logic of the dispositional strategy, a researcher would begin by asking if there are categories of people that may be contrasted in terms of their propensities to adopt either the high or the low self-monitoring interpersonal orientation.

Clearly, the first generation of research on self-monitoring embodied the dispositional strategy. It began by articulating, at the theoretical level, the contrasting categories typified by prototypes of the high self-monitor and the low self-monitor (see Chapter 1). It then proceeded to develop an empirical assessment procedure, the Self-Monitoring Scale, to reliably and validly identify members of these contrasting categories (see Chapter 2). Later, probes of the underlying structure of the Self-Monitoring Scale corroborated the fundamental assumption of this strategy. At an underlying level, people do in fact come in two types: They are members of either the discrete class of high self-monitors or the contrasting discrete class of low self-monitors (see Chapter 12). In fact, the underlying dichotomous nature of self-monitoring may have made it an ideal candidate for applications of the dispositional strategy.

Documenting Characteristic Interpersonal Orientations   In this (as in any) application of the dispositional strategy, identifying these contrasting categories was *not* an end in and of itself. Rather, it served as a means toward the end of understanding the interpersonal styles associated with self-monitoring propensities. Having identified these contrasting categories, researchers were in a position to document the consequences of self-monitoring in far-ranging domains. They were able to discover two characteristic social orientations—the high self-monitoring "Who does this situation want me to be and how can I be that person?" and the low self-monitoring "Who am I and how can I be me in this situation?" (see Chapter 3). Moreover, researchers were able to propose two contrasting conceptions of self—the high self-monitoring pragmatic self and the low self-monitoring principled self—associated with these social styles (see Chapter 4).

The results of this application of the dispositional strategy have been most productive. And in its application of the dispositional strategy, research on self-monitoring is in good company. Just as studying prejudiced people has revealed much about the nature of prejudice, studying those with high needs for approval has been very informative about the dynamics of approval seeking, and studying Machiavellians has been most instructive about interpersonal manipulation (for reviews, see Snyder and Ickes, 1985), so too has studying people with pragmatic and principled selves provided much insight into the nature of the self.

Self-Monitoring and the Interactional Strategy

The dispositional strategy has produced some very vivid and graphic portraits of personality and social behavior. Yet, the extent of its ability to predict the behavior of *all* people in *all* domains of psychological functioning and in *all* social contexts has been a source of some concern and frustration. In fact, the road that researchers have travelled in search of predictabilities in human social behavior is littered with causes for genuine concern and frustration.

The Search for Behavioral Consistency   For generations, behavioral scientists have tried to chart the links between actions in life situations and relevant attitudes, traits, and dispositions. Yet, time and again, personality researchers have found that trait measures are distressingly poor predictors of actual behavior, that actions are unreliable clues to underlying dispositions, and that observed cross-situational correlations are minimal (e.g., Mischel, 1968). All too often, social psychologists have encountered weak and inconsistent relations between measures of personal attitudes and observations of relevant behavior (e.g., Wicker, 1969). Equally often, they have been disappointed to find that hard-won changes in attitude are not translated into corresponding changes in behavior (e.g., Festinger, 1964).

Perhaps the lesson to be learned from generations of research in personality and social psychology is a negative one. Long-standing assumptions to the contrary, there may not necessarily be consistencies between the private worlds of attitudes and dispositions and the public worlds of behavior and action. In the face of the empirical crises of confidence that have plagued the concepts of attitude and trait, it should come as no surprise to learn that some researchers have grown disenchanted with the dispositional strategy. In spite of its evident successes, many have sought other ways that would account for more of the variability in social behavior and predict more of the people more of the time (e.g., Bem and Allen, 1974; Bem and Funder, 1978; Kenrick and Stringfield, 1980).

Out of these concerns and frustrations (the immodesty of the goals that produced them notwithstanding), emerged the interactional strategy, designed to maximize the predictive relations between dispositional measures and social behavior. The *interactional* strategy is guided by a theoretical perspective that assumes that much of the variation in social behavior is due to interactions between personal dispositions and situational factors. It is also directed by an empirical orientation that seeks moderating variables to specify instances in which dispositions will or will not predict behavior (Snyder and Ickes, 1985).

The Role of Moderating Variables   Moderating variables may be classified according to which one of four questions about predictability they answer: (1) *Which traits* will be good predictors of behavior? (2) *Which behaviors* are dispositions likely to predict? (3) For *which people* will traits predict behavior? and (4) In *which situations* will dispositions predict behavior? (For details of this classification scheme, see Snyder and Ickes, 1985.) That is, the interactional strategy proposes that behavioral consistency, rather than being a pervasive phenomenon, is localized in particular types of traits, classes of behaviors, categories of people, and sets of situations. Only when these particulars are properly specified with appropriate moderating variables is it possible to identify the behavioral consistencies of personality.

In its second generation, theory and research on self-monitoring addressed the nature and origins of behavioral consistency. Unlike the general evolutionary trend in research on personality and social behavior, the evolutionary sequence for self-monitoring reflected no frustrations with the dispositional strategy. To the contrary, that tactic had worked well for self-monitoring. However, there was no denying the general concerns about issues of prediction associated with this strategy. Moreover, it was becoming increasingly apparent that self-monitoring had something to say about personality and prediction.

In fact, research on the behavioral consequences of self-monitoring (see Chapter 3) suggests that self-monitoring does perform effectively as a moderating variable, providing theoretically informed answers to the "Which people?" question. The social behavior of low self-monitors characteristically embodies the regularities and consistencies thought to constitute personality. Unlike high self-monitors, their behavior is rarely shaped and molded to fit their surroundings. Instead, they typically display substantial correspondence between private attitudes and public behaviors.

Strategies for Personality and Prediction   Self-monitoring, this evidence suggests, provides a vehicle for identifying relatively dispositional (i.e., low self-monitoring) and relatively situational (i.e., high self-monitoring) people. Identifying such categories allows researchers to choose their strategies for predicting and understanding people. To predict and understand low self-monitors, a researcher would seek information about their attitudes, traits, and dispositions. It is as if the low self-monitoring psychology is one (perhaps reflecting a principled conception of self) of attitudes, dispositions, and other inner traits and states. By contrast, to predict and understand the behavior of high self-monitors, a researcher would seek information about characteristics of their situations. It is as if theirs is a psychology (in keeping, perhaps, with a pragmatic conception of self) of social situations and interpersonal surroundings.

Self-monitoring is, of course, but one of many vehicles for identifying relatively dispositional and relatively situational people. Indeed, measures of, among others, action control (Kuhl, 1981), anxiety (Grooms and Endler, 1960), ascription of responsibility (Schwartz, 1973), defensiveness (Kogan and Wallach, 1964), empathy (Hogan, 1969; Mills and Hogan, 1978), locus of control (Phares, 1976; Rotter, 1966), neuroticism (Endler, 1973), personal identity (Cheek, 1982; Hogan and Cheek, 1983), psychological androgyny (Bem, 1975), repression-sensitization (Byrne, 1964), and self-consciousness (Fenigstein, Scheier, and Buss, 1975) have proved their ability to function as personal moderating variables.

What, then, are the criteria that define successful moderating variables. Self-monitoring works as a moderating variable because it differentiates people whose behavior is an expression of inner feelings, attitudes, and beliefs from those who, in different situations and with different people, act like very different people. To generalize from the case of self-monitoring, a moderating variable will perform well to the extent that it taps processes by which information about the self and about social situations is attended to and used in guiding behavior. (For elaboration on these arguments, see Snyder and Ickes, 1985.)

Self-Monitoring and the Situational Strategy

As the issues that absorbed self-monitoring researchers evolved from predictabilities in social behavior to the motivational underpinnings of people's interpersonal styles, the investigative strategy also evolved—from the interactional to the situational. The *situational* strategy was born of desires to come to grips with the dynamic interplay between people and situations. It is guided by a theoretical perspective that proposes that regularities and consistencies in people's behavior are products of regularities and consistencies in their situations and by an empirical orientation that seeks to understand how people choose and influence situations (Snyder and Ickes, 1985).

Choosing Situations: Antecedents and Consequences   The situational strategy begins with the premise that in the natural course of events, people typically have considerable freedom to choose where to be, when to be there, and with whom to be there. Accordingly, the situations in which people find themselves are partially of their own choosing. Moreover, once in a situation—whether of their choosing or not—much of what transpires is determined by their own actions. For, in social situations, how people are treated by others is often determined by their own actions.

Why are people's choices of situations important? Choices of settings may reflect features of personal identity—conceptions of self, beliefs, attitudes, values, traits, dispositions, and other attributes of personal identity (e.g., Snyder, 1981b, 1983; Snyder and Ickes, 1985). For example, some people may choose situations that promote gregarious behaviors (e.g., parties) precisely because they are by nature gregarious. Moreover, when they find themselves in situations that do not foster gregarious behaviors (e.g., academic seminars), such people may try to transform those situations into gregarious ones (perhaps by suggesting that the seminar move down to the local tavern). Thus, gregarious people may be defined as those who choose to enter gregarious situations and who try to maximize the gregarious character of their situations. In so doing, they construct social worlds particularly conducive to their own dispositions where they would have ample opportunity to display gregarious behaviors.

Two features of the situational strategy should be noted. Although its theoretical orientation views *situations* as entities that dispose *behaviors,* one should *not* regard situations and behaviors as equivalent. Thus, the situations "at a party" and "in a bar" can be defined independently (e.g., spatial and temporal location, physical setting, social and demographic structure, etc.) of the behaviors of "dancing" and "drinking" that may occur in those situations. One ready criterion for distinguishing situations from behaviors is that situations, but not behaviors, are specified by phrases of the form "at...," "in...," or "on...." In addition, no necessary theoretical distinction is drawn between *approaching* situations that facilitate and *avoiding* those that impede characteristic behavioral orientations. Both activities are viewed as manifestations of choosing social situations.

How would investigators use the situational strategy to study the motivational underpinnings of self-monitoring? First, they would identify situations that elicit the high self-monitoring interpersonal style and others that elicit the low self-monitoring orientation. Next, they would identify categories of people who typically are found in these types of situation. Then, they would determine whether the people found in high or low self-monitoring situations are themselves high or low in self-monitoring.

Moreover, researchers would ask why some people find themselves in situations that let them behave in high self-monitoring fashion and others find themselves in situations that allow them to act in low self-monitoring ways. To answer this question, researchers would find out if people actively choose situations that foster their own self-monitoring orientation and avoid those that promote the contrasting one. In addition, they would determine whether people influence situations to make them better suited to their self-monitoring propensities.

In point of fact, the situational strategy has guided the third generation of theory and research on self-monitoring. Studies of choosing and influencing social situations have followed the dictates of the situational strategy and have revealed the motivational underpinnings of self-monitoring. People high and low in self-monitoring may create worlds that encourage them to be the pragmatic or principled beings they believe themselves to be by making a variety of choices, for instance, about the situations in which they operate (see Chapter 4), the friends with whom they associate (see Chapter 5), the romantic partners with whom they are involved (see Chapter 6), the work they do (see Chapter 7), the places they live, and the organizations they join.

The Nature and Origins of Predictability   Choosing social situations may be implicated in domains other than self-monitoring. Choices of situations may constitute fundamental sources of congruence between properties of people (attitudes, dispositions, self-conceptions, values, motives, affects) and their behavior. By considering choices of situations, researchers may learn how attitudes come to be reflected in action, how conceptions of self guide social behavior, how personal dispositions organize behavior across situations and over time, and how affective states come to be expressed in behavior. (For reviews of the relevant empirical evidence, see Snyder and Ickes, 1985.)

How might choices of situations lead to behavioral consistencies? Much evidence indicates that people gravitate toward situations that encourage behavioral expressions of their characteristic dispositions.

Evidence may be found in domains as diverse as extraversion (e.g., Furnham, 1981), sensation-seeking (e.g., Zuckerman, 1974), authoritarianism (e.g., Stern, Stein, and Bloom, 1956), locus of control (e.g., Kahle, 1980), need for achievement (e.g., Atkinson, 1957), gender (e.g., Eddy and Sinnett, 1973), sex role orientation (e.g., Lippa and Beauvais, 1980), and repression-sensitization (e.g., Olson and Zanna, 1979). Moreover, actively choosing situations effectively enhances predictive relations between measured dispositions and actual behavior. That is, for people who have chosen their situations, the relations between dispositional predictors and behavioral criteria are substantially larger than for people who have had no opportunity to choose their situations (e.g., Monson, Hesley, and Chernick, 1982; Monson, McDaniel, Menteer, and Williams, 1983).

It is also possible to identify people who will behave in accord with relevant attitudes by identifying those with an extended history of seeking out situations that permit them to act upon their attitudes (e.g., DeBono and Snyder, 1984). Histories of seeking out situations may be particularly important in the context of temporal consistencies. Such consistencies (of the kind often revealed in longitudinal studies; e.g., Block, 1971, 1977) may be products of extended histories of choosing conducive situations (cf. Endler, 1981, 1982). Indeed, we already have seen (in Chapter 11) how choosing situations may play an influential role in divergent causality scenarios for the socialization of self-monitoring.

Over and above these revelations, the situational strategy has helped researchers understand the links among personality, motivation, and social behavior. In fact, from specific concerns with self-monitoring a general strategy for investigating the reciprocal influences and mutual interplay of people and situations has emerged. To that strategy, a strategy for understanding individuals and their social worlds, we now turn.

Understanding Individuals
and Their Social Worlds

■

WHAT ARE THE links among personality, motivation, and social behavior? How do these links provide the foundation for a general approach to understanding individuals and their social worlds? Some answers to these questions are provided by theory and research on self-monitoring. People's active structuring of their social circumstances reminds us that, at its core, there is a fundamentally *motivational* feature to self-monitoring. It is a motivational feature rooted in the interactions between people and social situations—in the strategic uses people make of situations to create opportunities to act out their conceptions of self.

To witness the motivational aspects of self-monitoring (or, for that matter, any evidence of social motivation) people must be considered in their social contexts. For it is these contexts that provide the reference groups, norms, standards and goals that are such potent sources of social motivation. But these same contexts are, to a great extent, chosen and structured by people themselves, who are motivated largely by their personal identities. Thus, the mutual interplay between people and their social contexts may be the key to understanding personality, motivation, and social behavior.

The Person and the Situation: Reciprocal Influences

Considering how actively people are involved in choosing their situations, it may not be sufficient, if we are to fully understand people, to restrict ourselves to examining the behaviors that occur in social situations. We should also find out how and why people find themselves in those situations in the first place. After all, people can hardly react to situations without first encountering them. If the situations people encounter are of their own choosing (Chapter 15), then an understanding of the reasons behind their choices is essential to understanding the events that subsequently transpire. If so, the familiar Lewinian (1936) proposition that behavior is determined by the person and the situation should be amended to propose that behavior is a function of the person, the situation, and why the person gets into the situation.

Theory and research on self-monitoring apply this amended proposition to derive and test hypotheses about the reciprocal influences of people and situations. Investigators could apply the logic of this approach to virtually any other psychological phenomenon concerned (as is self-monitoring) with relations between people and their social worlds. As examples of the logic of this approach, consider hypotheses about:

1. the role of choosing situations in *social perception and interpersonal relationships* (e.g., that what we see of other people and how they behave toward us may depend on the situations in which we choose to interact with them);
2. the role of choosing situations in *social communication and interpersonal influence* (e.g., that people who seek to influence attitudes and change behavior may find the means to these ends by selecting the situations in which to place the targets of their attempts to influence);
3. the role of choosing situations in *socialization and social development* (e.g., that the types of people we grow up to be may be channeled by the kinds of situations in which we are thrust by our own choices and by those of significant agents of our socialization); and
4. the role of choosing situations in *mood states and affective experiences* (e.g., that people who suffer from sadness and depression may prolong their suffering by remaining in situations that contain the causes of their troubles and may, by escaping these situations, leave their sorrows behind them).

The Person and the Situation: Paradigms for Research

How are hypotheses about people and their social worlds to be investigated? Research paradigms for studying the impact of person on situation must cast features of the *person* (e.g., self-conceptions, values, attitudes, traits, motives, dispositions) in the role of *independent* variables and features of the *situation* (e.g., choice of situations, influence on situations) in the role of *dependent* variables. Within such paradigms, it is possible to document the manner in which characteristics of people are reflected in their social worlds. As well, such paradigms provide a vehicle for understanding the complex involvement of personality in interpersonal relationships.

One example of such an approach is provided by research on the *interpersonal consequences of person perception*. Often, what people learn about others is a function of how they, by their own actions, structure the circumstances in which they learn about them. One person's preconceived notions about another can exert powerful channeling influences on his or her subsequent interactions with that person, to the extent that the other's behavior actually confirms these preconceptions. These processes of *behavioral confirmation,* by which people create their own reality through their beliefs about the social world, have been the subject of numerous experimental investigations (for reviews, see Snyder, 1981*a, b, c, d*, 1984).

One investigation of behavioral confirmation revealed the impact of stereotypes about physical attractiveness (i.e., "beautiful people are good people") on the dynamics of social relationships (Snyder, Tanke, and Berscheid, 1977). Previously unacquainted couples participated in a "getting acquainted" situation (a telephone conversation) designed to permit control over the information that one member of the couple (in this study, the man) received about the physical attractiveness of the other (the woman). In anticipation of their upcoming conversations, the men fashioned erroneous images of their partners, images that reflected stereotypes about physical attractiveness. Men who anticipated physically attractive partners expected comparatively sociable, poised, humorous, and socially adept women. By contrast, men faced with the prospect of getting acquainted with relatively unattractive partners fashioned images of rather unsociable, awkward, serious, and socially inept creatures. Moreover, the men had very different styles of interacting with the women they thought were physically attractive and with those they thought were physically unattractive. These differences in interaction style, in turn, elicited and nurtured behaviors in the women consistent with the men's preconceived expectations. Women perceived (unknown to them) to be physically attractive actually came to behave in a friendly, likable, and sociable manner. Not incidentally, when the roles are reversed, precisely the same behavioral confirmation effect occurs; that is, when it is the women who have preconceptions about their male partners' attractiveness, they too treat their partners in ways that turn beliefs into realities (Andersen and Bem, 1981).

Other important and widespread stereotypes can and do channel social interaction to create their own reality within the context of individual relationships. Researchers have documented behavioral confirmation of stereotypes associated with race (Word, Zanna, and Cooper, 1974) and gender (Skrypnek and Snyder, 1982; Zanna and Pack, 1975). Moreover, the very act of labeling a person may initiate a chain of events that induces that person to behave in accord with the label. Investigators have demonstrated the self-fulfilling effects of labeling other people, for example, hostile (Snyder and Swann, 1978a), intelligent (Rosenthal and Jacobson, 1968), or competent (King, 1971).

Even when people attempt to use social interaction to evaluate the accuracy of beliefs, their "reality-testing" procedures often channel events in ways that provide behavioral confirmation for the beliefs under scrutiny (e.g., Snyder, 1981d; Snyder and Swann, 1978b; Snyder, Campbell, and Preston, 1982). Moreover, when people choose situations in which to assess the accuracy of hypothetical beliefs about others, they often choose situations that may constrain targets to provide behavioral confirmation for the beliefs under scrutiny (e.g., Glick, 1982).

The consequences of behavioral confirmation in social interaction may be both profound and pervasive. People may turn their social relationships into ones that verify, maintain, and justify their pre-existing conceptions of other people, including many highly stereotyped assumptions about human nature. Accordingly, behavioral confirmation prompted by beliefs about other people may operate hand in hand with choices of situations guided by conceptions of self. In either case, people actively construct social worlds fashioned in their own images (for a related perspective, see Aronoff and Wilson, 1985; Battistich, Assor, Messé, and Aronoff, 1985).

The Marriage of Personality and Social Psychology

Together, the theoretical perspective and methodological orientation of my approach to understanding individuals and their social worlds constitute a "marriage" of personality and social psychology. In this union, personality has provided a concern with regularities and consistencies in social behavior as phenomena to be understood; social psychology has offered a focus on regularities and consistencies in social situations as a mechanism for explaining these phenomena. Together these elements of personality and social psychology reveal the two-way street that joins people and situations in a relationship of mutual and reciprocal influences.

As a hybrid of personality and social psychology, my approach owes debts to its intellectual ancestors. The classical pragmatist philosophers and self-theorists, most notably Mead, recognized early on the interplay of people and society. For example, Mead (1934) proposed that people play an active role in shaping their destinies. He also regarded people as both causes and consequences of society:

> As a man adjusts himself to a certain environment he becomes a different individual; but in becoming a different individual he has affected the community in which he lives....[I]nsofar as he has adjusted himself, the adjustments have changed the type of environment to which he can respond, and the world is accordingly a different world. There is always a mutual relationship of the individual and the community in which the individual lives (p. 215).

More contemporary statements in the sociology of identity echo Mead's message. Many have proposed (and some have offered confirming evidence) that people are sensitive to the identities acquired and maintained by choosing specific social situations and social roles (e.g., Alexander and Knight, 1971; Alexander and Lauderdale, 1977; Goffman, 1959; McCall and Simmons, 1978; Secord and Backman, 1965; Stryker, 1980; Turner, 1968, 1975; and Weinstein, 1966).

Furthermore, interpretations (my own not excluded) of people as active agents who both influence and are influenced by their circum-

stances owe much to Lewin's (1935, 1936, 1951) propositions about
the interplay of people, environments, and behaviors. In addition, they
owe much to Kantor's (1924, 1926) earlier assertions about the reciprocal influences of people and environments and to Murray's (1938,
1951) views on the reciprocity of "needs" (i.e., characteristics of
the person) and "press" (i.e., characteristics of the environment).
Similarly, any attempt to understand people in terms of their chosen
settings is more than faintly reminiscent of Sullivan's interpersonal
theory of psychiatry (e.g., 1953, 1964). He regarded personality as
"the relatively enduring pattern of recurrent interpersonal situations
which characterize a human life" (1953, p. 111).

My strategy for understanding people and their social worlds reflects not only its intellectual ancestors but also its present company.
Indeed, it draws much of its spirit from those contemporary theorists
in personality and social psychology who have offered propositions
about the interactions of people and situations: "Behavior partly creates the environment, and the environment influences behavior in a
reciprocal fashion"(Bandura, 1974, p. 866); "The person continuously
influences the 'situations' of his life as well as being affected by them
in a mutual, organic, two-way interaction" (Mischel, 1973, p. 278);
"The understanding of any one person's behavior in an interpersonal
situation solely in terms of the stimuli *presented* to him gives only a
partial and misleading picture. For to a very large extent, these stimuli
are *created* by him" (Wachtel, 1973, p. 330).

As a hybrid of personality and social psychology, my approach may
prove to be of considerable relevance to concerns traditionally associated with either discipline. It preserves the personality psychologist's
fundamental concern with studying people as individuals. Indeed, it
goes at least one step further to propose that with an understanding
of the person will come an understanding of his or her surroundings.
Moreover, it preserves the personality psychologist's special concern
with inner psychological structures such as traits and dispositions. In
fact, it ascribes major causal influences to these and other features of
personal identity in guiding and directing the mutual interplay of people and their social circumstances.

Moreover, the approach I am outlining speaks directly to the defining concern of the social psychologist—the impact of social situations
on people and their behavior. By virtue of their choices of situations,

people may allow and use these situations to influence their behavior. For example, those of us who have chosen to live our lives in the intellectual and academic settings provided by university communities, in effect, have allowed such settings to bring out the intellectual and the academic in us. Such situations may be able to elicit such behaviors precisely because, typically, only the intellectually and academically inclined choose to place themselves in such situations. More generally, I believe the fact that people choose their social situations constitutes a fundamental source of the "power" of situations to influence behavior. From my perspective, the "power" of situations may be a power *granted* them by the people who choose them.

Motivation in Personality and Social Psychology

This union of personality and social psychology ought to be particularly appealing to those readers who feel that personality and social psychology have strayed from their motivational "roots." The theories of Lewin (e.g., 1935, 1936, 1951), who was so influential that he is claimed as a founding father by both personality and social psychologists, are fundamentally motivational in nature. His theories feature the concept of "psychological tension" and ascribe powerful motivational forces to conflicting goal states within the life space. Moreover, in Lewin's theories, motivational forces not only have a driving impact on behavior but also exert a directive influence on cognitive and perceptual processes.

Somehow, along the way from Lewin's time to our own, events in the evolution of personality and social psychology seem to have relegated motivational constructs to the sidelines. To some extent, the reduced prominence of motivational perspectives may be traced to the shift away from the group as the unit of analysis, a shift in emphasis chronicled by Steiner (1974). When people are not studied in the context of groups (or, at least, dyadic relationships), it becomes all too easy to think of them as entities unto themselves, removed from the context of important motivating influences. Norms, expectations, incentives, sanctions, role models and the like are all motivating influences that operate in the context of relationships and groups. Furthermore, when theorists think about people in isolation from their social contexts, and when researchers study people as islands unto themselves, they may lose sight of the motivational impact of people's goals and plans—an impact that occurs, almost by definition, in relationships and in groups.

To a considerable extent, this sidelining of motivational perspectives has been exacerbated by the rising prominence of cognitive perspectives in personality and social psychology. For whatever reason, cognitive perspectives often seem to be at odds (although they need not be) with motivational perspectives. Witness, for example, all of the theoretical and empirical energy expended to determine whether such seemingly motivated phenomena as prejudicial stereotyping of outgroups and self-serving perceptions of ingroups can be accounted for by mundane, run-of-the-mill cognitive activities in the absence of any motivational processes at all (e.g., Miller and Ross, 1975; Weary-Bradley, 1978). Even when cognitive perspectives have not been cast in the role of adversaries to motivational ones, they have tended to focus on the machinery of information processing to the relative neglect of the motivational impact of social beliefs on subsequent thoughts, feelings, and actions (a neglect noted by, among others, Kelley, 1973).

Although a focus on the individual and a concern for cognition have tended to relegate motivational considerations to the sidelines, this unfortunate effect is not necessary. The approach I have described here is decidedly motivational. Yet, it focuses substantially on the activities of the person and it ascribes an important role to cognitive activities. And it does each of these things from a fundamentally motivational perspective. It focuses on the person as an active agent, involved in motivated activities designed to structure his or her social circumstances. It holds that people and their social worlds can best be understood in terms of features of personal identity and the processes by which people construct worlds conducive to their identities.

Challenges and Prospects

As appealing as this partnership of personality and social psychology may be, it still faces major theoretical and methodological challenges. At the theoretical level, it must (as must all dynamic theories; cf. Snyder and Ickes, 1985) articulate a more precise account of the interrelations among personality, motivation, behavior, and situations. These variables must be joined in bidirectional, dynamic causal linkages that permit each to function both as cause and effect. At an empirical level, it must avail itself of (or, if necessary, develop) methodological paradigms for investigating personality and motivation in ongoing social interaction (Ickes, 1982), experimental and statistical techniques for studying reciprocal influences of people and situations (e.g., Kenny and Nasby, 1980; Mendoza and Graziano, 1982; Thomas and Malone, 1979), and measuring devices for assessing not only people and behavior but also social situations (Snyder, 1981c, d).

Even though this union of personality and social psychology must still meet many theoretical and empirical challenges, I believe that its potential is considerable. Its contributions may include understanding the processes of personality, motivation, and social behavior as they typically operate. As well, it may provide insights into "disordered" versions of these processes and their role in personal problems and pathological conditions.

At the most basic level, the proposition that people allow and use situations to influence their behavior suggests that when we witness instances of situations influencing people, we ought to ask: "To what extent has the person chosen to be in the situation, to allow it to influence his or her behavior?" "What actions of the person may have created the situation that confronts him or her?" "How might the situation facilitate the expression of characteristics of the person?"

The answers to such questions may be particularly revealing in cases where people point to circumstances as justifications and excuses for their actions. The would-be dieter who claims never to cheat on her diet at home but who somehow manages to get invited out to dinner night after night, the problem drinker who claims not to be alcoholic because he never drinks alone but who always manages to be in the company of someone who is willing to pour a drink, and the sadistic person who takes a job as a prison guard because physical brutality may be part of the job of restraining dangerous prisoners are but three of the more blatant examples of people who engineer life situations that permit them to succumb to their temptations.

Less blatant perhaps, but no less psychologically intriguing, are the self-handicapping strategies by which people arrange circumstances to create "no lose" situations for themselves. Jones and Berglas (1978) have proposed that people strive to protect their self-competence images by actions that make it easy to explain away their failures and take credit for their successes. In an experiment, Berglas and Jones

(1978) observed that male college students who anticipated they would not perform well on a problem-solving task chose to take drugs that would interfere with their performance. Should they then perform poorly, they would have a readily available explanation (the drug) for their failure. Should they actually perform well, they would be able to credit themselves with being sufficiently competent to have overcome the handicap of the drug. For other demonstrations of self-handicapping, see Kolditz and Arkin (1982), Rhodewalt, Saltzman, and Wittmer (1984), Smith, Snyder, and Handelsman (1982), Smith, Snyder, and Perkins (1983), Snyder and Smith (1982), Snyder, Smith, Angelli, and Ingram (1985), and Tucker, Vuchinich, and Sobell (1981).

These cases—the would-be dieter, the problem drinker, the sadistic person, and the self-handicapper—all have something in common. By choosing to enter a "legitimizing" situation, they effectively transfer (in their own eyes, at least) the reasons for their behavior from personal properties to situational pressures. One of them claims to eat only when invited out to dinner, one claims to drink only because someone else offers drinks, one claims to beat and torture prisoners only because it's all in a day's work, and one claims to fail only because of a drug. But, as analyses of each of these cases readily reveal, what appears to be the influence of the situation on the person is in fact the influence of the person in creating the very situation that allows him or her to act on personal dispositions.

In fact, examples such as these point to the clinical and therapeutic utility of considering the influence of people on their situations. Carson (1969), for one, has written about the role of congruency-maintaining processes (of the type described by Secord and Backman, 1965) in creating psychopathological conceptions of self. In his analysis of "games people play," Berne (1964) has pointed to the ways that troubled people often evoke responses from others that feed their neurotic tendencies. Furthermore, in clinical and therapeutic contexts, considerable benefits may accrue from educating people about how their own actions generate the problematic situations that they feel are the sources of their troubles.

The following are examples of such therapeutic applications. Wachtel (1973) has described the case of "the man who complains about the problems in dealing with his wife's nagging but fails to understand how this situation, which presents itself to him, derives in turn from his own procrastinating, unresponsible behavior" (p. 330).

Similarly, some depressives who complain that they stay depressed because they keep hearing about the unhappy lives led by others may benefit from learning that, if only they were less quick to tell others about the sad events of their lives, other people would be less likely to reciprocate these revelations with disclosures of the unpleasant aspects of their own lives (Snyder and White, 1982). And, some of those people who bemoan the lack of friendliness, warmth, and kindliness in the world may profit from learning just how effectively a few sociable overtures on their part can bring out reciprocal expressions of the warmth, friendliness, and kindliness that they crave (Snyder, Tanke, and Berscheid, 1977).

Conclusion

This book, as I characterized it at the outset, is something of a chronicle of a journey. It is a journey that began with questions about the relations between public appearances and private realities, questions that spawned a program of inquiries into the nature of the self. Throughout this journey, the concept of self-monitoring has served as a vehicle for these inquiries. As the journey progressed, these ventures grew and evolved into analyses of the ties that bind personality and social behavior, analyses which in turn have generated the beginnings of a new approach to understanding the thematic unity of individuals and their social circumstances.

What then, to bring this journey to a close, are the prescriptions of my approach to understanding people and their social worlds? In a nutshell, and in the most general of terms, we, as students of human nature, must go beyond asking about behavior in social situations. We must also ask why people happen to be in particular situations in the first place and what they have done to produce their situations. Only then will we see which of the situations that seem to influence behavior are created by people themselves. Only then will the reciprocal interaction between people and situations be fully apparent. Only then will it be possible to construct a psychology that fully captures the mutual interplay of people and their social worlds—a true union of personality and social psychology.

References

Abelson, R. P. (1976). Script processing in attitude formation and decision making. In J. S. Carroll & J. W. Payne (Eds.), *Cognition and social behavior*. Hillsdale, N.J.: Erlbaum.

Abston, N. (1980). Clinical confidence and self-monitoring behavior. *Perceptual and Motor Skills,* 51: 1021–1022.

Adorno, T. W., Frenkel-Brunswik, E., Levinson, D. J., & Sanford, R. N. (1950). *The authoritarian personality.* New York: Harper & Row.

Ajzen, I., Timko, C., & White, J. B. (1982). Self-monitoring and the attitude-behavior relation. *Journal of Personality and Social Psychology,* 42:426–435.

Alexander, C. N., Jr., & Knight, G. W. (1971). Situated identities and social psychological experimentation. *Sociometry,* 34:65–82.

Alexander, C. N., Jr., & Lauderdale, P. (1977). Situated identities and social influence. *Sociometry,* 40: 225–233.

Alexander, C. N., Jr., & Sagatun, L. (1973). An attributional analysis of experimental norms. *Sociometry,* 36: 127–142.

Allport, G. W. (1937). *Personality: A psychological interpretation.* New York: Holt, Rinehart & Winston.

Allport, G. W. (1961). *Pattern and growth in personality.* New York: Holt, Rinehart & Winston.

Altman, I., & Taylor, D. A. (1973). *Social penetration: The development of interpersonal relationships.* New York: Holt, Rinehart & Winston.

Anastasi, A. (1968). *Psychological testing.* New York: Macmillan.

Andersen, S., & Bem, S. L. (1981). Sex typing and androgyny in dyadic interaction. *Journal of Personality and Social Psychology,* 41:74–86.

Anderson, L. R. (1981). *Self-monitoring and managerial effectiveness.* Unpublished manuscript, Wayne State University.

Aristotle. (1968). *The basic works of Aristotle.* R. McKeon (Ed.). New York: Random House.

Arkin, R. M., Gabrenya, W. K., Jr., Appelman, A., & Cochran, S. E. (1979). Self-presentation, self-monitoring, and the self-serving bias in causal attribution. *Personality and Social Psychology Bulletin,* 5:73–76.

Arnold, V. (1976). *Further explication of the self-monitoring construct: Its relationship to coping and vocational choice.* Unpublished doctoral dissertation, University of Minnesota.

Aronoff, J., & Wilson, J. P. (1985). *Personality in the social process.* Hillsdale, N.J.: Erlbaum.

Arvey, R. D. (1979). Unfair discrimination in the employment interview: Legal and psychological aspects. *Psychological Bulletin,* 86: 736–765.

Arvey, R. D., & Campion, J. E. (1982). The employment interview: A summary and review of recent research. *Personnel Psychology,* 35: 281–321.

Atkinson, J. W. (1957). Motivational determinants of risk-taking behavior. *Psychological Review,* 64: 359–372.

Bachman, J. G., & Johnston, L. D. (1979). The freshman, 1979. *Psychology Today,* 13:79–87.

Bandura, A. (1971). *Social learning theory.* Morristown, N.J.: General Learning Press.

Bandura, A. (1974). Behavior therapy and the models of man. *American Psychologist,* 29:859–869.

Barnes, R. D., & Ickes, W. (1979). *Styles of self-monitoring: Assimilative versus accommodative.* Unpublished manuscript, University of Wisconsin.

Barzini, L. G. (1967). *The Italians.* New York: Atheneum.

Battistich, V. A., & Aronoff, J. (1985). Perceiver, target, and situational influences on social cognition: An interactional analysis. *Journal of Personality and Social Psychology,* 49:788–798.

Battistich, V., Assor, A., Messe, L. A., & Aronoff, J. (1985). Personality and person perception. In P. Shaver (Ed.), *Review of personality and social psychology* (Vol. 6). Beverly Hills, Calif.: Sage.

Bearden, W. O., Teel, J. E., & Beno, C. (1982). *Self-monitoring as a moderator of consumer satisfaction and complaining behavior.* Unpublished manuscript, College of Business Administration, University of South Carolina.

Becherer, R. C., & Richard, L. M. (1978). Self-monitoring as a moderating variable in consumer behavior. *Journal of Consumer Research,* 5: 159–162.

Beck, A. T., Ward, C. H., Mendelson, M., Mock, J., & Erbaugh, J. (1961). An inventory for measuring depression. *Archives of General Psychiatry,* 4:561–571.

Becker, H. S. (1968). The self and adult socialization. In E. Norbeck, D. Price-Williams, & W. M. McCord (Eds.), *The study of personality: An interdisciplinary appraisal* (pp. 194–208). New York: Holt, Rinehart & Winston.

Becker, H. S. (1975). The self as a locus of linguistic causality. In D. Brissett & C. Edgley (Eds.), *Life as the-*

ater (pp. 58–67). Chicago: Aldine.

Beckwith, L. (1979). Prediction of emotional and social behavior. In J. Osofsky (Ed.), *Handbook of infant development*. New York: Wiley.

Beehr, T. A., & Gilmore, D. C. (1982). Applicant attractiveness as a perceived job-relevant variable in selection of management trainees. *Academy of Management Journal,* 25:607–617.

Bell, R. Q. (1968). A reinterpretation of the direction of effects in studies of socialization. *Psychological Review,* 75:81–95.

Bell, R. Q. (1971). Stimulus control of parent or caretaker behavior of offspring. *Developmental Psychology,* 4:63–72.

Bem, D. J. (1972). Self-perception theory. In L. Berkowitz (Ed.), *Advances in experimental social psychology* (Vol. 6). New York: Academic Press.

Bem, D. J., & Allen, A. (1974). On predicting some of the people some of the time: The search for cross-situational consistencies in behavior. *Psychological Review,* 81: 506–520.

Bem, D. J., & Funder, D. C. (1978). Predicting more of the people more of the time: Assessing the personality of situations. *Psychological Review,* 85:485–501.

Bem, S. L. (1974). The measurement of psychological androgyny. *Journal of Consulting and Clinical Psychology,* 42:155–162.

Bem, S. L. (1975). Sex role adaptability: One consequence of psychological androgyny. *Journal of Personality and Social Psychology,* 31: 634–643.

Benedict, R. (1967). *The chrysanthemum and the sword*. London: Routledge & Kegan Paul (1st ed., 1946).

Berger, C. R., & Douglas, W. (1981). Studies in interpersonal epistemology: III. Anticipated interaction, self-monitoring, and observational context selection. *Communication Monographs,* 48:183–196.

Berglas, S., & Jones, E. E. (1978). Drug choice as an externalization strategy in response to noncontingent success. *Journal of Personality and Social Psychology,* 36:405–417.

Berne, E. (1964). *Games people play*. New York: Grove Press.

Berscheid, E. (1983). Emotion. In *Close relationships*. New York: W. H. Freeman and Company.

Berscheid, E. (1985). Interpersonal attraction. In G. Lindzey & E. Aronson (Eds.), *Handbook of social psychology* (3rd ed.). New York: Random House.

Berscheid, E., Graziano, W. G., Monson, T., & Dermer, M. (1976). Outcome dependency: Attention, attribution and attraction. *Journal of Personality and Social Psychology,* 34: 978–989.

Biddle, B. J., & Thomas, E. J. (Eds.). (1966). *Role theory: Concepts and research*. New York: Wiley.

Block, J. (1961). Ego identity, role variability, and adjustment. *Journal of Consulting Psychology*, 25: 392–397.

Block, J. (1971). *Lives through time.* Berkeley, Calif.: Bancroft.

Block, J. (1977). Advancing the psychology of personality: Paradigmatic shift or improving the quality of research. In D. Magnusson & N. S. Endler (Eds.), *Personality at the crossroads: Current issues in interactional psychology.* Hillsdale, N.J.: Erlbaum.

Block, S. (1983). *Advertising for love: How to play the personals.* West Caldwell, N.J.: Morrow.

Bosse, J. J., Croghan, L. M., Greenstein, M. B., Katz, N. W., Oliver, J. M., Powell, D. A., & Smith, W. R. (1975). Frequency of depression in the freshman year as measured in a random sample by a retrospective version of the Beck Depression Inventory. *Journal of Consulting and Clinical Psychology*, 43:746–747.

Braginsky, B. M., Braginsky, D. D., & Ring, K. (1969). *Methods of madness: The mental hospital as a last resort.* New York: Holt, Rinehart & Winston.

Braginsky, D. D., & Braginsky, B. M. (1971). *Hansels and Gretels: Studies of children in institutions for the mentally retarded.* New York: Holt, Rinehart & Winston.

Brandt, D. R., Miller, G. R., & Hocking, J. E. (1980a). Effects of self-monitoring and familiarity on deception detection. *Communication Quarterly*, 28:3–10.

Brandt, D. R., Miller, G. R., & Hocking, J. E. (1980b). The truth-deception attribution: Effects of familiarity on deception detection. *Human Communication Research*, 6:99–110.

Briggs, S. R., Cheek, J. M., & Buss, A. H. (1980). An analysis of the Self-Monitoring Scale. *Journal of Personality and Social Psychology*, 38:679–686.

Brissett, D., & Edgley, C. (1975). *Life as theater: A dramaturgical sourcebook.* Chicago: Aldine.

Brockner, J., & Eckenrode, J. (1978). Self-monitoring and the actor-observer bias. *Representative Research in Social Psychology*, 9:81–88.

Brunswik, E. (1956). *Perception and the representative design of experiments.* Berkeley: University of California Press.

Buss, A. H. (1980). *Self-consciousness and social anxiety.* New York: W. H. Freeman and Company.

Buss, A. H., & Briggs, S. R. (1984). Drama and the self in social interaction. *Journal of Personality and Social Psychology*, 47:1310–1324.

Buss, A. H., & Plomin, R. (1984). *Temperament: Early developing personality traits.* Hillsdale, N.J.: Erlbaum.

Buss, D. M., & Craik, K. H. (1983a). The act frequency approach to personality. *Psychological Review*, 90: 105–126.

Buss, D. M., & Craik, K. H. (1983*b*). The dispositional analysis of everyday conduct. *Journal of Personality,* 51:393–412.

Byrne, D. (1964). Repression-sensitization as a dimension of personality. In B. A. Maher (Ed.), *Progress in experimental personality research* (Vol. 1). New York: Academic Press.

Cairns, R. B. (1966). Attachment behavior of mammals. *Psychological Review,* 73:409–426.

Caldwell, D. F., & O'Reilly, C. A. (1982). Boundary spanning and individual performance: The impact of self-monitoring. *Journal of Applied Psychology,* 67:124–127.

Campbell, D. T. (1960). Recommendations for APA test standards regarding construct, trait, and discriminant validity. *American Psychologist,* 15:546–553.

Campbell, D. T., & Fiske, D. W. (1959). Convergent and discriminant validation by the multitrait-multimethod matrix. *Psychological Bulletin,* 56:81–105.

Cann, A., Siegfried, W. D., & Pearce, L. (1981). Forced attention to specific applicant qualifications: Impact of physical attractiveness and sex of applicant biases. *Personnel Psychology,* 34:65–75.

Cantor, N., & Mischel, W. (1979). Prototypes in person perception. In L. Berkowitz (Ed.), *Advances in experimental social psychology* (Vol. 12). New York: Academic Press.

Cappella, J. N. (1985). *Reciprocal and compensatory reactions to violations of distance norms for high and low self-monitors.* Paper presented at the International Communication Association Conference, Honolulu.

Carnegie, D. (1936). *How to win friends and influence people.* New York: Simon & Schuster.

Carson, R. C. (1969). *Interaction concepts of personality.* Chicago: Aldine.

Carver, C. S., & Scheier, M. F. (1981). *Attention and self-regulation: A control theory approach to human behavior.* New York: Springer-Verlag.

Cash, T. P., Gillen, B., & Burns, D. S. (1977). Sexism and "beautyism" in personnel consultant decision making. *Journal of Applied Psychology,* 62:301–310.

Chaiken, S. (1980). Heuristic versus systematic information processing and the use of source versus message cues in persuasion. *Journal of Personality and Social Psychology,* 39:752–766.

Charlesworth, R., & Hartup, W. W. (1967). Positive social reinforcement in the nursery school peer group. *Child Development,* 38: 993–1002.

Cheek, J. M. (1982). Aggregation, moderator variables, and the validity of personality tests: A peer-rating study. *Journal of Personality and*

Social Psychology, 43:1254–1269.

Cheek, J. M., & Briggs, S. R. (1981). *Self-consciousness, self-monitoring, and aspects of identity.* Paper presented at the meetings of the American Psychological Association, Los Angeles.

Cheek, J. M., & Busch, M. (1982). *Self-monitoring and the inner-outer metaphor: Principled versus pragmatic self?* Paper presented at the annual meeting of the American Psychological Association, Washington, D.C.

Chemers, M., & Ayman, R. (1985). Unpublished research, University of Utah.

Christie, R., & Geis, F. L. (1970). *Studies in Machiavellianism.* New York: Academic Press.

Clark, L., & Lippa, R. (1980). *Self-monitoring and self-disclosure.* Paper presented at the annual meetings of the American Psychological Association, Montreal.

Cooley, C. H. (1902). *Human nature and the social order.* New York: Scribner.

Corsini, R. J. (Ed.). (1979). *Current psychotherapies.* Itasca, Ill.: Peacock.

Craighead, W. E. (1981). Issues resulting from treatment studies. In L. P. Rehm (Ed.), *Behavior therapy for depression: Present status and future directions.* New York: Academic Press.

Cronbach, L. J. (1955). Processes affecting scores on "understanding of others" and "assumed similarity." *Psychological Bulletin,* 52:177–193.

Cronbach, L. J., & Meehl, P. E. (1955). Construct validity in psychological tests. *Psychological Bulletin,* 52:281–302.

Crowne, D. P., & Marlowe, D. (1964). *The Approval Motive.* New York: Wiley.

Culbertson, F. M. (1957). Modification of an emotionally-held attitude through role playing. *Journal of Abnormal and Social Psychology,* 54:230–233.

Dabbs, J. M., Evans, M. S., Hopper, C. H., & Purvis, J. A. (1980). Self-monitors in conversation: What do they monitor? *Journal of Personality and Social Psychology,* 39:278–284.

Danheiser, P. R., & Graziano, W. G. (1982). Self-monitoring and cooperation as a self-presentational strategy. *Journal of Personality and Social Psychology,* 42:497–505.

Davis, J. D. (1978). When boy meets girl: Sex roles and the negotiation of intimacy in an acquaintance exercise. *Journal of Personality and Social Psychology,* 36:684–692.

Davis, L. D., & Lennon, S. J. (1985). Self-monitoring, fashion opinion leadership, and attitudes toward clothing. In M. Solomon (Ed.), *Psychology of Fashion.* Lexington, Mass.: Heath.

Dawis, R. V., & Lofquist, L. H. (1984). *A psychological theory of work adjustment: An individual-differences model and its applications.* Minneapolis: University of Minnesota Press.

DeBono, K. G. (1985). *Attitudes and persuasion: Functional theories revisited.* Doctoral dissertation, University of Minnesota.

DeBono, K. G., & Omoto, A. M. (1984). Unpublished research, University of Minnesota.

DeBono, K. G., & Snyder, M. (1984). *Acting on one's attitudes: The role of a history of choosing situations.* Unpublished manuscript, University of Minnesota.

Deutsch, H. (1965). *Neuroses and character types.* New York: International Universities Press.

Dipboye, R. L. (1982). Self-fulfilling prophecies in the selection-recruitment interview. *Academy of Management Review,* 7:579–586.

Dipboye, R. L., Arvey, R. D., & Terpstra, D. E. (1977). Sex and physical attractiveness of raters and applicants as determinants of resumé evaluations. *Journal of Applied Psychology,* 62:288–294.

Dipboye, R. L., Fromkin, H. L., & Wiback, K. (1975). Relative importance of applicant sex, attractiveness, and scholastic standing in evaluation of job applicant resumés. *Journal of Applied Psychology,* 60:39–43.

Duck, S. (1983). *Friends for life.* New York: St. Martin's Press.

Dunn, J. F. (1980). Individual differences in temperament. In M. Rutter (Ed.), *The scientific foundations of developmental psychiatry.* London: Heinemann.

Dunnette, M. D., & Borman, W. C. (1979). Personnel selection and classification systems. *Annual Review of Psychology,* 30:477–525.

Duval, S., & Wicklund, R. A. (1972). *A theory of objective self-awareness.* New York: Academic Press.

Dworkin, R. H. (1977). *Genetic influences on cross-situational consistency.* Paper presented at the Second International Congress on Twin Studies, Washington, D.C.

Dworkin, R. H. (in press). Genetic influences on cross-situational consistency. In W. E. Nance, G. Allen, & P. Parisi (Eds.), *Twin studies.* New York: Alan R. Liss.

Eddy, G. L., & Sinnett, R. E. (1973). Behavior settings utilization by emotionally disturbed college students. *Journal of Consulting and Clinical Psychology,* 40:210–216.

Eder, R. (1984). Unpublished research, University of Minnesota and Southern Methodist University.

Edwards, A. L. (1966). Relationship between probability of endorsement and social desirability scale value for a set of 2824 personality statements. *Journal of Applied Psychology,* 54:238–239.

Ekman, P., & Friesen, W. V. (1969). Nonverbal leakage and clues to deception. *Psychiatry,* 32:88–106.

Ekman, P., & Friesen, W. V. (1974). Detecting deception from the body or face. *Journal of Personality and Social Psychology,* 29:288–298.

Elliott, G. C. (1977). *A cognitive theory of impression management: Some experimental evidence.* Unpublished doctoral dissertation, University of Wisconsin.

Elliott, G. C. (1979). Some effects of deception and level of self-monitoring on planning and reacting to a self-presentation. *Journal of Personality and Social Psychology,* 37: 1282–1292.

Ellis, A. (1970). *Reason and emotion in psychotherapy.* New York: Lyle Stuart.

Elms, A. C. (1976). *Personality and politics.* New York: Harcourt Brace Jovanovich.

Endler, N. S. (1973). The person versus the situation—a pseudo issue? A response to Alker. *Journal of Personality,* 41:287–303.

Endler, N. S. (1981). Situational aspects of interactional psychology. In D. Magnusson (Ed.), *Toward a psychology of situation: An interactional perspective.* Hillsdale, N.J.: Erlbaum.

Endler, N. S. (1982). Interactionism comes of age. In M. P. Zanna, E. T. Higgins, & C. P. Herman (Eds.), *Consistency in social behavior: The Ontario symposium* (Vol. 2). Hillsale, N.J.: Erlbaum.

Engle, J. F., Wales, H. G., & Warshaw, M. R. (1975). *Promotional strategy* (3rd ed.). Homewood, Ill.: Irwin.

Epstein, S. (1973). The self-concept revisited: Or a theory of a theory. *American Psychologist,* 28:404–416.

Everitt, B. S. (1974). *Cluster analysis.* London: Heinemann.

Eysenck, H. J. (1950). Criterion analysis—an application of the hypothetico-deductive method of factor analysis. *Psychological Review,* 57: 38–53.

Eysenck, H. J., & Eysenck, S. B. G. (1968). *Manual for the Eysenck Personality Inventory.* San Diego: Educational and Industrial Testing Service.

Farber, S. L. (1981). *Identical twins reared apart: A reanalysis.* New York: Basic Books.

Farris, J. S. (1979). On the naturalness of phylogenetic classification. *Systematic Zoology,* 28:200–214.

Fenigstein, A., Scheier, M. F., & Buss, A. H. (1975). Public and private self-consciousness: Assessment and theory. *Journal of Consulting and Clinical Psychology,* 43:522–527.

Ferguson, P. N. (1984). *Self-monitoring, openness, and social world composition: A study of gay men and lesbians.* Unpublished manuscript, Carleton College.

Festinger, L. (1964). Behavioral support for opinion change. *Public Opinion Quarterly,* 28:404–417.

Ford, M. E. (1979). The construct validity of egocentrism. *Psychological Bulletin,* 86:1169–1188.

Fox, S. (1984). *The Mirror Makers.* New York: Morrow.

Frazier, R. B., & Fatis, M. (1980). Sex differences in self-monitoring. *Psychological Reports,* 47:597–598.

Freud, S. (1914). *The history of the psychoanalytic movement.* (Standard Edition, Vol. 14, pp. 7–66.)

Freud, S. (1959). Fragment of an analysis of a case of hysteria (1905). In *Collected papers* (Vol. 3). New York: Basic Books.

Furnham, A. (1981). Personality and activity preference. *British Journal of Social and Clinical Psychology,* 20:57–68.

Furnham, A., & Capon, M. (1983). Social skills and self-monitoring processes. *Personality and Individual Differences,* 4:171–178.

Furnham, A., & Henderson, M. (1982). The good, the bad, and the mad: Response bias in self-report measures. *Personality and Individual Differences,* 3:311–320.

Gabrenya, W. K., Jr., & Arkin, R. M. (1980). Factor structure and factor correlates of the Self-Monitoring Scale. *Personality and Social Psychology Bulletin,* 6:13–22.

Gangestad, S. (1984). *On the etiology of individual differences in self-monitoring and expressive self-control: Testing the case of strong genetic influence.* Doctoral dissertation, University of Minnesota.

Gangestad, S., & Snyder, M. (1985). "To carve nature at its joints": On the existence of discrete classes in personality. *Psychological Review,* 92:317–349.

Garfield, S. L. (1978). Research on client variables in psychotherapy. In S. L. Garfield & A. E. Bergin (Eds.), *Handbook of psychotherapy and behavior change: An empirical analysis* (2nd ed.). New York: Wiley.

Garland, J., & Beard, J. F. (1979). Relationship between self-monitoring and leader emergence across two task situations. *Journal of Applied Psychology,* 64:72–76.

Geizer, R. S., Rarick, D. L., & Soldow, G. F. (1977). Deception and judgment accuracy: A study in person perception. *Personality and Social Psychology Bulletin,* 3:446–449.

Gergen, K. J. (1971). *The concept of self.* New York: Holt, Rinehart & Winston.

Gergen, K. J. (1977). The social construction of self-knowledge. In T. Mischel (Ed.), *The self: Psychological and philosophical issues.* Totowa, N.J.: Rowman & Littlefield.

Gerstein, L. H., Ginter, E. J., & Graziano, W. G. (1985). Self-monitoring, impression management, and interpersonal evaluations. *Journal of Social Psychology,* 125:379–389.

Giacalone, R. A., & Falvo, R. (1985). Self-presentation, self-monitoring, and organizational commitment. Paper presented at the annual meetings of the American Psychological Association, Los Angeles.

Gladstein, G. A. (1983). Understanding empathy: Integrating counseling, developmental, and social psychology perspectives. *Journal of Counseling Psychology,* 30:467–482.

Glick, P. S. (1982). Unpublished research, University of Minnesota.

Glick, P. S. (1983). Unpublished research, University of Minnesota.

Glick, P. S. (1984). *Orientations toward relationships: Choosing a situation in which to begin a relationship.* Unpublished manuscript, University of Minnesota.

Goffman, E. (1955). On face-work: An analysis of ritual elements in social interaction. *Psychiatry,* 18: 213–221.

Goffman, E. (1959). *The presentation of self in everyday life.* Garden City, N.Y.: Doubleday (Anchor Books).

Goffman, E. (1963). *Stigma: Notes on the management of spoiled identity.* Englewood Cliffs, N.J.: Prentice Hall.

Goffman, E. (1967). *Interaction ritual: Essays on face-to-face behavior.* Garden City, N.Y.: Doubleday (Anchor Books).

Goldberg, L. R. (1972). Man *vs.* mean: The exploitation of group profiles for the construction of diagnostic classification systems. *Journal of Abnormal Psychology,* 79:121–131.

Goldsmith, H. H., & Campos, J. J. (1982). Toward a theory of infant temperament. In R. N. Emde & R. J. Harmon (Eds.), *The development of attachment and affiliative systems: Psychobiological aspects.* New York: Plenum.

Goldsmith, H. H., & Gottesman, I. I. (1981). Origins of variation in behavioral style: A longitudinal study of temperament in young twins. *Child Development,* 52:91–103.

Gordon, C., & Gergen, K. J. (1968). *The self in social interaction.* New York: Wiley.

Gottman, J. M., & McFall, R. M. (1972). Self-monitoring effects in a program for potential high school dropouts: A time-series analysis. *Journal of Consulting and Clinical Psychology,* 39:273–281.

Graziano, W. G., Leone, C., Musser, L. M., & Lautenschlager, G. J. (1985). Self-monitoring in children: A differential approach to development. Unpublished manuscript, University of Georgia.

Greaner, J. L., & Penner, L. A. (1982). The reliability and validity of Bem and Allen's measure of cross-situational consistency. *Social Behavior and Personality,* 10: 241–244.

Greenwald, A. G. (1980). The totalitarian ego: Fabrication and revision of personal history. *American Psychologist,* 35:603–618.

Greenwald, A. G. (1981). Self and memory. In G. H. Bower (Ed.), *The psychology of learning and motivation* (Vol. 15). New York: Academic Press.

Greenwald, A. G. (1982). Ego task analysis: An integration of research on ego-involvement and self-awareness. In A. Hastorf & A. M. Isen (Eds.), *Cognitive social psychology.* New York: Elsevier.

Greenwald, A. G., & Breckler, S. J. (1985). To whom is the self presented? In B. R. Schlenker (Ed.), *The self in social life.* New York: McGraw-Hill.

Greenwald, A. G., & Pratkanis, A. R. (1984). The self. In R. S. Wyer & T. K. Srull (Eds.), *Handbook of social cognition* (Vol. 3). Hillsdale, N.J.: Erlbaum.

Grooms, R. R., & Endler, N. S. (1960). The effect of anxiety on academic achievement. *Journal of Educational Psychology,* 51:299–309.

Guilford, J. P., & Zimmerman, W. S. (1963). Some variable-sampling problems in the rotation of axes in factor analysis. *Psychological Bulletin,* 60:289–301.

Guthrie, T. (1971). *Tyrone Guthrie on acting.* London: Studio Vista.

Gutkin, D. C., & Suls, J. (1979). The relation between the ethics of personal conscience: Social responsibility and principled moral reasoning. *Journal of Youth and Adolescence,* 8:433–441.

Hacker, A. (1984). Poets of packaging, sculptors of desire. *New York Times Book Review,* June 24, p. 1.

Hamilton, J. C., & Baumeister, R. F. (1984). Biasing evaluations to appear unbiased: A self-presentational paradox. *Journal of Experimental Social Psychology,* 20:552–566.

Harris, E. L., & Rose, R. J. (1977). *Personality resemblance in twin children: Comparison of self-descriptions with mothers' ratings.* Paper presented at the meeting of the 2nd International Congress on Twin Studies, Washington, D.C.

Harter, S. (1983). Developmental perspectives on the self-system. In P. H. Mussen (Ed.), E. M. Hetherington (Vol. Ed.), *Carmichael's manual of child psychology: Socialization, personality, and social development* (4th ed., Vol. 4). New York: Wiley.

Heider, F. (1958). *The psychology of interpersonal relations.* New York: Wiley.

Heilman, M. E., & Saruwatari, L. R. (1979). When beauty is beastly: The effects of appearance and sex on evaluations of job applicants for managerial and nonmanagerial jobs. *Organizational Behavior and Human Performance,* 23:360–372.

Henderson, N. D. (1982). Human behavior genetics. *Annual Review of Psychology,* 33:403–440.

Herek, G. M. (1984). *The functions of attitudes: A new approach to an old perspective.* Unpublished manuscript, Yale University.

Higgins, E. T., Feldman, N. S., & Ruble, D. N. (1980). Accuracy and differentiation in social prediction: A developmental study. *Journal of Personality,* 48:520–540.

Hogan, R. (1969). Development of

an empathy scale. *Journal of Consulting and Clinical Psychology*, 33:307–316.

Hogan, R. (1976). *Personality theory.* Englewood Cliffs, N.J.: Prentice-Hall.

Hogan, R., & Cheek, J. M. (1983). Identity, authenticity, and maturity. In T. R. Sarbin & K. E. Scheibe (Eds.), *Studies in social identity.* New York: Praeger.

Hogan, R., DeSoto, C. B., & Solano, C. (1977). Traits, tests, and personality research. *American Psychologist,* 32:255–264.

Holland, J. L. (1966). *The psychology of vocational choice.* Waltham, Mass.: Blaisdell.

Holland, J. L. (1973). *Making vocational choices: A theory of careers.* Englewood Cliffs, N.J.: Prentice-Hall.

Holland, J. L. (1976). Vocational preferences. In M. D. Dunnette (Ed.), *Handbook of industrial and organizational psychology.* Chicago, Ill.: Rand McNally.

Hollon, S. D., & Beck, A. T. (1978). Psychotherapy and drug therapy: Comparison and combinations. In S. L. Garfield & A. E. Bergin (Eds.), *The handbook of psychotherapy and behavior change: An empirical analysis* (2nd ed.). New York: Wiley.

Hollon, S. D., & Beck, A. T. (1979). Cognitive therapy for depression. In P. C. Kendall & S. D. Hollon (Eds.), *Cognitive-behavioral interventions: Theory, research, and procedures.* New York: Academic Press.

Hormuth, S. E. (1984a). *An ecological approach to self-concept change.* Paper presented at the 23rd International Congress of Psychology, Acapulco.

Hormuth, S. E. (1984b). *Restructuring the ecology of the self: A model for self-concept change.* Paper presented at the International Conference on Self and Identity, University College, Cardiff, Wales.

Hormuth, S. E. (1984c). Transitions in commitments to roles and self-concept change: Relocation as a paradigm. In V. L. Allen & E. van de Vliert (Eds.), *Role transitions: Explorations and explanations.* New York: Plenum.

Hormuth, S. E., & Lalli, M. (1984). *The role of urban environments for the self-concept: A research example using an autophotographical approach.* Paper presented at the 8th International Conference on "Environment and Human Action" of the International Association for the Study of People and their Physical Surroundings, Berlin, West Germany.

Hosch, H. M., & Cooper, D. S. (1981). *Victimization and self-monitoring as determinants of eyewitness accuracy.* Unpublished manuscript, University of Texas at El Paso.

Hosch, H. M., Leippe, M. R., Marchioni, P. M., & Cooper, D. S. (1984). Victimization, self-monitoring, and eyewitness identification. *Journal of Applied Psychology,* 69: 280–288.

Hosch, H. M., & Platz, S. J. (1984). Self-monitoring and eyewitness accuracy. *Personality and Social Psychology Bulletin,* 10:289–292.

Hubert, N., Wachs, T. D., Peters-Martin, P., & Gandour, M. (1982). The study of early temperament: Measurement and conceptual issues. *Child Development,* 53:571–600.

Ickes, W. (1982). A basic paradigm for the study of personality, roles, and social behavior. In W. Ickes & E. S. Knowles (Eds.), *Personality, roles, and social behavior.* New York: Springer-Verlag.

Ickes, W. J., & Barnes, R. D. (1977). The role of sex and self-monitoring in unstructured dyadic interactions. *Journal of Personality and Social Psychology,* 35:315–330.

Ickes, W., & Barnes, R. D. (1978). Boys and girls together—and alienated: On enacting stereotyped sex roles in mixed-sex dyads. *Journal of Personality and Social Psychology,* 36:669–683.

Ickes, W. J., Layden, M. A., & Barnes, R. D. (1978). Objective self-awareness and individuation: An empirical link. *Journal of Personality,* 46: 146–161.

Ickes, W., Reidhead, S., & Patterson, M. (1985). *Machiavellianism and self-monitoring: As different as "me"*

and "you." Unpublished manuscript, University of Texas at Arlington and University of Missouri—St. Louis.

Insko, C. A. (1967). *Theories of attitude change.* New York: Appleton-Century-Crofts.

Iwabuchi, C., Tanada, K., & Nakazato, K. (1982). A study of the Self-Monitoring Scale. *The Japanese Journal of Psychology,* 53:54–57.

Jackson, D. N. (1971). Structured personality tests: 1971. *Psychological Review,* 78:229–248.

Jackson, D. N. (1974). *Personality Research Form manual.* New York: Research Psychologists Press.

James, W. (1890). *The principles of psychology* (Vols. 1 and 2). New York: Henry Holt and Co.

Jamieson, D. W., Lydon, J., & Zanna, M. P. (1984). *Similarity of attitudes versus activity preferences: A differential basis of interpersonal attraction for low and high self-monitors?* Paper presented at the annual meetings of the Canadian Psychological Association, Ottawa.

Jones, E. E. (1964). *Ingratiation.* New York: Appleton-Century-Crofts.

Jones, E. E., & Baumeister, R. (1976). The self-monitor looks at the ingratiator. *Journal of Personality,* 44: 654–674.

Jones, E. E., & Berglas, S. (1978). Control of attributions about the self through self-handicapping strategies: The appeal of alcohol and the role of underachievement. *Personality and Social Psychology Bulletin,* 4:200–206.

Judd, C. M., & Kulik, J. A. (1980). Schematic effects of social attitudes on information processing and recall. *Journal of Personality and Social Psychology,* 38:569–578.

Jung, C. (1909). *The psychology of dementia praecox.* New York: Nervous and Mental Disease Publishing Co.

Kahle, L. R. (1980). Stimulus condition self-selection by males in the interaction of locus of control and skill-chance situations. *Journal of Personality and Social Psychology,* 38:50–56.

Kantor, J. R. (1924). *Principles of psychology* (Vol. 1). Bloomington: Principia Press.

Kantor, J. R. (1926). *Principles of psychology* (Vol. 2). Bloomington: Principia Press.

Kassarjian, W. M. (1962). A study of Riesman's theory of social character. *Sociometry,* 25:213–230.

Katz, D. (1960). The functional approach to the study of attitudes. *Public Opinion Quarterly,* 24:163–204.

Katz, D., McClintock, C., & Sarnoff, I. (1957). The measurement of ego-defense as related to attitude change. *Journal of Personality,* 25: 465–474.

Katz, D., Sarnoff, I., & McClintock, C. (1956). Ego-defense and attitude change. *Human Relations,* 9:27–46.

Kazdin, A. E. (1974). Self-monitoring and behavior change. In M. J. Mahoney & C. E. Thoresen (Eds.), *Self-control: Power to the person,* (pp. 218–246). Monterey, Calif.: Brooks/Cole.

Keating, D. (1980). Thinking processes in adolescence. In J. Adelson (Ed.), *Handbook of adolescent psychology.* New York: Wiley.

Kelley, H. H. (1972). Attribution in social interaction. In E. E. Jones, D. Kanouse, H. H. Kelley, R. E. Nisbett, S. Valins, & B. Weiner (Eds.), *Attribution: Perceiving the causes of behavior.* New York: General Learning Press.

Kelley, H. H. (1973). The process of causal attribution. *American Psychologist,* 28:107–128.

Kelley, H. H. (1980). The causes of behavior: Their perception and regulation. In L. Festinger (Ed.), *Retrospections on social psychology.* New York: Oxford University Press.

Kelley, H. H. (1983). Love and commitment. In *Close relationships.* New York: W. H. Freeman and Company.

Kelley, H. H., Berscheid, E., Christensen, A., Harvey, J., Huston, T. L., Levinger, G., McClintock, E., Peplau, L. A., & Peterson, D. R. (1983). *Close relationships.* New York: W. H. Freeman and Company.

Kelly, G. A. (1955). *The psychology of personal constructs.* New York: Norton.

Kelman, H. C. (1961). Processes of opinion change. *Public Opinion Quarterly,* 25:57–78.

Kendler, K. S. (1983). Overview: A current perspective on twin studies of schizophrenia. *American Journal of Psychiatry,* 140:1413–1425.

Kendzierski, D. (1982a). *Acting on attitudes: The effects of feedback about past behavior.* Doctoral dissertation, University of Minnesota.

Kendzierski, D. (1982b). Unpublished research, Northwestern University.

Kenny, D. A., & Nasby, W. (1980). Splitting the reciprocity correlation. *Journal of Personality and Social Psychology,* 38:249–256.

Kenrick, D. T., & Stringfield, D. O. (1980). Personality traits and the eye of the beholder: Crossing some traditional philosophical boundaries in the search for consistency in all of the people. *Psychological Review,* 87:88–104.

Kiesler, C. A., Collins, B. E., & Miller, N. (1969). *Attitude change: A critical analysis of theoretical approaches.* New York: Wiley.

King, A. S. (1971). Self-fulfilling prophecies in training the hard-core: Supervisors' expectations and the underprivileged workers' performance. *Social Science Quarterly,* 52: 369–378.

Klinger, E. (1977). *Meaning and void: Inner experience and the incentives in people's lives.* Minneapolis: University of Minnesota Press.

Kogan, N., & Wallach, M. A. (1964). *Risk taking: A study in cognition and personality.* New York: Holt, Rinehart & Winston.

Kolditz, T. A., & Arkin, R. M. (1982). An impression management interpretation of the self-handicapping strategy. *Journal of Personality and Social Psychology,* 43:492–502.

Krantz, D. S. (1978). The social context of obesity research: Another perspective on its place in the field of social psychology. *Personality and Social Psychology Bulletin,* 4: 177–184.

Krauss, R. M., Geller, V., & Olson, C. (1976). *Modalities and cues in perceiving deception.* Paper presented at the annual meetings of the American Psychological Association, Washington, D.C.

Kuhl, J. (1981). Action- *vs.* state-orientation as a mediator between motivation and action. In W. Hacker, W. Volpert, & M. von Cranach (Eds.), *Cognitive and motivational aspects of action.* Amsterdam: North Holland.

Kulik, J. A., & Taylor, S. E. (1981). Self-monitoring and the use of consensus information. *Journal of Personality,* 49:75–84.

Langmuir, I. (1943). Science, common sense, and decency. *Science,* 97:1–7.

Latham, V. M. (1985). *The role of personality in the job search process.* Paper presented at the annual meetings of the Midwestern Psychological Association, Chicago.

Lecky, P. (1969). *Self-consistency: A*

theory of personality. Garden City, N.Y.: Doubleday (Anchor Books). (Originally published, 1945.)

Lee, A. G., & Scheurer, V. L. (1983). Psychological androgyny and aspects of self-image in women and men. *Sex Roles,* 9:289–306.

Lehrman, D. S. (1970). Semantic and conceptual issues in the nature-nurture problem. In L. R. Aronson, N. Tobach, & E. Shaw (Eds.), *Developmental evolution of behavior.* New York: W. H. Freeman and Company.

Lennox, R., & Wolfe, R. (1984). Revision of the Self-Monitoring Scale. *Journal of Personality and Social Psychology,* 46:1349–1364.

Leone, C. (1979). *Recall and attributions in dating situations: An outcome dependency, prospect of future interaction, situational structure, by locus of control analysis.* Doctoral dissertation, University of Georgia.

Leone, C., Musser, L. M., Graziano, W. G., & Lautenschlager, G. (1984). *Individual differences in attention to social comparison information: Self-monitoring in children.* Paper presented at the annual meetings of the Society for Research in Child Development, Toronto.

Levinger, G. (1974). A three-level view of attraction: Toward an understanding of pair relatedness. In T. L. Huston (Ed.), *Foundations of interpersonal attraction.* New York: Academic Press.

Lewin, K. (1935). *A dynamic theory of personality.* New York: McGraw-Hill.

Lewin, K. (1936). *Principles of topological psychology.* New York: McGraw-Hill.

Lewin, K. (1951). *Field theory in social science: Selected theoretical papers.* New York: Harper & Row.

Lewis, M., & Starr, M. (1979). Developmental continuity. In J. Osofsky (Ed.), *Handbook of infant development.* New York: Wiley.

Lewontin, R. C., Rose, S., & Kamin, L. (1984). *Not in our genes.* New York: Pantheon Books.

Liberman, R. P. (1981). A model for individualizing treatment. In L. P. Rehm (Ed.), *Behavior therapy for depression.* New York: Academic Press.

Lippa, R. A. (1976a). *The effect of expressive control on expressive consistency and on the relation between expressive behavior and personality.* Doctoral dissertation, Stanford University.

Lippa, R. (1976b). Expressive control and the leakage of dispositional introversion-extraversion during role-played teaching. *Journal of Personality,* 44:541–559.

Lippa, R. (1978a). Expressive control, expressive consistency, and the correspondence between expressive behavior and personality. *Journal of Personality,* 46:438–461.

Lippa, R. (1978b). *Self-presentation and the expressive display of personality.* Paper presented at the meeting of the American Psychological Association, Toronto.

Lippa, R., & Beauvais, C. (1980). *Gender jeopardy: The effects of gender, assessed femininity and masculinity, and false success/failure feedback on performance in an experimental quiz game.* Unpublished manuscript, California State University at Fullerton.

Lippa, R., & Mash, M. (1981). The effects of self-monitoring and self-reported consistency of personality statements made by strangers and intimates. *Journal of Research in Personality,* 15:172–181.

Lippa, R., Valdez, E., & Jolly, A. (1979). *Self-monitoring and the consistency of masculinity-femininity cues.* Paper presented at the annual meetings of the American Psychological Association, New York City.

Livesley, W., & Bromley, D. (1973). *Person perception in childhood and adolescence.* London: Wiley.

Loehlin, J. C., & Nichols, R. C. (1976). *Heredity, environment, and personality.* Austin: University of Texas Press.

Loevinger, J. (1957). Objective tests as instruments of psychological theory. *Psychological Reports,* 3:635–694.

London, I. D. (1946). Some consequences for history and psychology of Langmuir's concepts of convergence and divergence of phenomena. *Psychological Review,* 53:170–188.

Luborsky, L., Singer, B., & Luborsky, L. (1975). Cooperative studies of psychotherapies: Is it true that "everybody has won and all must have prizes?" *Archives of General Psychiatry,* 32:995–1008.

Ludwig, D., Franco, J. N., & Malloy, T. E. (in press). Effects of reciprocity, self-monitoring, and hedonic incentive on self-disclosure with a new acquaintance. *Journal of Personality and Social Psychology.*

Lutsky, N., Woodworth, W., & Clayton, S. (1980). *Actions–attitudes–actions: A multivariate, longitudinal study of attitude–behavior consistency.* Paper presented at Midwestern Psychological Association, St. Louis.

Lykken, D. T., Tellegen, A., & Bouchard, T. (1984). Unpublished data, University of Minnesota.

Markus, H. (1977). Self-schemata and processing information about the self. *Journal of Personality and Social Psychology,* 35:63–78.

Markus, H. (1980). The self in thought and memory. In D. M. Wegner & R. R. Vallacher (Eds.), *The self in social psychology.* New York: Oxford University Press.

Marrow, A. J. (1969). *The practical theorist: The life and works of Kurt Lewin.* New York: Basic Books.

Matheny, A. P. (1980). Bayley's infant behavior record: Behavioral components and twin analyses. *Child Development,* 51:1157–1161.

Matheny, A. P., Wilson, R. S., &

Dolan, A. B. (1976). Relations between twins' similarity in appearance and behavioral similarity: Testing an assumption. *Behavior Genetics,* 6:343–352.

Matwychuk, A., & Snyder, M. (1982). Unpublished research, University of Minnesota.

McCall, G. J., & Simmons, J. T. (1978). *Identities and interactions* (2nd ed.). New York: Free Press.

McCann, D., & Hancock, R. D. (1983). Self-monitoring in communicative interactions: Social cognitive consequences of goal-directed message modification. *Journal of Experimental Social Psychology,* 19: 109–121.

McClintock, C. (1958). Personality syndromes and attitude change. *Journal of Personality,* 26:479–493.

McFall, R. M. (1970). Effects of self-monitoring on normal smoking behavior. *Journal of Consulting and Clinical Psychology,* 35:135–142.

McFall, R. M., & Hammen, C. L. (1971). Motivation, structure, and self-monitoring: Role of nonspecific factors in smoking reduction. *Journal of Consulting and Clinical Psychology,* 37:80–86.

McGinnis, J. (1970). *The selling of the president, 1968.* New York: Pocket Books.

Mead, G. H. (1934). *Mind, self, and society.* Chicago: University of Chicago Press.

Meehl, P. E. (1972). Specific genetic etiology, psychodynamics, and thera-peutic nihilism. *International Journal of Mental Health,* 1:10–27.

Meehl, P. E. (1978). Theoretical risks and tabular asterisks: Sir Karl, Sir Ronald, and the slow progress of soft psychology. *Journal of Consulting and Clinical Psychology,* 46: 806–834.

Meehl, P. E., & Golden, R. R. (1982). Taxometric methods. In J. N. Butcher & P. C. Kendall (Eds.), *The handbook of research methods in clinical psychology* (pp. 127–181). New York: Wiley.

Mendelsohn, G. A., Weiss, D. S., & Feimer, N. R. (1982). Conceptual and empirical analysis of the typological implications of patterns of socialization and femininity. *Journal of Personality and Social Psychology,* 42:1157–1170.

Mendoza, J., & Graziano, W. G. (1982). The statistical analysis of dyadic social behavior: A multivariate approach. *Psychological Bulletin,* 92:532–540.

Metcalf, J. T. (1931). Empathy and the actor's emotion. *Journal of Social Psychology,* 2:235–238.

Miell, D., & Le Voi, M. (1985). *Self-monitoring and control in dyadic interactions.* Unpublished manuscript, The Open University, Milton Keynes, England.

Mill, J. (1984). High and low self-monitoring individuals: Their decoding skills and empathic expression. *Journal of Personality,* 52: 372–388.

Miller, D. T., & Ross, M. (1975). Self-serving biases in the attribution of causality: Fact or fiction? *Psychological Bulletin,* 82: 213–225.

Miller, G. A., Galanter, E., & Pribram, K. H. (1960). *Plans and the structure of behavior.* New York: Holt, Rinehart & Winston.

Miller, G. R., de Turch, M. A., & Kalbfleisch, P. J. (1983). Self-monitoring, rehearsal, and deceptive communication. *Human Communication Research,* 10:97–117.

Miller, L. E. (1984). *Self-monitoring and leadership.* Paper presented at the annual meetings of the Midwestern Psychological Association, Chicago.

Mills, C., & Hogan, R. (1978). A role theoretical interpretation of personality scale item responses. *Journal of Personality,* 46:778–785.

Mischel, W. (1968). *Personality and assessment.* New York: Wiley.

Mischel, W. (1973). Toward a cognitive social learning reconceptualization of personality. *Psychological Review,* 80: 252–283.

Mischel, W. (1976) *Introduction to personality* (2nd. ed.). New York: Holt, Rinehart & Winston.

Monson, T. C., Hesley, J. W., & Chernick, L. (1981). Specifying when personality traits can and cannot predict behavior: An alternative to abandoning the attempt to predict single-act criteria. *Journal of Personality and Social Psychology,* 43:385–399.

Monson, T. C., McDaniel, R., Menteer, L., & Williams, C. (1983). *The self-selection of persons to situations: Its implications for the correlation between dispositions and behavior within a situation.* Unpublished manuscript, University of Texas at Arlington.

Moos, R. H. (1968). Situational analysis of a therapeutic community milieu. *Journal of Abnormal Psychology,* 73:49–61.

Murray, H. A. (1938). *Explorations in personality.* New York: Oxford University Press.

Murray, H. A. (1951). Toward a classification of interaction. In T. Parsons & E. A. Shils (Eds.), *Toward a general theory of action.* Cambridge: Harvard University Press.

Murstein, B. I. (1970). Stimulus–value–role: A theory of marital choice. *Journal of Marriage and the Family,* 32:465–481.

Nelson, K. (1973). Structure and strategy in learning how to talk. *Monographs of the Society for Research in Child Development.* 38 (1–2, Serial No. 149).

Nelson, K. (1981). Individual differences in language development: Implications for development and language. *Developmental Psychology,* 17:170–187.

Nicholls, J. G., Licht, B. G., & Pearl, R. A. (1982). Some dangers of using personality questionnaires to study personality. *Psychological Bulletin,* 92:572–580.

Nowack, W., & Kammer, D. (1984). *Towards a reconceptualization of self-monitoring.* Unpublished manuscript, University of Bielefeld, Bielefeld, West Germany.

Nunnally, J. C. (1967). *Psychometric theory.* New York: McGraw-Hill.

Olson, J. M., & Zanna, M. P. (1979). A new look at selective exposure. *Journal of Experimental Social Psychology,* 15:1–15.

Olson, J. M., Zanna, M. P., & Fazio, R. H. (1978). *Attitude-behavior consistency: An individual difference perspective.* Paper presented at the annual meetings of the American Psychological Association, Washington, D. C.

Omoto, A. M., DeBono, K. G., & Snyder, M. (1985). *Getting what you want: Appearance and relationship initiation.* Paper presented at the annual meetings of the Midwestern Psychological Association, Chicago.

Overall, J. (1964). Note on the scientific status of factors. *Psychological Bulletin,* 61:270–276.

Parloff, M. B., Wolfe, B., Hadley, S., & Waskow, I. E. (1978). *Assessment of psychosocial treatment of mental disorders: Current status and prospects.* NIMH Working Group: Advisory Committee on Mental Health, Institute of Medicine, National Academy of Sciences, Washington, D.C.

Paulhus, D. (1982). Individual differences, self-presentation, and cognitive dissonance: Their concurrent operation in forced compliance. *Journal of Personality and Social Psychology,* 43:838–852.

Paulhus, D. (1984). Two component models of socially desirable responding. *Journal of Personality and Social Psychology,* 46:598–609.

Peevers, B. H., & Secord, P. F. (1973). Developmental changes in attribution of descriptive concepts to persons. *Journal of Personality and Social Psychology,* 27:120–128.

Perry, H. S. (1982). *Psychiatrist of America: The life of Harry Stack Sullivan.* Cambridge: Harvard University Press (Bellknap Press).

Petty, R. E., & Cacioppo, J. T. (1981). *Attitudes and persuasion: Classic and contemporary approaches.* Dubuque, Ia.: Wm. C. Brown.

Phares, E. J. (1976). *Locus of control in personality.* Morristown, N.J.: General Learning Press.

Piaget, J. (1970). Piaget's theory. In P. H. Mussen (Ed.), *Carmichael's manual of child psychology* (3rd ed., Vol. 1). New York: Wiley.

Pilkonis, P. A. (1977). Shyness, public and private, and its relationship to other measures of social behavior. *Journal of Personality,* 45:585–595.

Plomin, R., DeFries, J. C., & Loehlin, J. C. (1977). Genotype-environment interaction and correlation in the analysis of human behavior. *Psychological Bulletin,* 84:309–322.

Plomin, R., DeFries, J. C., & Mc-Clearn, G. E. (1980). *Behavioral genetics: A primer.* New York: W. H. Freeman and Company.

Plomin, R., & Rowe, D. (1977). A twin study of temperament in young children. *Journal of Psychology,* 97: 107–113.

Plomin, R., Willerman, L., & Loehlin, J. C. (1976). Resemblance in appearance and the equal environments assumption in twin studies of personality traits. *Behavior Genetics,* 6:42–52.

Potter, D. M. (1954). *People of plenty: Economic abundance and the American character.* Chicago: University of Chicago Press.

Rahaim, S., Waid, L. R., Kennelly, K. J., & Stricklin, A. (1980). Differences in self-monitoring of expressive behavior in depressed and nondepressed individuals. *Psychological Reports,* 46:1051–1056.

Rarick, D. L., Soldow, G. F., & Geizer, R. S. (1976). Self-monitoring as a mediator of conformity. *Central States Speech Journal,* 27: 267–271.

Rehm, L. P., & Kornblith, S. J. (1979). Behavior therapy for depression: A review of recent developments. In M. Hersen, R. M. Eisler, & P. M. Miller (Eds.), *Progress in behavior modification* (Vol. 7). New York: Academic Press.

Rhodewalt, F., & Comer, R. (1981). The role of self-attribution differences in the utilization of social comparison information. *Journal of Research in Personality,* 15:210–220.

Rhodewalt, F., Saltzman, A. T., & Wittmer, J. (1984). Self-handicapping among competitive athletes: The role of practice in self-esteem protection. *Basic and Applied Social Psychology,* 5:197–209.

Riesman, D. (1950). *The lonely crowd.* New Haven: Yale University Press.

Riggio, R. E., & Friedman, H. S. (1982). The interrelationships of self-monitoring factors, personality traits, and nonverbal social skills. *Journal of Personality and Social Psychology,* 40:627–634.

Riggio, R. E., Friedman, H. S., & DiMatteo, M. R. (1981). Nonverbal greetings: Effects of the situation and personality. *Personality and Social Psychology Bulletin,* 7: 682–689.

Rim, Y. (1982). Self-monitoring, ethical position, personality, values, and cognitive performance. *Personality and Individual Differences,* 3: 219–220.

Ring, K., & Wallston, K. (1968). A test to measure performance styles in interpersonal relations. *Psychological Reports,* 22:147–154.

Rogers, C. R. (1942). *Counseling and psychotherapy.* Boston: Houghton Mifflin.

Rogers, C. R. (1951). *Client-centered therapy.* Boston: Houghton Mifflin.

Rogers, C. R. (1954). *Psychotherapy and personality change.* Chicago:

University of Chicago Press.

Rogers, T. B. (1981). A model of the self as an aspect of the human information processing system. In N. Cantor & J. Kihlstrom (Eds.), *Personality, cognition, and social interaction.* Hillsdale, N.J.: Erlbaum.

Rokeach, M. (1968). *Beliefs, attitudes, and values.* San Francisco: Jossey-Bass.

Ronchi, D., & Sparacino, J. (1982). Density of dormitory living and stress: Mediating effects of sex, self-monitoring, and environmental affective qualities. *Perceptual and Motor Skills,* 55:759–770.

Rosenblatt, P. C. (1977). Needed research on commitment in marriage. In G. Levinger & H. L. Rausch (Eds.), *Close relationships: Perspectives on the meaning of intimacy.* Amherst: University of Massachusetts Press.

Rosenthal, R., & DePaulo, B. M. (1979). Sex differences in accommodatingness in nonverbal communication. In R. Rosenthal (Ed.), *Skill in nonverbal communication: Individual differences.* Cambridge, Mass.: Oelgeschlager, Gunn, & Hain.

Rosenthal, R., & Jacobson, L. (1968). *Pygmalion in the classroom.* New York: Holt, Rinehart & Winston.

Ross, M., McFarland, C., & Fletcher, G. J. O. (1981). The effect of attitude on the recall of personal histories. *Journal of Personality and Social Psychology,* 40:627–634.

Rotter, J. B. (1966). Generalized expectancies for internal versus external control of reinforcement. *Psychological Monographs,* 80(Whole No. 609).

Ruble, D. N. (1983). The development of social-comparison processes. In E. T. Higgins, D. N. Ruble, & W. W. Hartup (Eds.), *Social cognition and social development.* New York: Cambridge University Press.

Ruble, D. N., Feldman, N. S., Higgins, E. T., & Karlovac, M. (1979). Locus of causality and the use of information in the development of causal attributions. *Journal of Personality,* 47:595–614.

Rummel, R. J. (1970). *Applied factor analysis.* Evanston: Northwestern University Press.

Sampson, E. E. (1978). Personality and the location of identity. *Journal of Personality,* 46:552–568.

Sansom, W. (1956). *A contest of ladies.* London: Hogarth.

Santee, R. T., & Maslach, C. (1982). To agree or not to agree: Personal dissent amid social pressure to conform. *Journal of Personality and Social Psychology,* 42:690–700.

Sara, N. G. (1982). *A validation study of the Self-Monitoring Scale in Lebanon.* Unpublished manuscript, American University of Beirut.

Sarbin, T. R., & Allen, V. L. (1968). Role theory. In G. Lindzey & E. Aronson (Eds.), *The handbook of social psychology* (2nd ed., Vol. 1). Reading, Mass.: Addison-Wesley.

Scarr, S. (1968). Environmental bias in twin studies. In S. Vandenberg (Ed.), *Progress in human behavior genetics*. Baltimore: Johns Hopkins University Press.

Scarr, S., & Carter-Saltzman, L. (1979). Twin method: Defense of a critical assumption. *Behavior Genetics,* 9:527–542.

Scarr, S., & Kidd, K. K. (1983). Developmental behavior genetics. In P. H. Mussen (Ed.), *Handbook of child psychology* (Vol. 2). New York: Wiley.

Schachter, S. (1971). Some extraordinary facts about obese humans and rats. *American Psychologist,* 26: 129–144.

Schachter, S., & Singer, J. (1962). Cognitive, social, and physiological determinants of emotional state. *Psychological Review,* 69:379–399.

Schank, R., & Abelson, R. P. (1977). *Scripts, plans, goals, and understanding: An inquiry into human knowledge structures.* Hillsdale, N.J.: Erlbaum.

Scheibe, K. E. (1985). Historical perspectives on the presented self. In B. Schlenker (Ed.), *The self and social life.* New York: McGraw-Hill.

Schlenker, B. R. (1980). *Impression management: The self-concept, social identity, and interpersonal relations.* Monterey, Calif.: Brooks/ Cole.

Schlenker, B. R. (1985). *The self and social life.* New York: McGraw-Hill.

Schlenker, B., Miller, R. S., & Leary, M. R. (1983). Self-presentation as a function of self-monitoring and the validity and quality of past performance. *Representative Research in Social Psychology,* 13:2–14.

Schneiderman, W. (1980). A personality dimension of consistency versus variability without the use of self-reports or ratings. *Journal of Personality and Social Psychology,* 39: 158–164.

Schneiderman, W., Webb, W., Davis, B., & Thomas, S. (1981). *Self-monitoring and states of self-awareness.* Unpublished manuscript, Marshall University.

Schubot, D. B., & Kurecka, P. M. (1980). *Self-monitoring, gender, and coaching effects on group discussion performance.* Paper presented at the annual meeting of the American Psychological Association, Toronto.

Schubot, D. B., & Kurecka, P. M. (1981). *The interactive effects of self-monitoring, sex, and coaching on leaderless group discussion performance ratings.* Paper presented at the annual meeting of the Midwestern Psychological Association, Detroit.

Schwartz, S. H. (1973). Normative explanations of helping behavior: A critique, proposal, and empirical test. *Journal of Experimental Social Psychology,* 9:349–364.

Secord, P. F., & Backman, C. W. (1965). An interpersonal approach to personality. In B. Maher (Ed.), *Progress in experimental personality research* (Vol. 2, pp. 91–125). New York: Academic Press.

Secord, P. F., & Backman, C. W. (1974). *Social psychology* (2nd ed.). New York: McGraw-Hill.

Secunda, R., Friedman, R. J., & Schuyler, D. (1973). *Special report: The depressive disorders* (DHEW Publication No. HSM 73-9125). Washington, D.C.: U.S. Government Printing Office.

Selman, R. L. (1980). *The growth of interpersonal understanding.* New York: Academic Press.

Shaffer, D. R., Ogden, J. K., & Wu, C. (1985). *Effects of self-monitoring and prospect of future interaction on self-disclosure reciprocity during the acquaintance process.* Unpublished manuscript, University of Georgia at Athens.

Shaffer, D. R., Smith, J. E., & Tomarelli, M. (1982). Self-monitoring as a determinant of self-disclosure reciprocity during the acquaintance process. *Journal of Personality and Social Psychology,* 43:163–175.

Shaw, B. F. (1981). Matching treatment to patient characteristics in an inpatient setting. In L. P. Rehm (Ed.), *Behavior therapy for depression.* New York: Academic Press.

Shrum, R. (1977). Symbols of our times. *New Times,* February 18, p. 6.

Siegman, A. W., & Reynolds, M. A. (1983). Self-monitoring and speech in feigned and unfeigned lying. *Journal of Personality and Social Psychology,* 45:1325–1333.

Sigall, J., & Landy, D. (1973). Radiating beauty: Effects of having a physically attractive partner on person perception. *Journal of Personality and Social Psychology,* 28:218–224.

Skinner, B. F. (1953). *Science and human behavior.* New York: Macmillan.

Skrypnek, B. J., & Snyder, M. (1982). On the self-perpetuating nature of stereotypes about women and men. *Journal of Experimental Social Psychology,* 18:277–291.

Smith, A., & Davidson, J., Jr. (1983). *Personality and situational variables in the evaluation screening process.* Unpublished manuscript, Boston University and University of Utah.

Smith, M. B., Bruner, J. S., & White, R. W. (1956). *Opinions and personality.* New York: Wiley.

Smith, R. T. (1965). A comparison of socio-environmental factors in monozygotic and dizygotic twins: Testing an assumption. In S. Vandenberg (Ed.), *Methods and goals in behavior genetics.* New York: Academic Press.

Smith, T. W., Snyder, C. R., & Handelsman, M. M. (1982). On the self-serving function of an academic wooden leg: Test anxiety as a self-handicapping strategy. *Journal of Personality and Social Psychology,* 42:314–321.

Smith, T. W., Snyder, C. R., & Perkins, S. C. (1983). The self-serving function of hypochondriacal complaints: Physical symptoms as self-handicapping strategies. *Journal of Personality and Social Psychology,* 44: 787–797.

Snyder, C. R., & Smith, T. W. (1982). Symptoms as self-handicapping strategies: The virtues of old wine in new bottles. In G. Weary & H. L. Mirels (Eds.), *Integrations of clinical and social psychology* (pp. 104–127). New York: Oxford University Press.

Snyder, C. R., Smith, T. W., Angelli, R. W., & Ingram, R. E. (1985). On the self-serving function of social anxiety: Shyness as a self-handicapping strategy. *Journal of Personality and Social Psychology,* 48:970–980.

Snyder, M. (1972). Individual differences and the self-control of expressive behavior (Doctoral dissertation, Stanford University, 1972). *Dissertation Abstracts International,* 33:4533A–4534A (University Microfilms No. 73-4598).

Snyder, M. (1974). The self-monitoring of expressive behavior. *Journal of Personality and Social Psychology,* 30:526–537.

Snyder, M. (1976). Attribution and behavior: Social perception and social causation. In J. H. Harvey, W. J. Ickes, & R. F. Kidd (Eds.), *New directions in attribution research.* Hillsdale, N.J.: Erlbaum.

Snyder, M. (1979a). Cognitive, behavioral, and interpersonal consequences of self-monitoring. In P. Pliner, K. R. Blankstein, & I. M. Spigel (Eds.), *Advances in the study of communication and affect* (Vol. 5). *Perception of emotion in self and others.* New York: Plenum.

Snyder, M. (1979b). Self-monitoring processes. In L. Berkowitz (Ed.), *Advances in experimental social psychology* (Vol. 12). New York: Academic Press.

Snyder, M. (1981a). Impression management: The self in social interaction. In Wrightsman, L. S., & Deaux, K., *Social psychology in the 80s* (3rd ed.). Monterey, Calif.: Brooks/Cole.

Snyder, M. (1981b). On the influence of individuals on situations. In N. Cantor & J. F. Kihlstrom (Eds.), *Personality, cognition, and social interaction.* Hillsdale, N.J.: Erlbaum.

Snyder, M. (1981c). On the self-perpetuating nature of social stereotypes. In D. L. Hamilton (Ed.), *Cognitive processes in stereotyping and intergroup behavior.* Hillsdale, N.J.: Erlbaum.

Snyder, M. (1981d). Seek, and ye shall find: Testing hypotheses about other people. In E. T. Higgins, C. P. Herman, & M. P. Zanna (Eds.), *Social cognition: The Ontario symposium* (Vol. 1). Hillsdale, N.J.: Erlbaum.

Snyder, M. (1982). When believing means doing: Creating links between attitudes and behavior. In M. P. Zanna, E. T. Higgins, & C. P.

Herman (Eds.), *Consistency in social behavior: The Ontario symposium* (Vol. 2). Hillsdale N.J.: Erlbaum.

Snyder, M. (1983). The influence of individuals on situations: Implications for understanding the links between personality and social behavior. *Journal of Personality,* 51: 497–516.

Snyder, M. (1984). When belief creates reality. In L. Berkowitz (Ed.), *Advances in experimental social psychology* (Vol. 18). New York: Academic Press.

Snyder, M. (1986). *Self-monitoring bibliography.* Unpublished manuscript, University of Minnesota.

Snyder, M., Berscheid, E., & Glick, P. (1985). Focusing on the exterior and the interior: Two investigations of the initiation of personal relationships. *Journal of Personality and Social Psychology,* 48:1427–1439.

Snyder, M., Berscheid, E., & Matwychuk, A. (1985). Unpublished research, University of Minnesota.

Snyder, M., Campbell, B., & Preston, E. (1982). Testing hypotheses about human nature: Assessing the accuracy of social stereotypes. *Social Cognition,* 1:256–272.

Snyder, M., & Cantor, N. (1980). Thinking about ourselves and others: Self-monitoring and social knowledge. *Journal of Personality and Social Psychology,* 39:222–234.

Snyder, M., & DeBono, K. G. (1984). Unpublished research, University of Minnesota.

Snyder, M., & DeBono, K. G. (1985a). Unpublished research, University of Minnesota.

Snyder, M., & DeBono, K.G. (1985b). Appeals to images and claims about quality: Understanding the psychology of advertising. *Journal of Personality and Social Psychology.* 49: 586–597.

Snyder, M., & DeBono, K. G. (in press). A functional approach to attitudes and persuasion. In M. P. Zanna, J. M. Olson, & C. P. Herman (Eds.), *Social influence: The Ontario symposium* (Vol. 5). Hillsdale, N.J.: Erlbaum.

Snyder, M., & Gangestad, S. (1982). Choosing social situations: Two investigations of self-monitoring processes. *Journal of Personality and Social Psychology,* 43:123–135.

Snyder, M., & Gangestad, S. (1986). On the nature of self-monitoring: Matters of assessment, matters of validity. *Journal of Personality and Social Psychology.*

Snyder, M., Gangestad, S., & Simpson, J. A. (1983). Choosing friends as activity partners: The role of self-monitoring. *Journal of Personality and Social Psychology,* 45:1061–1072.

Snyder, M., & Harkness, A. R. (1984). $E = f(p)$: *The impact of personality on choice of situation.* Paper presented at the annual meetings of the Midwestern Psychological Association, Chicago.

Snyder, M., & Ickes, W. (1985). Personality and social behavior. In

G. Lindzey & E. Aronson (Eds.), *Handbook of social psychology* (3rd ed.). New York: Random House.

Snyder, M., & Kendzierski, D. (1982a). Acting on one's attitudes: Procedures for linking attitude and behavior. *Journal of Experimental Social Psychology,* 18:165–183.

Snyder, M., & Kendzierski, D. (1982b). Choosing social situations: A strategy for generating correspondence between attitudes and behavior. *Journal of Personality,* 50: 280–295.

Snyder, M., & Monson, T. C. (1975). Persons, situations, and the control of social behavior. *Journal of Personality and Social Psychology,* 32: 637–644.

Snyder, M., Nettle, R., & DeBono, K. G. (1985). Unpublished research, University of Minnesota.

Snyder, M., & Simpson, J. A. (1983). Unpublished research, University of Minnesota.

Snyder, M., & Simpson, J. A. (1984a). Self-monitoring and dating relationships. *Journal of Personality and Social Psychology,* 47:1281–1291.

Snyder, M., & Simpson, J. A. (1984b). Unpublished research, University of Minnesota.

Snyder, M., & Simpson, J. A. (in press). Orientations toward romantic relationships. In S. Duck & D. Perlman (Eds.), *Intimate relationships: Development, dynamics, and deterioration.* Beverly Hills: Sage.

Snyder, M., Simpson, J. A., & Gangestad, S. (in press). Personality and sexual relations. *Journal of Personality and Social Psychology.*

Snyder, M., Simpson, J. A., & Smith, D. (1984). *Personality and friendship: The role of self-monitoring in choosing close and casual friends.* Paper presented at the annual meetings of the Midwestern Psychological Association, Chicago.

Snyder, M., & Smith, D. (1984). *Self-monitoring and conceptions of friendship.* Paper presented at the annual meetings of the Midwestern Psychological Association, Chicago.

Snyder, M., & Smith, D. (1985). *Self-monitoring and depression: Precipitating events and coping strategies.* Paper presented at the annual meetings of the Midwestern Psychological Association, Chicago.

Snyder, M., & Smith, D. (in press). Personality and friendship: The friendship worlds of self-monitoring. In V. Derlega & B. Winstead (Eds.), *Friendship and social interaction.* New York: Springer-Verlag.

Snyder, M., & Swann, W. B., Jr. (1976). When actions reflect attitudes: The politics of impression management. *Journal of Personality and Social Psychology,* 34: 1034–1042.

Snyder, M., & Swann, W. B., Jr. (1978a). Behavioral confirmation in social interaction: From social perception to social reality. *Journal of Experimental Social Psychology,* 14:148–162.

Snyder, M., & Swann, W. B., Jr. (1978*b*). Hypothesis testing processes in social interaction. *Journal of Personality and Social Psychology,* 36:1202–1212.

Snyder, M., & Tanke, E. D. (1974). Unpublished research, University of Minnesota.

Snyder, M., & Tanke, E. D. (1976). Behavior and attitude: Some people are more consistent than others. *Journal of Personality,* 44:510–517.

Snyder, M., Tanke, E. D., & Berscheid, E. (1977). Social perception and interpersonal behavior: On the self-fulfilling nature of social stereotypes. *Journal of Personality and Social Psychology,* 35:656–666.

Snyder, M., & White, P. (1982). Moods and memories: Elation, depression, and the remembering of the events of one's life. *Journal of Personality,* 50:149–167.

Solomon, L., & Berzon, B. (Eds.). (1972). *New perspectives on encounter groups.* San Francisco: Jossey-Bass.

Sparacino, J. (1981). Self-monitoring and psychotherapy: A comment. *Perceptual and Motor Skills,* 52:974.

Sparacino, J., Ronchi, D., Bigley, T. K., Flesch, A. L., & Kuhn, J. W. (1983). Self-monitoring and blood pressure. *Journal of Personality and Social Psychology,* 44:365–375.

Steiner, I. D. (1974). Whatever happened to the group in social psychol-ogy? *Journal of Experimental Social Psychology,* 10:94–108.

Stern, G., Stein, M., & Bloom, B. (1956). *Methods in personality assessment: Human behaviour in complex social settings.* New York: Free Press.

Stotland, E., Katz, D., & Patchen, M. (1959). The reduction of prejudice through the arousal of self-insight. *Journal of Personality,* 27:507–531.

Stryker, S. (1979). Symbolic interactionism: Themes and variations. In M. Rosenberg & R. H. Turner (Eds.), *Social Psychology: Sociological perspectives.* New York: Basic Books.

Stryker, S. (1980). *Symbolic interactionism: A social structural version.* Palo Alto: Benjamin/Cummings.

Stryker, S., & Stratham, A. (1985). Symbolic interaction and role theory. In G. Lindzey & E. Aronson (Eds.), *Handbook of social psychology* (3rd ed.). New York: Random House.

Sullivan, H. S. (1953). *The interpersonal theory of psychiatry.* New York: Norton.

Sullivan, H. S. (1964). *The fusion of psychiatry and social science.* New York: Norton.

Suls, J. (1982). *Psychological perspectives on the self* (Vol. 1). Hillsdale, N.J.: Erlbaum.

Suls, J., & Greenwald, A. G. (1983). *Psychological perspectives on the self* (Vol. 2). Hillsdale, N.J.: Erlbaum.

Super, D. E., Starishesky, R., Matlin, N., & Jordann, J. P. (1963). *Career development: Self-concept theory.* New York: College Entrance Examination Board.

Swann, W. B., Jr. (1983). Self-verification: Bringing social reality into harmony with the self. In J. Suls & A. G. Greenwald (Eds.), *Psychological perspectives on the self* (Vol. 2). Hillsdale, N.J.: Erlbaum.

Swann, W. B., Jr. (1985). The self as architect of social reality. In B. R. Schlenker (Ed.), *The self and social life.* New York: McGraw-Hill.

Swann, W. B., Jr., & Read, S. J. (1981). Self-verification processes: How we sustain our self-conceptions. *Journal of Experimental Social Psychology,* 17:351–372.

Sypher, B. D., & Sypher, H. H. (1981). *Individual differences and perceptions of communication abilities in an organizational setting.* Paper presented at the annual meetings of the International Communication Association, Minneapolis.

Sypher, B. D., & Sypher, H. H. (1983). Self-monitoring and perceptions of communication ability in an organizational setting. *Personality and Social Psychology Bulletin,* 9:297–304.

Tardy, C., & Hasman, L. (1982). Self-monitoring and self-disclosure flexibility: A research note. *Western Journal of Speech Communication,* 46:92–97.

Taylor, S. E., & Crocker, J. (1981). Schematic bases of social information processing. In E. T. Higgins, C. P. Herman, & M. P. Zanna (Eds.), *Social cognition: The Ontario symposium* (Vol. 1). Hillsdale, N.J.: Erlbaum.

Thomas, A., Chess, S., & Birch, H. (1968). *Temperament and behavior disorders in children.* New York: New York University Press.

Thomas, E. A. C., & Malone, T. W. (1979). On the dynamics of two-person interactions. *Psychological Review,* 86:331–360.

Thomas, W. I. (1923). *The unadjusted girl.* Boston: Little, Brown.

Thurstone, L. L. (1947). *Multiple factor analysis.* Chicago: University of Chicago Press.

Tobey, E. L., & Tunnell, G. (1981). Predicting our impressions on others: Effects of public self-consciousness and acting, a Self-Monitoring subscale. *Personality and Social Psychology Bulletin,* 7:661–669.

Tomarelli, M. M., & Graziano, W. G. (1981). *When opposites may attract: Self-monitoring and dating relationships.* Paper presented at the annual meetings of the Southeastern Psychological Association, Atlanta.

Tomarelli, M. M., & Shaffer, D. R. (in press). What aspects of self do self-monitors monitor? *Bulletin of the Psychonomic Society.*

Tucker, J. A., Vuchinich, R. E., & Sobell, M. B. (1981). Alcohol consumption as a self-handicapping strategy. *Journal of Abnormal Psy-*

chology, 90:220–230.

Tunnell, G. (1980). Intraindividual consistency in personality assessment: The effect of self-monitoring. *Journal of Personality,* 48:220–232.

Turner, R. G. (1979). *Self-monitoring and private versus public impressions of others.* Paper presented at the American Psychological Association, New York City.

Turner, R. G. (1980). Self-monitoring and humor production. *Journal of Personality,* 48:163–172.

Turner, R. G., Scheier, M. F., Carver, C. S., & Ickes, W. (1978). Correlates of self-consciousness. *Journal of Personality Assessment,* 42:285–289.

Turner, R. H. (1968). The self-conception in social interaction. In C. Gordon & K. J. Gergen (Eds.), *The self in social interaction.* New York: Wiley.

Turner, R. H. (1975). The real self: From institution to impulse. *American Journal of Sociology,* 81: 989–1015.

Tybout, A. M., & Scott, C. A. (1983). Availability of well-defined internal knowledge and the attitude formation process: Information aggregation versus self-perception. *Journal of Personality and Social Psychology,* 44:474–491.

U.S. Bureau of the Census. (1976). *Statistical abstract of the United States: 1975* (96th ed.). Washington, D.C.: U.S. Government Printing Office.

Wachtel, P. (1973). Psychodynamics, behavior therapy, and the implacable experimenter: An inquiry into the consistency of personality. *Journal of Abnormal Psychology,* 82: 324–334.

Wagman, M. (1955). Attitude change and authoritarian personality. *Journal of Psychology,* 40:3–24.

Weary-Bradley, G. (1978). Self-serving biases in the attribution process: A re-examination of the fact or fiction question. *Journal of Personality and Social Psychology,* 36:56–71.

Weinstein, E. A. (1966). Toward a theory of interpersonal tactics. In C. W. Backman & P. F. Secord (Eds.), *Problems in social psychology.* New York: McGraw-Hill.

White-Phelan, P. (1983). Unpublished research, University of Minnesota.

Whitmore, M. D., & Klimoski, R. J. (1984). *Leader emergence and self-monitoring behavior under conditions of high and low motivation.* Paper presented at the annual meetings of the Midwestern Psychological Association, Chicago.

Wicker, A. W. (1969). Attitudes versus actions: The relationship of verbal and overt behavioral responses to attitude objects. *Journal of Social Issues,* 25:41–78.

Wicklund, R. A. (1975). Objective self-awareness. In L. Berkowitz (Ed.), *Advances in experimental social psychology* (Vol. 8). New York: Academic Press.

Wiggins, J. S. (1974). *In defense of*

traits. Paper presented at the Ninth Annual Symposium of the MMPI, Los Angeles.

Wilkinson, J. A. (1982). *The evaluation of involvement in developmental drama and its relationship to self-monitoring and hemisphericity.* Doctoral dissertation, University of Minnesota.

Witcover, J. (1970). *The resurrection of Richard Nixon.* New York: Putnam.

Wojciszke, B. (1982). (An introduction to self-monitoring theory for Polish scholars.) Przeglad Psychologiczny.

Wolf, D., & Gardner, H. (1979). Style and sequence in early symbolic play. In N. Smith & M. Franklin (Eds.), *Symbolic functioning in childhood* (pp. 117–138). Hillsdale, N.J.: Erlbaum.

Wolfe, R., Lennox, R., & Hudiburg, R. (1983). Self-monitoring and sex as moderator variables in the statistical explanation of self-reported marijuana and alcohol use. *Journal of Personality and Social Psychology,* 44:1069–1074.

Wolpe, J. (1958). *Psychotherapy by reciprocal inhibition.* Stanford, Calif.: Stanford University Press.

Word, C. O., Zanna, M. P., & Cooper, J. (1974). The nonverbal mediation of self-fulfilling prophecies in interracial interaction. *Journal of Experimental Social Psychology,* 10: 109–120.

Wright, H. F. (1967). *Recording and analyzing child behavior.* New York: Harper & Row.

Wylie, R. (1974). *The self-concept* (Vol. 1). *A review of methodological considerations and measuring instruments* (rev. ed.). Lincoln: University of Nebraska Press.

Wylie, R. (1979). *The self-concept* (Vol. 2). *Theory and research on selected topics.* Lincoln: University of Nebraska Press.

Younger, J. C., & Pliner, P. (1976). Obese–normal differences in the self-monitoring of expressive behavior. *Journal of Research in Personality,* 10:112–115.

Zaidel, S., & Mehrabian, A. (1969). The ability to communicate and infer positive and negative attitudes facially and vocally. *Journal of Experimental Research in Personality,* 3:233–241.

Zaidman, B., & Snyder, M. (1983). Unpublished research, University of Minnesota.

Zanna, M. P., & Olson, J. M. (1982). Individual differences in attitudinal relations. In M. P. Zanna, E. T. Higgins, & C. P. Herman (Eds.), *Consistency in social behavior: The Ontario symposium* (Vol. 2). Hillsdale, N.J.: Erlbaum.

Zanna, M. P., Olson, J. M., & Fazio, R. H. (1980). Attitude–behavior consistency: An individual difference perspective. *Journal of Personality and Social Psychology,* 38: 432–440.

Zanna, M. P., & Pack, S. J. (1975). On the self-fulfilling nature of apparent sex differences in behavior. *Journal of Experimental Social Psychology,* 11:583–591.

Zedeck, S., & Cascio, W. F. (1984). Psychological issues in personnel decisions. *Annual Review of Psychology,* 35:461–518.

Ziller, R. C., & Lewis, D. (1981). Orientations: Self, social, and environmental percepts through autophotography. *Personality and Social Psychology Bulletin,* 7:338–343.

Ziller, R. C., & Smith, D. E. (1977). A phenomenological utilization of photographs. *Journal of Phenomenological Psychology,* 7:172–185.

Zimbardo, P. G. (1969). The human choice: Individuation, reason, and order versus deindividuation, impulse, and chaos. In W. J. Arnold & D. Levine (Eds.), *Nebraska Symposium on Motivation.* Lincoln: University of Nebraska Press.

Zuckerman, M. (1974). The sensation seeking motive. In B. Maher (Ed.), *Progress in experimental personality research* (Vol. 7, pp. 79–148). New York: Academic Press.

Zuckerman, M., & Reis, H. T. (1978). A comparison of three models for predicting altruistic behavior. *Journal of Personality and Social Psychology,* 36:498–510.

Author Index

Subject Index

Academic achievement, 28
Acting, 185–187
Action control, 205
Actors, professional, 21, 186
Adjustment, problems of, 111
Adolescence, 148–149
Advertising, 97
  claims, 101
  "hard-sell" in, 98, 104
  image-oriented, 98–105
  and persuasion, 102–103
  quality-oriented, 98–105
  reactions to appeals, 99–105
  "soft-sell" in, 98, 104
Alka-Seltzer, 105
Alternative partners, 78–79
Androgyny, 205
Anxiety, 28, 112, 164n, 205
Aristotle, 69
Arrow shirt collars, 98
Ascription of responsibility, 205
As-if personality, 113n
Assortative mating, 80

Attention to others, 34–35
Attitude functions, 108–110
  and persuasion, 109–110
  research strategy for, 110
Attitude–behavior links, 39–41, 101–102, 190, 203
Auden, W. H., 1
Audience segregation, 62–63
Audio magazine, 106
Authoritarian personality, 113, 120, 208
Autophotography, 151–152

Base rates, estimates of, 161–162, 169
Beck Depression Inventory, 115
Behavior, prediction of, 204–205
Behavioral confirmation, 211–212
Bem Sex Role Inventory, 19n
Beneffectance, 192
Biochemical determinants, 134
Biological influence (*see* Genetic influence)
Birth order, 28
Boundary-spanning, 88